KENWOOD

Recipes for the Kenwood Chef & Major

MAKING GREAT
FOOD SIMPLE

Jennie Shapter

Published for Kenwood Ltd.
By The Romsey Group 2003

Design: Turquoise Creative
Editor: Jennie Shapter
Photography: Dave King
Food Stylist: Jennie Shapter
Prop Stylist: Jo Harris

A CIP catalogue record for this book is available from the British Library.

ISBN 0-9526262-1-7

Cookery Notes

For all the recipes, quantities are given in metric and imperial measures. Follow one set only, but not a mixture in any one recipe as they are not interchangeable.

All spoon measurements are level unless otherwise stated.

Use medium eggs unless otherwise stated.

Cooking times may vary slightly depending on each individual oven. Start to check to see whether a dish is cooked towards the end of the cooking time.

Place dishes in the centre of the oven unless otherwise stated in the recipe.

Preparation and Cooking Times are included as a general guide. In particular the preparation times given are approximate and are rounded up to the nearest 5 minutes. They do not include the time taken to make any basic recipe.

Raw eggs are used in a few recipes. Make sure the eggs are as fresh as possible. Pregnant women, small children and any one susceptible to infection should avoid dishes containing raw eggs.

CONTENTS

INTRODUCTION

Congratulations, you are now the proud owner of a Kenwood Chef or Major Kitchen Machine. With today's busy lifestyle, the Kitchen Machine is the perfect appliance to help make cooking easier, quicker and extremely pleasurable.

The Kenwood Chef and Major Machines, along with the vast selection of attachments, make light work of so many repetitive preparation tasks. The K Beater, Whisk and Dough Hook tools will help prepare cakes, desserts, biscuits, pastry and bread as well as mash vegetables, mix pâté, stuffings, meat loaves, burgers, fish cakes and vegetable nut roasts; whilst the list of uses for the attachments is almost endless. They can help prepare vegetables for crisp salads and stir-fries, purée fruit and vegetables for soups and sauces, mix and shape both flat and tubular pasta, make sausages, mill coffee beans or spices for marinades, whiz up smoothies, juice most fruits and vegetables for healthy drinks or mix and freeze ice cream.

This book has been written especially for the range of Kenwood Kitchen Machines, and contains nearly 200 recipes to illustrate some of the many uses. The front section of the book explains in detail about the Kenwood Chef and Major, the tools and attachments. Each tool and attachment is individually described with useful information on how and when to use them, what foods or recipes they are best for, plus helpful hints and tips. Where appropriate, photographs help to illustrate the techniques throughout this section.

The recipe section is divided into chapters, just like a cookery book, enabling you to refer to whichever section you require. It includes recipes for soups and starters and eggs and cheese, many of which are equally suitable for snacks or main meals; or perhaps you wish to cook a main course fish or meat recipe or a cake dessert or bread recipe, the choice is yours. The recipes are International, using a wide range of ingredients and vary from quick and easy to more sophisticated recipes, perfect for showing off your culinary skills made so much easier with the help of your Kitchen Machine.

Every recipe in the book has been tested using a Kenwood Kitchen Machine. If you wish to select a recipe for a particular tool or attachment, there is a separate index on pages 172-3. There is a glossary on pages 168-171 which offers a guide to any cookery terms, methods or ingredients you may be unfamiliar with.

Don't limit yourself to the recipes in this book, but use them and the additional information at the front of the book as a guideline and adapt your favourite recipes as well. Whatever you choose to make with your Kenwood Chef or Major, may you have many hours of satisfaction and enjoy sampling the end results.

The history of Kenwood began more than half a century ago when Mr. Kenneth Wood founded his first company in Woking, Surrey. He started a business in 1947 making electrical appliances called the Kenwood Manufacturing Company Limited. He wanted to manufacture and sell appliances, which people desired as luxury items, but indeed would soon become every-day essentials.

His first product was a toaster, closely followed by a twin beater mixer. The mixer sold extremely well, but competition, particularly from America meant he needed to invent something new and innovative to keep ahead. Together with his team of design engineers he started to re-design the mixer into what was to be the beginning of over 50 years of the Kenwood Chef generation.

In March 1950 he launched the new machine at the renowned Ideal Home exhibition in London. The functions of this new machine were too diverse to be just called a mixer, so he renamed it the Kenwood Electric Chef A 700. It first sold for the grand sum of £19 10s 10d.

Its reputation grew fast and soon the Chef was being exported around the World to Western Europe, Canada, South America and the USA.

The appeal for the Chef has continued to grow and it is now sold to over a hundred countries around the World. Over fifty years of food preparation experience and continuous product development have gone into producing the latest Kenwood Kitchen Machines. Since the first Kenwood Chefs rolled off the production line over 10 million machines have been sold worldwide. The current range now offers the consumer even more choice with new attachments, the highest specification of design and engineering and also a range of sizes and colours. With power output from 700 watts to an exceptional 1200 watts the Kenwood Chef is still a firm favourite both in the home and with semi-professionals.

Top Left: *Kenneth Wood*
Above: *Kenwood Range from 1950 to 1976*

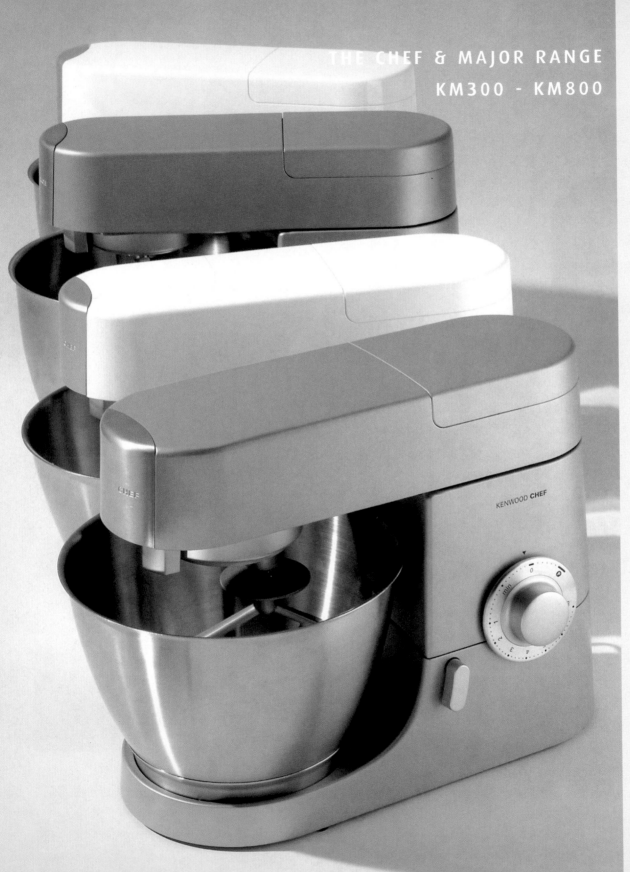

The KM300-KM800 range offers the consumer design in both Chef and Major size capacity. All the models in this range have a front slow speed outlet, and top high speed outlet for operating the range of versatile attachments.

KENWOOD **CHEF**

The KM001-KM007 range boasts a design incorporating a gearbox creating a medium speed outlet for use with the latest citrus juicing attachment and a comprehensive food processing unit. Additional product features include a metal exterior finish, cord storage, a quieter running sound and superior power of 1000 – 1200 watts.

THE CHEF AND MAJOR RANGE
KM001 - KM007

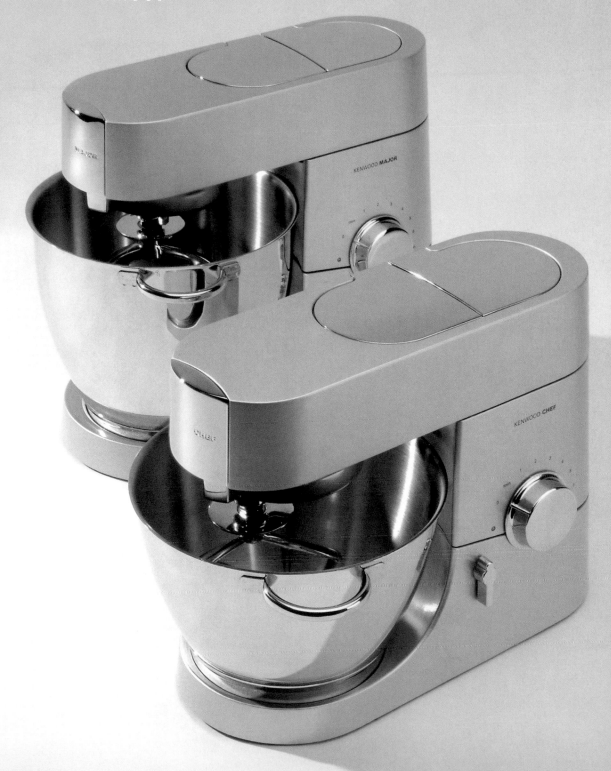

Whichever size or style of Kitchen Machine you have purchased the mixing tools will carry out similar functions, the main difference between the machines being the maximum capacity each can handle. The Major has a larger bowl and a more powerful motor to cope with the extra quantity. For maximum capacities check the instruction booklet supplied with your Kitchen Machine.

THE MIXING TOOLS

Every mixing function from cakes, biscuits, pastry and yeast doughs to cream, eggs, soufflés, meringues and mousses can be successfully achieved using the K Beater, Whisk or Dough Hook provided with your machine.

The Kitchen Machines have a unique movement that enables the tools to rotate whilst travelling around the inside of the bowl. This is known as the Planetary Action. It ensures that the K Beater, Whisk or Dough Hook can reach all areas of the bowl, to ensure complete and even mixing of the ingredients.

More detailed information on mixing, kneading and whisking can be found on pages 9-11.

THE BOWLS

There is a selection of bowls, which are supplied with different Kenwood Chef and Major models. There is the Round Bowl; or a Stainless Steel Round Bowl. These can be purchased in addition, if wished.

Each can be interchanged on any of the models in the range and provide different benefits.

The Stainless Steel Bowl in either matt or polished finish is available for both the Chef and Major and offers the advantage of remaining cool. This is especially helpful when making pastry, whipping cream or whisking egg whites.

The KM001-KM007 range of models comes with Stainless Steel Bowls, complete with handles for easier lifting and pouring.

ACCESSORIES

The Splashguard

The Splashguard locates on the machine, above the tool, so any tool can easily be changed without removing the Splashguard. It also has a hinged section, so that during mixing ingredients can easily be added directly to the bowl.

The Splashguard will not only prevent liquids splashing out of the bowl, it will also contain powders, like flour, which have a tendency to produce a cloud of dust when added to the Kenwood Bowl during mixing.

The Spatula

An extremely useful tool, it is very flexible and will easily scrape every last morsel from the bowl.

The Cover

An attractive wipe-clean, hygienic cover which slips over your Kitchen Machine, to keep it dust free and clean whilst not in use.

K BEATER

The K Beater is likely to be the most frequently used tool; it is so versatile in the preparation of many sweet and savoury foods. The angled fins of the K Beater along with the planetary action ensures that it will reach every area of the Bowl, whether creaming cake mixtures, making pastry or gently stirring ingredients together for stuffings and fillings.

WHEN TO USE

Creamed Mixtures

The traditional method used to make a classic Victoria sandwich as well as fruit cakes, chocolate cakes, sponge puddings and some biscuit mixes. The K Beater makes creaming the fat and sugar easy to achieve, increasing the volume to give a fluffy light mixture.

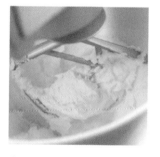

The K Beater can then beat in the eggs, on maximum speed. The efficiency of the Beater minimises the likelihood of the mixture curdling, which results in a dense cake. Reduce to minimum to fold in the flour.

Crumbing Biscuits

The K Beater may be used to crush digestive biscuits for making cheesecake bases, flan cases and no-bake chocolate cakes. Use the K Beater on speeds 1 to 2 to crush the biscuits, and then mix in the melted butter for the crumb base, or other ingredients as required.

Icing

Buttercream icing is perhaps the most frequently used icing and topping for cakes. The K Beater will cream the butter until soft and then beat in the icing sugar and flavourings to form a smooth fluffy icing. The K Beater also takes the hard work out of making royal icing and almond paste used for celebration cakes.

Mashing Vegetables

Use the K Beater to mash potatoes, swede or parsnips. Cook the vegetables in boiling water until soft, then drain and place in the Kenwood Bowl. Using the K Beater on speed 2, mix until they are mashed. Beat in a little milk, butter and seasoning as desired.

Mixing and Blending

Melted mixtures for cakes like gingerbread, honey cake and some tea breads can be easily blended using the K Beater, as can all-in-one cake mixes using soft margarine and quick mix muffin mixtures. Use the K Beater to beat the eggs into choux pastry or for making biscuit dough and shortbread. The versatility of the K Beater is almost endless; it has many uses in the preparation of savoury dishes, from mixing together pâté ingredients, or stuffing mixes for vegetables or

poultry to blending together burger, meatball and sausage mixes. Meat loaves, nut roast and fish cake fillings are just a few more examples.

Rubbed-In Mixtures

The K Beater is perfect for blending flour and fat to a crumb-like mix, known as a 'rubbed-in' mixture.

This is the basis for plain cakes, scones, pastry, many biscuits, streusel topped cakes, tea breads, rock cakes and crumble topped desserts. The K Beater will also mix the crumb mixture into the final cake mix, biscuit mix, scone or pastry dough. The K Beater, being metal, adds a coolness to the mixing; essential for making pastry. Use speeds minimum to 2.

HINTS AND TIPS

❶ For best results make sure the fat for creamed mixtures is at room temperature, unless a recipe states otherwise.

❷ Use the Splashguard to keep flour, icing sugar and other powders contained during mixing.

BALLOON WHISK

The Balloon Whisk is perfect for creating foamy whipped mixtures; it is shaped to trap air easily whilst mixing, to create maximum volume in the ingredients being whisked. It can successfully whisk just a single egg white, but is also able to handle up to 12 or 16 if using the Major Kitchen Machine.

Batters

Flour, milk and egg batters for pancakes, crepes, dropped scones, toad-in-the-hole and Yorkshire Puddings can be made in seconds using the Whisk. Add the flour, eggs and about half the milk, and using the Whisk on minimum up to speed 3, mix to a thick, smooth batter, then gradually whisk in the remaining liquid.

Egg Whites

Whether you are making a pavlova, nut meringue, meringue pie or pudding topping or whisking egg whites for soufflés and mousses, the Whisk will produce perfect results every time. Whisk egg whites on maximum speed. When whisking egg whites they first become foamy, then increase in volume and become stiffer, although still having a wet appearance, known as soft peak stage. Recipes where egg whites are folded in, such as mousses and soufflés often refer to a soft peak. If you lift the Whisk from the bowl

at this stage, the egg white will hold its shape, but the peak will flop. If a recipe calls for stiff peaks, meringue for instance, the egg whites will appear dry and the peak will not flop.

Mayonnaise

Mayonnaise is often considered difficult to make, probably because without an electric whisk, it can often curdle. By adding the olive oil to the egg yolks whilst the Whisk is running on maximum, you can be sure they will emulsify.

Whipped Desserts

There is a whole multitude of recipes you can make with the Whisk. For example, whisking

cream and egg whites for soufflés; cream and wine, or sherry, for syllabubs or egg yolks and fruit purées for mousse.

Whipping Cream

The Whisk is perfect for whipping cream to top tarts and trifles, fill sponges, cakes and profiteroles, or for adding to mousses, soufflés and cheesecakes. Use the Stainless Steel Bowl if you have one, to keep the cream cool. Whip the cream to soft peaks using as low a speed from minimum up to speed 2 to 3. It is better not to whip it too quickly to ensure that it does not over whisk to become butter.

Whisked Sponges

Whether making a fatless sponge, Swiss roll, roulade or butter enriched Genoese sponge, this method of making a cake relies entirely on the volume of air trapped in the egg mixture, to make it rise. To achieve a good sponge, the eggs and sugar must be whisked until really thick and

creamy; the mixture should be thick enough to leave a trail on the surface when the Whisk is lifted.

Start the Whisk on minimum speed and fairly quickly increase to maximum. Make sure you lightly fold in the flour and any other remaining ingredients to keep as much air in the mixture as possible.

HINTS AND TIPS

❶ Keep eggs at room temperature, or remove from the refrigerator 30 minutes before whisking for best results.

❷ Always ensure that the Whisk and Bowl are scrupulously clean before whisking egg whites. Any grease will prevent the egg whites whisking to full volume.

❸ Make sure that the Splashguard is removed before whisking, so that the air can circulate freely.

DOUGH HOOK

Making bread using the Kenwood Chef is one of the most popular uses. The Dough Hook takes all the hard work out of making bread. It perfectly combines the ingredients to produce a soft dough after which it requires vigorous kneading to make the dough elastic. This develops the gluten in the flour, and ultimately produces a well risen loaf. The Dough Hook carries out this kneading process; the planetary action ensures that the Hook is gentle, yet firm, producing perfectly smooth and elastic dough.

Breads, Rolls, Buns, Pizza and Sweet Dough

Whichever type of bread you wish to make, the Dough Hook will mix and knead it for you. Start the Dough Hook on minimum to mix the ingredients, then increase to speed 1 for kneading. Once you have mastered basic white bread, try wholemeal, granary or rye, or

sweet breads such as brioche, stollen, Chelsea buns, as well as shaped rolls, Danish pastries, and of course pizza bases.

Soft Yeast Doughs and Batter

Some yeast based cakes and desserts, such as savarin, kugelhopf and rum babas are made with a thick batter or very soft dough. These confections

benefit from being mixed with the Dough Hook, as the beating process is necessary to develop the gluten.

The Dough Hook can also be used to mix in extra ingredients such as dried fruit, or nuts after the initial rising.

Use the Dough Hook to mix the batter for blinis - Russian pancakes made from buckwheat flour and yeast.

Using Fresh Yeast

Most yeast based recipes now recommend using fast action dried yeast. It has revolutionised bread making because it can be directly sprinkled into the flour, before the liquid is added and the dough kneaded together, using the Dough Hook. It is, however, completely interchangeable with fresh yeast, which can give better results for heavily fruited and egg and fat enriched doughs. Fresh yeast can be bought from some

Supermarkets, which have in-store bakeries, bakers' shops and good health food shops. It should be stored in the refrigerator and used within about 3 days. However it may be frozen - freeze in usable quantities and use within 3 months. As a rough guide 15g (½oz) fresh yeast or a 7g sachet (1½ tsp) fast action dried yeast is sufficient to raise 750g (1½lb) flour. Enriched dough recipes may suggest a little more yeast as the rise is more difficult. To use fresh yeast simply blend with a little of the liquid specified

in the recipe, then mix into the flour with the remaining liquids.

Pasta Dough

If you are making Pasta Dough for use with the Italian Pasta Maker, or for pasta dough to roll out, then use the Dough Hook on speed 3 to 4 to mix the ingredients for the pasta dough. For details see page 80.

HINTS AND TIPS

❶ Never exceed the maximum capacities or you will overload the motor. For maximum quantities, check the instructions booklet with your particular model.

❷ Always use liquid which is lukewarm; if it is too hot it could kill the yeast, and if too cold, the yeast will not work.

❸ Keep the yeast mix in the Kenwood Bowl to rise, then the Dough Hook can easily be re-inserted, to knock back the dough before shaping.

LIQUIDISER

The Liquidiser or blender as it is sometimes known, is used for puréeing and blending a multitude of ingredients. It has extremely sharp stainless steel blades that rotate at very high speed. The food items placed in the Liquidiser jug are forced to move around and across the blades. This either finely chops or if continued purées the contents to a smooth texture. The Liquidiser usually purées food more finely than a food processor.

The range of Kenwood Liquidisers includes stainless steel, glass and acrylic jugs. The stainless steel version, in addition to being extremely stylish has the bonus of keeping ingredients cool, which is fantastic for cocktails, fruit drinks and milkshakes. It also has a larger capacity and can blend up to 1.5 litres (2½ pints).

The glass and acrylic jugs will process up to 1.5 litres. The acrylic jug makes a light and easy to handle version. Both are transparent so are excellent for seeing exactly what is happening during operation. The glass is also scratch resistant, which is especially good with hard spices, sugar and ice. The uses for the Liquidiser are almost endless; below are some examples of how it can help you in food and recipe preparation.

Biscuit Crumbs

Biscuits for dessert bases and cheesecakes can be briefly processed in the Liquidiser to make crumbs. It is best to break them into pieces and add to the Liquidiser Jug, through the filler cap opening whilst the machine is running. Make in batches, rather than over-fill the jug.

Breadcrumbs

You may use the Liquidiser to make fresh breadcrumbs from either white or brown bread. Cut the crusts off the slices of bread and cut into cubes or tear into pieces, small enough to fit through the filler cap. Turn the Liquidiser to maximum speed and drop the bread pieces through the filler cap.

Avoid using very fresh bread as it tends to cling together; one day old bread is best. If you wish to make a large quantity of breadcrumbs process in batches for best results.

Chopping Nuts

Use shelled nuts only. Add through the lid via the filler cap opening, whilst the Liquidiser is running. It is best for smaller quantities only. Use the Food Processing Attachment for larger quantities of nuts.

Crushing Ice

Ice cubes may be crushed for adding to drinks or as part of a drink. If crushing ice on its own, always add a little water with the ice cubes. Preferably use the glass or metal jug for drinks containing ice or crushing ice cubes.

Drinks

From milkshakes and smoothies to alcoholic cocktails the Liquidiser will blend you a drink within seconds. Just add milk, fresh fruit, such as strawberries or mango and a scoop of ice cream to the Liquidiser jug and blend to a thick, frothy shake; or try a banana nut shake. Add a sliced banana, an individual hazelnut yogurt and 300ml (½ pint) milk and whiz together.

Mayonnaise

The Liquidiser may be used to make mayonnaise, as an alternative to the Whisk, if wished. Add the egg yolks, seasoning and vinegar or lemon juice to the Liquidiser jug and then place on the Kenwood Chef or Major. With the machine running, remove the filler cap and pour the oil in a slow steady stream into the Liquidiser jug.

LIQUIDISER

The shearing action of the stainless steel blade will emulsify the egg yolks and oil to make a thick smooth mayonnaise. Make at least a two egg yolk quantity to ensure the blades are covered.

Pâtés

Smooth chicken liver pâté or vegetable pâtés and dips such as garlic and bean pâté, hummus or avocado dip are all successful in the Liquidiser. To make a quick avocado dip add 2 chopped ripe avocado pears with 60ml (4 tbsp) each of crème fraîche and mayonnaise and the juice of a lime or lemon to the Liquidiser jug and blend together. Season and chill to serve.

It is probably best to blend pâtés and dips on a slower speed or pulse and you may need to scrape down the contents of the jug with the Spatula.

Sauces

Savoury sauces such as mushroom, red pepper and tomato, for serving with pasta, fish, burgers, meatballs or steaks can be blended in the Liquidiser. Cook the sauce first then blend to a purée.

Soft fruits such as raspberries and strawberries or mangoes can be puréed from raw with a little sugar and fruit juice, wine or water, whilst hard fruits like apples, plums and cranberries are best cooked in a little water with sugar until tender before puréeing.

Even smooth sauces or gravies, which have inadvertently gone lumpy during making, can be rescued by a quick whiz in the Liquidiser!

Soups

Many vegetable soups like pea, carrot, mushroom, asparagus and artichoke are puréed after the vegetables are cooked to produce a smooth velvety soup. Add the cooked vegetables and liquor and blend until smooth on maximum speed. If necessary process the soup in two batches.

Cold vegetable soups like gazpacho are processed raw. Seafood bisques can also be liquidised in a similar fashion.

TO USE THE LIQUIDISER

❶ Make sure the sealing ring is in place in the blade unit to prevent any leaks, then place the jug in the blade unit and turn firmly to lock.

❷ Do not over-fill. It is often better to blend food in two or three batches, rather than add too much to the jug.

❸ Add the ingredients to the Liquidiser jug and place the lid with filler cap in place before attaching to the Kenwood Chef or Major high speed outlet.

❹ Always allow hot liquids to cool before blending just in case you haven't fitted the lid securely.

❺ Always add dry ingredients to the Liquidiser whilst it is running. Add through the filler cap.

❻ Process the ingredients in the Liquidiser on maximum speed unless stated otherwise in a specific recipe.

HINTS AND TIPS

❶ Never fit or remove the jug with the blade unit resting on a work surface or other flat surface as it will interfere with the safety interlock tabs, which need to drop down during assembly.

❷ It is worth wetting the sealing ring before fitting to the blade unit to ensure a good seal.

❸ Never run the Liquidiser for longer than one minute as it may overheat. Switch off as soon as you have processed the food.

❹ Always empty the jug before unscrewing the blade unit.

❺ Avoid processing hard spices, such as cloves, dill seeds and cumin seeds in the acrylic Liquidiser jug as they may damage it.

❻ Use the pulse setting for thick mixtures, to get the ingredients moving over the blades.

MULTI FOOD GRINDER

There are numerous delicious and tempting recipes for using minced meat; the Multi Food Grinder enables you to make your own mince and so control the type of meat and the amount of fat in the mince. Not only can you mince meat but also chicken, duck, fish, rabbit, nuts and vegetables to make pâtés, terrines, burgers, fish cakes and fillings for pasta, pasta dishes and pies.

GRINDER SCREENS

With the selection of mincing screens you can produce different thicknesses and textures. There are three different sizes: fine, medium and coarse.

Fine Screen

Use the fine screen for raw meat and fish when you want a fairly smooth texture in foods like sausages and pâtés. Fillings for snacks and starters, like Thai-style fish balls, Chinese wantons and filo parcels or for meat filled ravioli style pasta can all be made with finely minced fish, duck, beef or lamb. Use this screen for mincing cooked meat for beef or lamb kebbe, Shepherd's pie and for small nuts.

The fine screen is perfect for making a quick smoked salmon pâté. Mince smoked salmon trimmings and mix with a little cream, melted butter, lemon juice and seasoning. Chill for 30 minutes and you have a perfect salmon starter.

Medium Screen

The medium screen is the ideal size for mincing beef for burgers, chilli-con-carne, meat loaves, moussaka and to make the filling for Mexican taco shells; or mince

lamb for Shepherd's pie, meatballs and koftas. Try low fat chicken for burgers as an alternative to beef. This screen is also useful for vegetables, hard cheese and nuts.

Coarse Screen

Coarse textured sausage fillings are best made with this screen. You can also use the coarse screen for mincing raw pork, liver and onion for a coarse pâté or for meat terrines.

Candied peel can be minced through the coarse screen for use in puddings and cakes. Also try fresh citrus peels to use in marmalade making.

Hard cheese can be cut into pieces and passed through the Multi Food Grinder, before adding to quiches, fondues and sauces.

USING THE GRINDER

❶ Fit the scroll inside the Grinder body and then fit the cutter blade. It is important to make sure the cutting side is facing outwards.

❷ Fit the selected screen making sure the notch fits over the pin in the Grinder body and secure with the ring nut.

❸ Place the food to be minced in the tray and using the pusher, gently push the food through. Do not overload the Grinder; only push through one piece at a time. Meat should be cut into 2.5cm (1 inch) wide strips.

Other food items should be cut into similar sized pieces, if large.

HINTS AND TIPS

❶ Push a couple of pieces of bread through the Multi Food Grinder at the end of mincing to help push out any remaining meat or fish.

❷ Use the cover as a dish to collect the mince as it is extruded.

❸ Keep your Sausage Filler and Kebbe Maker with the extra screens inside the specially designed pusher, for easy storage.

MULTI FOOD GRINDER / SAUSAGE FILLER AND KEBBE MAKER

SAUSAGE FILLER

Across the World there is a vast array of different types of sausages, with each country making distinctive varieties. Countries like France, Germany and Italy have as many varieties as regions.

Fresh sausages are highly perishable, so what better than to make your own. You can also experiment and use any combination of meats and additional flavourings you prefer, including herbs like rosemary, sage and thyme to fennel seeds, garlic, chilli, ginger or lemon. It is also possible to make fish, seafood, nut or lentil sausages.

Most sausage fillings have breadcrumbs added to bulk the ingredients and lighten the texture and usually include egg to bind the ingredients together. You can find a selection of recipes in the recipe section of this book.

TO USE THE SAUSAGE FILLER

The filler is attached to the Mincer body, so after mincing the meat, remove the screen and cutter and replace with the base plate and nozzle. There are two nozzles, one for thin sausages, and the other for thick sausages.

You may use skins or roll sausages in breadcrumbs or seasoned flour before cooking.

If using skins it is often easier to feed the sausage skin on to the nozzle before attaching to the machine. Moisten the end of the nozzle with water and slip on the skin. Again there are two sizes, standard size casings for the large nozzle, are from pigs and small casings from sheep, for the small

nozzle. Your local butcher should be able to supply these. Keep the casings in a bowl of water in the fridge, as this makes them easier to use. Any left over may be frozen in a little water.

FILLING SAUSAGE SKINS

❶ Place the sausage filling on the feed tray. Switch the Chef or Major to speed 3 to 4.

❷ Using the pusher, gently push the filling into the Grinder body. Hold the end of the sausage casing and ease the skin off the Sausage Filler nozzle as it fills.

❸ When the casing is full and the filling has all been used, twist the casing to form sausages of approximately 10cm (4 inches) for standard sausages and 4cm (1½ inches) for cocktail sausages.

KEBBE MAKER

Kebbe is a traditional Middle Eastern dish comprising of a cylinder-like shell made from meat, usually lamb and bulghur

wheat, the centre is then stuffed with a spiced minced lamb filling and the ends are sealed to form a parcel. These are then deep-fried.

To make the outer shell requires great expertise; the Kebbe Maker will shape the outer shell ready for stuffing. Recipes for both meat and vegetarian kebbe can be found in the recipe section.

TO USE THE KEBBE MAKER

❶ After mincing the meat for the kebbe shells and filling, remove the mincing screen and blade and replace with the Kebbe Maker, fitting the notch over the pin in the Grinder body. Fit the cone and screw the ring nut on.

❷ Place the kebbe mixture on the feed tray. Switch the machine to speed 1. Using the pusher, gently push the mixture through.

❸ Cut the kebbe shells at 7.5cm (3 inch) intervals and lay each tube on a tray. When all the mixture has been shaped, fill and cook as desired.

PRO SLICER/GRATER

The Pro Slicer/Grater makes light work of preparing many foodstuffs, in particular vegetables and salad ingredients. The Pro Slicer/Grater consists of a flat plate which rotates and quickly slices or shreds food, ensuring a uniform size. It is the perfect attachment for producing large quantities of prepared food, as it is a continuous process where food is fed in through the feed tube and comes out through the outlet in the base into a collecting bowl.

THICK SLICING / COARSE SHREDDING PLATE

This is a reversible plate with a thick slicing blade on one side and coarse shredding cutters on the other. The thick slicer is perfect for slicing beetroot, carrots, cabbage, carrots, courgette, leeks, onions, peppers and potatoes as well as cheese and apples, bananas and pears. Place long thin foods like carrots and leeks vertically in the feed tube for even slicing and peel and cut the onions into quarters.

The coarse shredding side of this plate can be used for many of the ingredients suggested for slicing. It is especially good for cheese, carrots for salad and coleslaw, apples, courgettes and raw potatoes for rösti.

THIN SLICING / FINE SHREDDING PLATE

This is another reversible plate, like the one above, but with a thinner slicing blade and a finer shredder. The thin slicer is useful for potatoes or parsnips to make crisps and for thinly sliced onions and cucumber.

The fine shredder is suitable for any of the ingredients mentioned above, for the coarse shredder, but will give a finer shred.

Grated carrots tossed in lemon juice are perfect for adding to salads.

THIN CHIPPER PLATE

The thin chipper plate cuts thin 'julienne style' stick shapes. As well as producing super thin French fries, you can prepare thin sticks of carrots or courgettes for a stir-fry or cucumber or celeriac for salads and dips.

BEAN SLICER

The Pro Slicer/Grater has an additional feature, perfect for cutting green and runner beans. Runner beans need to be cut into long thin strips of similar thickness, so they all cook in the same amount of time.

This can be difficult and time consuming by hand. To prepare, just trim the beans and using the thick slicing shredding plate, slicing side uppermost, feed the beans through the bean slicer opening. Use the machine on minimum speed.

HOW TO USE THE PRO SLICER/GRATER

❶ Both the slicing shredding plates are reversible, with the slicer on one side and the shredder on the other; make sure you select the correct side and place uppermost on the shaft.

❷ Fit the lid and turn clockwise until it clicks into position. Attach to the Chef and place the Bowl underneath the food outlet to catch the sliced or shredded food.

❸ Place the food in the feed tube and process on minimum speed or speed 1.

HINTS AND TIPS

❶ Fill the feed tube before switching on the machine.

❷ Always use the pusher to push food down the feed tube.

❸ Fill the feed tube solidly to prevent it slipping sideways during operation and so ensure even slices or shreds.

ROTO FOOD CUTTER

Use as an alternative to the Pro Slicer/Grater for preparing vegetable and salad ingredients as well as cheese, nuts and chocolate. This is a more traditional Slicer Shredder and uses drums which slowly revolve to slice or shred the food. The slower shredding makes it particularly suitable for cheese and chocolate, because there is less friction and heat produced; especially important with chocolate, so that it does not begin to soften during shredding. There are four drums; two for slicing and two for shredding.

SHREDDING DRUMS

There is a fine shredding drum - number 1 and a coarse shredding drum - number 2. Both drums may be used for shredding cheese, but the fine one is best for hard cheese like Parmesan, Pecorino and Grana Padano.

Other cheeses suitable for shredding, mainly with the coarse shredding drum, include Cheddar Emmental, Gruyère and Manchego.

For chocolate, the coarse drum produces large shreds of chocolate; perfect for decorating cakes and desserts or sprinkling over hot milky drinks.

Nuts can be finely chopped using the coarse shredding drum or coarsely ground using the fine shredding drum. Use to prepare almonds, walnuts, hazelnuts and pecan nuts.

Carrots, potatoes, cucumber, parsnips and courgettes can all be shredded using the Roto Food Cutter. Cut carrots and courgettes, cucumber and parsnips into short lengths 5-6cm (2-2½ inches) long and place next to each other to fill the feed tube, leaving room for the pusher.

SLICING DRUMS

Again there are two drums; a thin slicing drum - number 3 and a thick slicing drum - number 4. Use the thin slicer for apples, nuts, chocolate, onions, cucumber and potatoes.

The thick slicing drum will also slice nuts, and vegetables. It is ideal for slicing beetroot and both red and white cabbage.

To prepare the cabbage, cut into wedges, remove the stalks. Place in the feed tube and keep upright. Apply a steady pressure with the pusher, and use the Roto Food Cutter on speed 3 to 4.

HOW TO USE THE ROTO FOOD CUTTER

❶ Select the drum required for slicing or shredding and fit into the body of the roto food cutter.

❷ Secure with the drum retainer, making sure it is locked into position.

❸ Insert into the slow speed outlet on the front of the machine, turning it both ways until it is located into position.

❹ Place the Kenwood Bowl beneath the outlet for collecting the prepared food.

❺ Fill the feed tube with the chosen ingredients and switch on. Use the pusher to gently push down. Use speeds 3 to 4.

HINTS AND TIPS

❶ Always make sure the feed tube is packed with the food to be shredded or sliced, so that it doesn't slip sideways during processing. This is especially important with the slicer drums for even slices.

❷ Fill the feed tube with food before switching on the Chef or Major, as this will give the best, most even results.

❸ Make sure the food only reaches about two-thirds of the way up the feed tube so there is still room to insert the pusher. This way you can locate the pusher and apply steady pressure, without it slipping.

POTATO PREP ATTACHMENT

Potatoes and other root vegetables are an essential part of a well balanced diet, but the regular preparation of these vegetables is not one that most people relish. The Potato Prep Attachment will as its name suggests, peel potatoes. It will also prepare other root vegetables, like turnips, carrots and parsnips.

The Potato Prep Attachment has a bowl with abrasive sides. The base rotates and moves the vegetables over the abrasive surfaces, gently removing the peel. You can stop the Potato Prep Attachment at any time, so if wished you could use it just to clean vegetables which is perfect for new potatoes.

As it removes only the slightest amount of skin, the maximum amount of nutrients are retained in the vegetables, especially as they are in maximum concentration just under the skin.

For an attractive vegetable accompaniment make ball shaped vegetables. Cut carrots and parsnips or potatoes into regular shaped pieces about 4cm (1½ inches) long, place them in the Potato Prep Attachment, with sufficient water to cover the base plate.

Switch the Potato Prep Attachment on and peel the vegetables to remove any skin, and they become rounded into the shape of balls. Rinse the shaped vegetables in cold water to remove any remains from the peeling and shaping. Cook in boiling water, steam, or roast as appropriate.

TO USE THE POTATO PREP

❶ Fit the rotating plate inside the bowl and add sufficient cold water to just cover it.

❷ Place the vegetables in the bowl and snap the lid on top.

❸ Fit the bowl, turning anticlockwise, to the Chef or Major, making sure the metal pin of the mixer head is located in the plastic hole at the top of the rotating plate.

❹ Switch on to speed 2-3 and leave to prepare and peel the chosen vegetables.

❺ Make sure you rinse the vegetables in cold water after peeling to clean off any loose peelings before cooking.

HINTS AND TIPS

❶ For best results do not overfill the Potato Prep Attachment. Peel the vegetables in batches, if necessary.

❷ Make sure potatoes are all roughly the same size. Baby new potatoes can be used whole, whilst large potatoes should be cut into even sized pieces.

❸ Cut large vegetables, such as carrots and turnips or parsnips, into even smaller sized pieces.

❹ New potatoes will peel more rapidly than old potatoes. It may only take a minute or so for new potatoes, but five minutes or more for old potatoes. The time taken will also vary depending on the quantity of vegetables in the Potato Prep Attachment.

COLANDER & SIEVE

The texture and appearance of food is just as important as the flavour. A perfectly smooth purée is part of the balance of colours, flavours and consistency within a meal. When smoothness and consistency of a dish is important, making sure you achieve this effect is essential.

The Colander and Sieve has a rotating paddle which gently pushes the food ingredients through the sieve screen to achieve this. The Colander and Sieve will purée fruit and vegetables, soup and sauces as well as making biscuit into crumb and sifting flour.

There is a choice of two screens for the Sieve; one fine and the other coarser. The screens may be used either rough side uppermost or smooth side uppermost, depending on the ingredients you wish to sieve.

FINE SCREEN SIEVE

The smooth side of the fine screen is perfect for sifting flour when making cakes and bread and can be sifted straight into the Kenwood Bowl for mixing.

The rough side of the fine screen is perfect for puréeing soft fruits such as raspberries and strawberries for making fresh fruit coulis, as not only will the fruit be puréed, but the pips are removed at the same time, a fiddly and time consuming job if done by hand. Sweeten the purée with icing sugar if wished.

COARSE SCREEN SIEVE

Poached fruits such as plums, apricots and damsons may be sieved through the smooth side of the Sieve. The purée is perfect for making fruit fools, mousses, whips and sauces.

The rough side is better for more fibrous foods such as rhubarb or banana. Use the rough side for potatoes, celeriac and sweet potatoes to make smooth lump free mash; just add a little butter and seasoning after sieving.

Digestive biscuits may be crushed using the Colander and Sieve to make crumbs for dessert bases and cheesecakes.

If you make preserves such as fruit butter or cheeses, pass the fruit pulp through the Sieve. Apples can be passed through either Sieve but use the fine Sieve for gooseberries or blackberries, to catch the seeds. Fruit curds, made from lemons, oranges or blueberries all need to be strained after cooking.

TO USE THE COLANDER AND SIEVE

❶ Place the Colander bowl on top of a round Kenwood Bowl, and insert the screen required.

❷ Fit the paddle to the Chef or Major Kitchen Machine and place the bowl and Sieve in position, then lower the paddle.

❸ Add the food to be sieved and process at minimum speed. Increase the speed to 1 or 2, but reduce it if the food starts to splash.

HINTS AND TIPS

❶ Make sure the paddle reaches far enough down onto the screen. The paddle blades should bend slightly against the Sieve screen, yet still retain a slight flex. Adjust the paddle if necessary using the nut at the top. Refer to your instruction leaflet for further details.

❷ The two screens may be used together to achieve an extra smooth result. This can be particularly useful if the food contains tiny pips.

❸ Allow cooked food to cool slightly, before passing through the Sieve.

❹ Add up to a maximum of 450g (1lb) of food. If necessary process in batches, cleaning the Sieve between each batch.

PASTA FRESCA

Home-made fresh pasta is the best pasta and is virtually impossible to beat. The flavour of freshly cooked pasta, made with eggs is incomparable. The best results are achieved if you use a special flour, such as the fine textured wheat flour type '00' which is available from Italian delicatessens and some large supermarkets. If this is not available, the nearest equivalent is strong plain white bread flour.

The pasta dough can be flavoured with herbs, tomato purée, spinach, squid ink or for a nuttier flavour use wholemeal flour. The herbs give a speckled effect, whilst the spinach is used for green pasta and the squid ink for black pasta.

Once you have made the pasta dough using the K Beater, the Pasta Fresca (model A910) will extrude the dough using the maccheroni rigati die.

PASTA FRESCA DIES

There are a wide variety of dies available to produce a selection of

pasta. The high quality bronze dies ensure home made pasta, has a rough textured surface to hold sauce for an authentic full flavour. Whichever type of pasta you select it is important to produce a dough of the correct consistency. The basic recipe for pasta dough is 125g (4½oz) plain wheat flour '00' grade to one medium egg. The mix should resemble fine breadcrumbs after mixing together with the K Beater.

There is a choice of 14 different pasta shapes and sizes from fusilli spiral tubes to pappardelle ribbons.

An optional biscuit maker die with stainless steel shaper can be used with this attachment to make home made biscuits in a variety of shapes.

HOW TO USE THE PASTA MAKER

❶ Fit the Pasta Fresca to the Kenwood Chef or Major with the preferred screen attached.

❷ With the machine running on speed 2 to 3 drop small amounts of the pasta dough mix into the feed tube. Do not overfill. Allow the dough to clear through before adding more.

❸ To encourage the dough mix through the Pasta Fresca softly push down into the scroll using

the spanner/spanner. Don't use anything else or press too hard otherwise you may damage the pasta machine.

❹ To change or remove the screen, remove the securing nut and switch on to speed 1. This will eject the screen.

HINTS AND TIPS

❶ Dough that is too dry or that is pushed through the machine too quickly may damage the machine. Make sure you follow the recipe given on page 80 or in your instruction booklet.

❷ Fresh pasta is best left to dry slightly for about 30 minutes before cooking, or can be left to completely dry. Rigatoni and macaroni are best cooked within 4 hours. Spaghetti, tagliatelle and lasagne may be placed in a plastic bag and frozen.

❸ The easiest way to clean the screens is to leave them to dry over-night or even place in the freezer for an hour, then use the cleaning tool provided to poke the pasta out of the extruder holes. The Maccheroni rigati, Maccheroni lisci and Bucatini dies can be pulled apart to assist with the cleaning process.

ITALIAN PASTA MAKER & ATTACHMENTS

Many pasta recipes use flat sheets or ribbons of pasta. The Italian Pasta Maker (model A970) makes the preparation of this type of pasta easy. It rolls out the dough to the correct thickness and cuts it into a range of different types of pasta with the help of the Attachments.

The dough for this machine is similar to the one for Pasta Maker opposite. It is important to make a dough of the correct consistency. Follow recipe on page 80. After mixing the flour and eggs with the Dough Hook to a crumbly consistency it is kneaded together to form a smooth dough.

HOW TO USE THE ITALIAN PASTA MAKER

❶ Fit the Italian Pasta Maker attachment to the slow speed outlet on the front of the Chef or Major, using the connecting adaptor. Refer to your instruction manual if necessary.

❷ Set the adjustable knob on the side of the Italian Pasta Maker to number 1, the thickest setting. Sprinkle a little flour over the rollers to make sure the pasta dough does not stick.

❸ Flatten a piece of dough, turn the machine on to speed 1 and feed the dough through the rollers. Fold the strips of dough in

three, rotate and pass through the machine again.

❹ Adjust the setting of the rollers by one to two numbers and guide the dough through the Italian Pasta Maker rollers again.

❺ Continue progressing up through the settings, re-rolling the pasta each time until you achieve the desired thickness.

A pasta thickness of 5 to 7 is recommended.

This dough can be cut into lengths and used for making lasagne, ravioli or cannelloni. For lasagne cut into rectangles approximately 10 x 15cm (4 x 6 inches), for ravioli 30-40cm (12-16 inch) long strips and for cannelloni 10cm

(4 inch) squares, add your chosen filling and roll up. For ribbon pasta and spaghetti use one of the additional Cutting Attachments.

ADDITIONAL CUTTING ATTACHMENTS

There is a choice of four optional extra Cutting Attachments which fit the Italian Pasta Maker. There are three varieties of thin ribbon pasta cutters. There is Trenette which is about 1.5mm ($\frac{1}{16}$ inch) wide, the slightly wider Tagliolini measuring 4mm ($\frac{1}{8}$ inch) wide and the universal Tagliatelle cutter which produces 7mm ($\frac{1}{3}$ inch) wide strips of pasta.

The remaining cutter is a traditional Spaghetti cutter.

TO USE THE CUTTING ATTACHMENTS

Whichever attachment you select, the pasta dough must first be rolled out using the Pasta Maker. Fit the chosen cutter and feed the rolled out pasta sheet through the Cutting Attachment which will cut the pasta into strips of Trenette, Tagliolini, Tagliatelle or Spaghetti.

You may find it easier to cut the pasta sheet first into 25-30cm (10-12 inch) lengths, before feeding through the Cutting Attachment.

HINTS AND TIPS

❶ Leave the pasta dough to rest for 10-15 minutes, wrapped in clear film or a clean tea towel. It will make rolling and cutting the pasta much easier.

❷ If the pasta starts to stick to the rollers, dust with a little flour.

❸ The thickness of the pasta depends on how you are going to serve it. It should be very thin for a butter sauce, slightly thicker for a cream sauce and slightly thicker still for a meat or tomato sauce. Experiment to find out which thickness you prefer.

❹ Always switch off the Chef or Major before changing the roller for any of the Cutting Attachments.

MULTI-MILL

The Multi-Mill is the perfect multi-task attachment for all small and often awkward or time-consuming food preparation processes. Not only will it mill or grind hard items, such as spices, the sharp blades make it the perfect mini chopper and blender.

CHOPPING

The Multi-Mill has sharp blades, ideal for chopping small quantities, which are awkward to chop by hand and insufficient to make good use of the other Kenwood attachments. This mini chopper will chop small quantities of fresh herbs, garlic and onion. Peel and quarter the onion before adding to the Multi-Mill.

It will also quickly chop or finely grind nuts for adding to cakes and biscuit mixes or for decorating and finishing desserts.

If you only need one to two spoonfuls of breadcrumbs use the Multi-Mill rather than the liquidiser or food processor.

MILLING AND GRINDING

The Multi-Mill will mill whole spices coarsely or to a powder; perfect for curries and marinades.

Whole black peppercorns can be coarsely milled for coating steaks and poultry or adding to sausage mixes; or finer for marinades and general seasoning.

The aroma and flavour of freshly ground coffee beans is hard to beat. Prepare the amount required for immediate use. The Multi-Mill can mill small amounts, just enough for one cup. Again use the mill to obtain the desired coarseness, fine for filter machines or medium ground for cafetières, percolators and jugs.

BLENDING

As a mini blender the Multi-Mill will purée small quantities of food, which would become lost in the base of a full-sized liquidiser. Fruit purées and sauces, baby food, curry and spice pastes, nut butters, pesto sauce and salad dressings can all be prepared within seconds.

Make a quick marinade, perfect for meat, poultry or fish; just place a peeled garlic clove, 1 small red chilli, 2 sprigs of parsley, 45ml (3 tbsp) lemon juice and 30ml (2 tbsp) olive oil in the Multi-Mill. Blend for a few seconds until the garlic, chilli and herbs are chopped, then pour over fish fillets, kebabs, pork chops or chicken breasts and leave to marinate before grilling or barbecuing.

The Multi-Mill comes complete with a set of three storage jars with lids, so after preparation the contents of the Multi-Mill can be transferred to one of the jars until required. As the jars are made of glass, strong aromas like garlic, aromatic spices and coffee will not taint them, unlike many plastic storage containers.

TO USE THE MULTI-MILL

1 Do not over-fill. Add ingredients up to the maximum level only.

2 Make sure the rubber seal is correctly in place on the blade unit to prevent any leaks and lower on to the top of the jar and screw together.

3 Use the Multi-Mill on maximum speed unless stated otherwise in a specific recipe.

HINTS AND TIPS

1 Never run the Multi-Mill for longer than two minutes as it may over-heat. Most processes take less than one minute.

2 If chopping herbs they are best chopped dry. If moist, dry on absorbent kitchen paper first. Do not over-fill. If necessary process the herbs in two batches.

3 When making baby foods add a little liquid to the cooked ingredients before blending and puréeing, for best results.

4 If chopping hard items, such as fresh ginger or lemon grass, cut into thick slices first.

GRAIN MILL

The Grain Mill attachment uses an authentic milling action to quickly process grains and pulses. It will mill them to any grain size you require, from coarse granules to a very fine flour.

By milling your own flour at home you can be sure of the initial quality of the grain and also that it is not contaminated by other grains; vital for anyone with an allergy to certain flours. Coeliacs are unable to eat grains containing gluten found in wheat, rye, barley and possibly oats and spelt grain. Spelt grain is an ancient grain, which has not been modified over the centuries, and although it contains gluten, many coeliac sufferers find they are able to tolerate this flour. However if you are allergic to gluten make sure you check with your Doctor before including spelt flour in your diet.

The Grain Mill makes it possible to produce alternative gluten free flours from rice, buckwheat, millet or chick peas.

Rice flour makes a great alternative for pastry; whilst buckwheat, bulghur wheat and chick pea flours are used extensively for traditional flat breads and pancakes in Eastern Europe and India. These flours are only available in specialist shops, but can easily be made using the Grain Mill. It will of course also mill the more traditional cereals such as wheat, rye, husked barley, pearl barley and oats.

TO MAKE BROWN RICE PASTRY

Both brown and white rice can be milled to make a flour, suitable as an alternative to wheat flour. Brown rice flour imparts a nuttier flavour and is ideal for making pastry for flans, tarts and pies, both sweet and savoury.

For a 23cm (9 inch) flan case

❶ Using the finest setting on the Grain Mill, mill 115g (4oz) brown rice straight into the Kenwood Bowl.

❷ Add 75g (3oz) butter or margarine, cut into small cubes and using the K Beater mix on minimum speed until it resembles fine breadcrumbs. Add 30-45ml (2-3 tbsp) cold water and mix to a soft dough.

❸ Either roll out on a surface dusted with rice flour and use to line 23cm (9 inch) flan tin, or press the mixture into the tin using your fingers and the back of a spoon.

❹ Bake blind at 190°C/375°F/Gas 5 for 15 minutes and use in the same way as a traditional flan case, with a sweet or savoury filling.

HINTS AND TIPS

❶ Sometimes grains left in the scroll of the Grain Mill prevent the removal of the attachment from the machine. Make sure all the grains have been milled before detaching, to prevent this occurring.

❷ For the freshest results always mill grains or pulses as required.

❸ Make sure the grains are dry before milling; otherwise the Mill may become clogged.

TO USE THE GRAIN MILL

❶ Fill the hopper with grains or pulses, then select the desired grain size from 1 for very fine flour through to 6 for a coarse grain.

❷ Place the Kenwood Bowl under the Grain Mill outlet. Switch the machine to maximum speed and collect the milled flour.

❸ Shake out any loose grains and if necessary take the Grain Mill apart and brush out the inside, but avoid immersing the internal parts in water.

THE CITRUS PRESS OR JUICER

The Citrus Press or Juicer makes squeezing citrus juice extremely easy and quick to prepare. Citrus juices are packed full of vitamins which are quickly lost on storage, so freshly squeezed is the perfect way to drink them.

The Citrus Press fits the KM series 300-800 range of Kenwood Kitchen Machines and stainless steel sieve.

The Citrus Juicer fits the KM001-KM007 range and includes a stainless steel sieve.

Whichever model you have they will both extract the citrus juice from oranges, lemons, limes and grapefruits. The cone or reamer rotates, which presses the juice from the citrus half, catching the pips in the sieve and the juice in the bowl beneath.

The juice can be used for drinks or for making desserts, such as pies, sorbets, soufflés and jellies. It can be used for preserves such as marmalades, curds and fruit butters. It is so quick to use the Citrus Press or Juicer for many food preparation tasks where the juice of a lemon, orange or lime is added as an ingredient such as dips, dressings and sauces, or to prevent the discolouration of fruits or vegetables.

The citrus reamer can also be used for extracting the pulp from large ripe tomatoes. Cut the top off the tomato then place on the reamer to remove the centres.

The shells can then be filled with a savoury mousse as an appetising starter, or stuffed with vegetables or rice and served as a main meal accompaniment or vegetarian alternative.

TO USE THE CITRUS PRESS OR JUICER

❶ If using the Citrus Press with models KM series 300-800 unscrew the outlet plug from your machine using the end of the cone before assembling your Juicer. Screw the connector and washer into the outlet.

❷ Assemble the bowl, sieve and finally the cone.

❸ Turn the machine on and hold a citrus half on top of the cone, pressing down gently.

HINTS AND TIPS

❶ Cut all the fruits to be juiced in half first.

❷ If preparing lots of fruit, juice in batches, switching the machine off after a couple of minutes.

❸ Use the stainless steel Citrus Juicer on speed 2 or the Citrus Press on speed 4.

❹ Empty regularly to prevent the juice level rising up to the base of the sieve.

NON-STOP CENTRIFUGAL JUICER

There is no other appliance or method, even by hand, that will transform fresh fruit and vegetables into tasty drinks nearly so well; the Non-Stop Centrifugal Juicer will process almost any ingredients to produce a juice packed full of goodness.

The Non-Stop Centrifugal Juicer operates at high speed, separating the juice from the pulp. There is no need to peel or core most fruit, vegetables or ginger before juicing because everything including the seeds and skins just get pulped. Only stones and tough skins need to be removed first.

Coconut flesh can be passed through the Juicer to give finely grated coconut for cooking.

MAKING JUICES

Always select the finest and freshest produce possible. Slightly under-ripe hard fruits are better than over-ripe fruit which may turn to pulp rather than juice due to lost moisture.

Some juices are quite thick, such as apricot, mango and peach; these can easily be diluted with water, if wished. Use individual fruits such as kiwi, grapes, currants or pineapple or a mix of fruits.

It is best to avoid too many flavours as the end result will be indistinct. Try two main ingredients only like peach and strawberry, raspberry and melon or pineapple and mango.

Try apples with mint or carrots with ginger for a refreshing pick-me-up. If adding herbs it is best to put a handful of herbs in the Non-Stop Centrifugal Juicer first and then the fruit or vegetables as these help to push the herbs through the machine.

Ginger, being coarse, can go through unpeeled, along with the carrots. Stir a little orange juice into the carrot juice. Beetroot combines well with apple and ginger or carrot. Process the beetroot first, then the apple or carrot which will help to clear the Juicer of beetroot.

A wide variety of vegetables can be juiced; try peppers, spinach, watercress, tomatoes, cauliflower and celery. Strongly flavoured ingredients like fennel, celery and broccoli are best used in small quantities in combination with other fruits or vegetables so they are not overpowering.

The pulp of potatoes can be used for rösti or for adding to breads and scones. The liquor contains the heavy starch which should be discarded. Use the pulp from carrots in cakes, or bread.

TO USE THE CONTINUOUS JUICE EXTRACTOR

1 Assemble the Non-Stop Centrifugal Juicer, making sure the filter and grater plate are screwed into position and the lid clipped shut.

2 Cut the food to fit the feed tube, removing any stones or tough skins with fruits such as melon or pineapple.

3 Make sure you place a container under each spout to collect the juice and pulp.

4 Use the Non-Stop Centrifugal Juicer on speed 1 unless a recipe states otherwise.

HINTS AND TIPS

1 Dismantle the Non-Stop Centrifugal Juicer before washing. Use the top of the pusher to unscrew the grater plate. Do not immerse the base in water.

2 Any discolouration from foods such as carrot juice can usually be removed by rubbing with a cloth dipped in vegetable oil.

3 If pulp stops coming out switch off and unclog the bowl before continuing.

4 Citrus fruits may be juiced using the Non-Stop Centrifugal Juicer but you must remove both the peel and white pith otherwise the juice will have a bitter taste. You may find it easier to use the Citrus Press or Juicer.

The Food Processing Attachment is extremely versatile. It can blend soup in seconds and purée fruits as well as chop, slice or shred a variety of ingredients. This attachment comes complete with a Knife Blade for mixing, chopping, mincing and puréeing; two dual Slicing and Shredding Plates of different thickness plus a julienne style Thin Chipper Plate. There are three optional plates; a standard chipper plate for thick French fries and vegetables; a rasping plate for vegetables and grated cheese and an extra coarse shredding plate for vegetables.

KNIFE BLADE
Chopping

The Knife Blade will chop both hard and soft foods. To obtain the best result, make sure ingredients of equal size are added. Use the pulse button to roughly chop meat, fish, fruit, vegetables and nuts. For fine or ground nuts process continuously on speed 2-3, for the desired texture. Use to chop onions, mushrooms, celery or tomatoes, taking care not to over-process. For chillies or garlic drop into the feed tube with the motor running. To make garlic butter place the garlic and parsley in the processing bowl and chop; then add cubes of butter.

Process to mix. Dry the herbs before processing. The Knife Blade can also be used to crumb bread; use bread cut into cubes or torn into pieces. Biscuits such as amaretti or digestives may be processed to produce a crumb for desserts and tart cases.

Puréeing
Fruit coulis, purées and sauces can be processed with the Knife Blade in seconds. Soft fruits such as summer berries, kiwi, mangoes and peaches can be processed raw. Stone large fruits, peel if necessary and cut into smaller even-sized pieces first. Poach hard fruits like apple, apricots, plums, pears and rhubarb in a little water and sugar until tender before puréeing. Use the Knife Blade to make smooth soups. Drain the ingredients and add to the Processing bowl. Add a little of the liquid and process to the desired consistency.

Add the purée to the remaining liquid in the pan and combine.

Mixing
Use the Knife Blade to mix ingredients for a marinade, salad dressing or mayonnaise. Use it to blend mixtures of soft cheese or yogurt with vegetables, spices and herbs for dips or to make batter for crêpes, or fritters. The Knife Blade may be used to make smaller quantities of shortcrust pastry or crumble topping. Put the flour and fat, straight from the fridge, into the bowl. Cut the fat into cubes first. Process for a few seconds until the mixture resembles breadcrumbs.

If making shortcrust pastry, add the water through the feed tube with the machine running.

THICK SLICING/COARSE SHREDDING PLATE

This is a reversible plate with a thick slicing blade on one side and coarse shredding on the other. Cut any large foods to fit the feed tube and fill evenly for the best results.

For long thin vegetables like leeks, courgettes and carrots, load vertically to produce neat slices.

If only slicing one item then use the small feed tube.

Load the carrot, leek, courgette or cucumber vertically as before.

The thick slicing blade can also be used for beetroot, celery, onions, peppers, fennel and potatoes. Peel and quarter the onions or halve if small. Cut peppers into two halves and remove the core and seeds, then fold into itself and place vertically in the feed tube.

Fruits like banana need to be placed upright for perfect slices, using the small tube if only slicing one. Core and quarter or halve fruits like pears and apples before placing in the large feed tube.

The coarse shredding side of this plate is suitable for a wide range of ingredients. Use it to grate cheese, vegetables like potatoes, courgettes, carrots and cabbage. Trim cabbage and remove the core. Cut into wedges to fit the feed tube and place upright. If making coleslaw shred the cabbage and follow with a couple of carrots.

Transfer to a serving bowl and just mix with a little mayonnaise or dressing.

THIN SLICING/FINE SHREDDING PLATE

This dual purpose plate also slices and shreds but with thin slices and fine shreds. The thin slicer is perfect for thin slices of celery, cucumber, mushrooms or radishes to use in salads. Use the small feed tube for celery and radishes.

Make sure mushrooms are placed horizontally, one on top of another, to fill the feed tube, for the best results.

The fine shredding side is ideal for hard cheese for sauces, salads and gratin toppings. It will also finely grate crisp apples perfect for strudel or fillings for individual pies and pastries.

Use the fine shredding cutters for carrots, courgettes or celeriac to incorporate in salads, fillings for pies and pastries or making stuffing or nut and meat loaves.

THIN CHIPPER PLATE

For slim French fries or fine strips of vegetables for stir-fries and salads, use this thin, julienne style cutter. It is suitable for beetroot, carrots, celeriac, courgettes, cucumber, peppers, potatoes and turnips.

For long thin vegetables such as carrots, courgettes and cucumber cut into 6.5cm (2½ inch) lengths and load horizontally in the feed tube. Place one on top of another, for the best results.

HINTS AND TIPS

❶ If using one of the cutting plates fill the feed tube before switching on the machine.

❷ Always use the pusher to push the food down the feed tube. Use the small feed tube for single or small items, to prevent them slipping sideways.

❸ Do not use the Food Processing Attachment for grinding coffee beans, use the Multi-Mill attachment for this.

❹ Liquids may leak out of the Processing bowl and could cause damage. When puréeing soups, leave to cool, then drain the ingredients and add to the Food Processing bowl. Blend and then return to the liquid and mix together. Reheat as necessary.

❺ Use the pulse setting for greater control over the final texture of the food being processed. Use for rough chopping and mixing to avoid over-blending the ingredients.

❻ Start on a low speed to avoid over-processing, as the Food Processing Attachment is very quick. Use low speed for slicing, shredding and chipping and higher speeds for puréeing and blending.

ICE CREAM MAKER

The Ice Cream Maker makes smooth textured ice creams and sorbets every time. It consists of a freezing bowl and a paddle, so that it will freeze and churn at the same time.

To make perfect ice cream and sorbets the mixture needs to be kept moving whilst it freezes, to prevent large ice-crystals forming. The rotating paddle within the Ice Cream Maker keeps the mixture moving and as it moves past the frozen bowl the mixture is chilled and frozen ensuring the texture remains velvety smooth. Within 20-30 minutes the ice cream mixture is frozen and ready to serve as a soft-scoop style ice cream, or for transferring to the freezer to become a little firmer, as desired.

The Ice Cream Maker allows you to make ice cream with completely natural additive free ingredients, from the simplest milk and cream based vanilla ice cream or fruit based ice cream with the addition of fresh fruit purées to yogurt ices and sugar syrup based fruit sorbets.

TO USE THE ICE CREAM MAKER

1 Always freeze the Ice Cream Maker freezing bowl for at least 24 hours before use.

2 Prepare the ice cream or sorbet mix and chill it thoroughly before starting. The colder the ingredients and equipment the better the results.

3 Assemble the Ice Cream Maker, complete with paddle and switch on before adding the chilled mixture, otherwise it may freeze immediately onto the inside of the bowl. Add the mix through the chute.

4 Continue mixing until the ice cream is frozen, this takes 20-30 minutes. It will have a consistency similar to freshly whipped cream.

5 It may be eaten straight away as a soft style ice cream, but is best if placed in the freezer for 20-30 minutes, before serving.

HINTS AND TIPS

1 The Ice Cream Maker will only operate successfully with the plastic bowl supplied with the Ice Cream Maker.

2 If you have sufficient room in your freezer it is worth keeping the freezing bowl stored in the freezer for immediate use. Place the paddle and cover in the fridge to chill before use.

3 Once the ice cream or sorbet is made, transfer it to a plastic container with a lid and store in the freezer until required.

4 To serve ice cream which has been stored in the freezer, transfer it to the refrigerator for 30 minutes before serving, to soften.

5 Never re-freeze ice cream that has partially defrosted.

TO MAKE SORBET

Fruits sorbets are successfully made in the Ice Cream Maker in a similar way to the more traditional cream based ices.

1 First make a sugar syrup using 125g (4½oz) sugar and 300ml (½ pint) water. Place both in a pan and heat gently until the sugar dissolves, stirring occasionally. Bring to the boil and boil for 2 minutes. Set aside to cool.

2 Using the Citrus Juicer, juice 3 lemons for lemon sorbet or 3 oranges for orange sorbet and stir into the syrup. Chill thoroughly.

3 Lightly whisk an egg white with a fork and add to the citrus syrup. Assemble the Ice Cream Maker and switch on. Pour the sorbet mix into the Ice Cream Maker through the chute.

4 Continue mixing the sorbet for 20-30 minutes until thickened and icy.

5 The finished sorbet will form small regular ice crystals and will be lighter in colour.

Note: If you prefer not to include raw egg white in your recipes, it may be omitted.

This section of the book contains a collection of recipes which help to illustrate just how versatile your Kenwood Kitchen Machine is, especially with the help of the various attachments. The recipes include traditional classics as well as new contemporary dishes to inspire you and are divided into twelve individual chapters, each covering a different subject, for easy reference.

There are ideas for soups and starters; fish, meat and poultry dishes and a range of recipes for vegetarians including eggs, cheese, rice, grains and pasta; a selection of tasty desserts, cakes pastries and breads and a final chapter covering some of the basic recipes you are sure to refer to time and again.

RECIPES

There is nothing as tasty as a really good homemade soup, bursting with flavour. Creamy soups can be processed within seconds in the Liquidiser, or for velvety smooth tomato soup the Colander and Sieve is a must to remove the tomato seeds. Use the Pro Slicer/Grater to quickly prepare vegetables for chunky soups.

The Multi Food Grinder is the perfect attachment for making meat pâtés for a tasty starter or meat fillings for filo parcels and savoury pastries. Quickly prepare crudités with the Pro Slicer/Grater and blend avocado or cheese dips in the Liquidiser or Food Processing Attachment as an accompaniment.

FISHERMAN'S BISQUE

SERVES 4   PREPARATION TIME: 10 MINUTES   COOKING TIME: 35 MINUTES
TOOLS LIQUIDISER

INGREDIENTS

30ml (2 tbsp) sunflower oil
2 potatoes, peeled and chopped
1 onion, peeled and chopped
2 tomatoes, halved
2 cloves garlic, peeled and chopped
600ml (1 pint) vegetable or
fish stock
300ml (½ pint) milk
225g (8oz) shelled shrimps or
prawns, defrosted, if frozen
salt and freshly ground black pepper

❶ Heat the oil in a heavy based saucepan, add the potatoes, onion and tomatoes and sauté for 10 minutes.

❷ Add the garlic, stock, milk and shrimps or prawns and bring to the boil. Cover and simmer gently for 20 minutes.

❸ Cool slightly, then blend in the Liquidiser in batches if necessary, until the soup is smooth.

❹ Season with salt and freshly ground black pepper, then return to the pan and reheat gently.

CARROT AND LEMON SOUP

SERVES 4   PREPARATION TIME: 10 MINUTES   COOKING TIME: 15-20 MINUTES
TOOLS PRO SLICER/GRATER OR FOOD PROCESSING ATTACHMENT

INGREDIENTS

1 leek, topped and tailed
325g (12oz) carrots, peeled or
scrapped
30ml (2 tbsp) sunflower oil
1 small clove garlic, crushed
grated rind and juice 1 lemon
700ml (1¼ pints) vegetable or
chicken stock
30ml (2 tbsp) freshly chopped
parsley
salt and freshly ground black pepper

❶ Fit the thick slicing plate to the Pro Slicer/Grater or to the Food Processing Attachment and slice the leek. Change to the thick shredding plate and shred the carrots.

❷ Heat the oil in a heavy based saucepan, add the leek, carrot and garlic, cover the pan and cook gently for 5-10 minutes or until the vegetables begin to soften, but not colour, stirring from time to time.

❸ Add the grated lemon rind and stock and simmer for 10 minutes. Remove from the heat, stir in the lemon juice and fresh parsley. Season with salt and black pepper and serve immediately.

CELERIAC AND BLUE CHEESE SOUP

INGREDIENTS
325g (12oz) celeriac
15ml (1 tbsp) lemon juice
25g (1oz) butter
1 potato, peeled and chopped
1 small onion, peeled and chopped
600ml (1 pint) vegetable stock
75g (3oz) Stilton cheese, crumbled
75ml (2½fl oz) double cream
2 rashers bacon, crisp fried, to garnish

SERVES 4   PREPARATION TIME: 15 MINUTES   COOKING TIME: 45 MINUTES
TOOLS LIQUIDISER

1 Peel the celeriac and cut into 1cm (½ inch) cubes. Place in a bowl of water with the lemon juice, to prevent discolouration.

2 Melt the butter in a saucepan over a low heat and add the potato and onion and sauté gently for 3-4 minutes. Drain the celeriac and add to the pan. Cook for a further 5 minutes.

3 Add the stock and simmer gently for 30 minutes, until the vegetables are soft. Remove the pan from the heat and stir in the Stilton and cream.

4 Allow to cool slightly then blend in the Liquidiser at low speed, until the soup is smooth. Transfer to a cleaned saucepan and season to taste. Reheat gently, but do not boil.

5 Serve in warm soup bowls. Break the crisp fried bacon into bite-sized pieces and scatter over the soup to garnish.

INSTANT SPRING VEGETABLE SOUP

INGREDIENTS
225g (8oz) cooked potatoes
1 carrot, thinly sliced
1 leek, trimmed and thinly sliced
1 stick celery, thinly sliced
1 tomato, quartered
600ml (1 pint) boiling hot vegetable, beef or chicken stock
salt and freshly ground black pepper
crusty bread, to serve

SERVES 4   PREPARATION TIME: 10 MINUTES
TOOLS LIQUIDISER

1 Place the cooked potatoes, carrot, leek, celery and tomato in the Liquidiser. Leave the stock to cool for 2 minutes then pour into the Liquidiser to cover the vegetables.

2 Blend at minimum speed for 2-3 minutes, until smooth, then season with salt and freshly ground black pepper. Serve immediately with chunks of crusty bread, for a quick snack.

Cook's Note Take great care when liquidising the soup, as it is very hot. Make sure the lid and filler cap are securely fitted.

GAZPACHO

SERVES 6   PREPARATION TIME: 15 MINUTES PLUS CHILLING
TOOLS LIQUIDISER OR FOOD PROCESSING ATTACHMENT

INGREDIENTS

450g (1lb) ripe tomatoes
1 clove garlic, peeled
2 sprigs fresh parsley or basil
15ml (1 tbsp) tomato purée
¼ cucumber, peeled and chopped
300ml (½ pint) tomato juice
2 spring onions, finely chopped
1 small green pepper, seeded and
very finely chopped
5cm (2 inch) piece cucumber, very
finely chopped
15ml (1 tbsp) lemon juice
30ml (2 tbsp) olive oil
salt and freshly ground black pepper
ice cubes and croûtons for serving,
optional

1 Immerse the tomatoes in a bowl of boiling water for 15 seconds; remove using a slotted spoon, cool slightly then peel away the skins and roughly chop.

2 Place the tomatoes in the Liquidiser or Food Processing bowl with the garlic and parsley or basil, tomato purée and cucumber and blend until smooth.

3 Strain through a nylon sieve into a bowl, pushing through as much as possible.

4 Stir in the spring onions, green pepper and finely chopped cucumber with the lemon juice and olive oil. Season with salt and pepper and leave to chill for 2 hours in the fridge.

5 Just before serving check the seasoning again as chilling will reduce the strength of the flavours. Spoon into chilled serving bowls, add one or two ice cubes to each bowl and serve garnished with croûtons, if wished.

WINTER VEGETABLE SOUP

SERVES 4   PREPARATION TIME: 10 MINUTES   COOKING TIME: 35 MINUTES
TOOLS FOOD PROCESSING ATTACHMENT OR PRO SLICER/GRATER / COLANDER AND SIEVE

INGREDIENTS

1 small onion, peeled and halved
lengthways
2 carrots, peeled
2 potatoes, peeled
175g (6oz) swede, peeled and diced
175g (6oz) turnip, peeled and diced
3 tomatoes, halved
15ml (1 tbsp) chopped fresh parsley
900ml (1½ pints) vegetable stock
salt and freshly ground black pepper

1 Fit the Food Processing Attachment or Pro Slicer/Grater with the thick slicing plate and slice the onion, carrots and potatoes. Place in a saucepan with the swede, turnip, tomatoes, parsley and stock.

2 Bring to the boil, cover and simmer for 30 minutes, until the vegetables are tender. Leave to cool for 5 minutes.

3 Fit the Sieve with the coarse screen, rough side uppermost and purée the vegetable soup. Return to the clean pan, reheat gently and season to taste with salt and freshly ground black pepper. Serve with chunks of fresh wholemeal bread, if wished.

FRESH TOMATO SOUP WITH BASIL OIL

SERVES 4-6   PREPARATION TIME: 15 MINUTES   COOKING TIME: 30-35 MINUTES
TOOLS FOOD PROCESSING ATTACHMENT / MULTI-MILL / COLANDER AND SIEVE

INGREDIENTS

2 onions, peeled and quartered
1 garlic clove, peeled
30ml (2 tbsp) olive oil
25g (1oz) butter
2 carrots, peeled
900g (2 lb) ripe tomatoes
600ml (1 pint) vegetable stock
30ml (2 tbsp) tomato purée
salt and freshly ground black pepper
Pecorino shavings, to garnish

FOR THE BASIL OIL:
12 basil leaves
90ml (6 tbsp) olive oil

1 Using the Food Processing Attachment, fitted with the knife blade, roughly chop the onions and garlic. Heat the oil and butter in a saucepan, add the onions and garlic and fry gently for 10-15 minutes, or until softened.

2 Using the Food Processing Attachment, roughly chop the carrots, then the tomatoes and add to the pan with the stock and tomato purée. Bring to the boil, cover and simmer gently for 15 minutes.

3 Meanwhile make the basil oil. Place the basil leaves and olive oil in the Multi-Mill and blend until smooth. Strain through a fine hand sieve and set the basil oil aside.

4 Using the Sieve fitted with the fine screen, rough side uppermost, sieve the soup. Return to the pan, season to taste and heat through. Serve in warm bowls, drizzled with basil oil and garnished with Pecorino shavings, if wished.

Illustrated on page 30.

BRUSCHETTA WITH GARLIC BRANDADE, TOMATO, ROCKET & MOZZARELLA

SERVES 4   PREPARATION TIME: 15 MINUTES   COOKING TIME: 5 MINUTES
TOOLS FOOD PROCESSING ATTACHMENT

INGREDIENTS

8 thick slices French or ciabatta bread
50g (2oz) rocket or mizuna and rocket leaves
15ml (1 tbsp) extra virgin olive oil
15ml (1 tbsp) balsamic vinegar
12 baby tomatoes, halved
12 baby mozzarella, each cut into 3
extra olive oil for drizzling

FOR THE BRANDADE:
6 sprigs fresh parsley
225g (8oz) drained, canned or freshly cooked butter beans
1 large clove garlic, peeled
15ml (1 tbsp) lemon juice
30ml (2 tbsp) olive oil
salt and freshly ground black pepper

1 To make the brandade, fit the knife blade to the Food Processing Attachment, add the parsley and chop finely. Remove and set aside.

2 Add the beans, garlic, lemon juice, olive oil and 15ml (1 tbsp) cold water and process to a rough paste. Add another 15ml (1 tbsp) of water if the mixture is too thick to process. Stir in the chopped parsley and season with salt and freshly ground black pepper, to taste.

3 Toast the bread on both sides and spread with the brandade. Meanwhile toss the rocket and mizuna leaves with the oil and balsamic vinegar.

4 Arrange the bruschetta on 4 serving plates and top each with baby tomato halves, mozzarella slices and a handful of dressed leaves. Drizzle with a little extra olive oil and sprinkle with freshly ground black pepper Serve immediately.

Illustrated on page 30.

ASPARAGUS WITH LIME HOLLANDAISE DRESSING

SERVES 4   PREPARATION TIME: 15 MINUTES   COOKING TIME: 10 MINUTES
TOOLS CITRUS JUICER / LIQUIDISER OR FOOD PROCESSING ATTACHMENT

INGREDIENTS

450g (1lb) asparagus, trimmed
lime halves or wedges and zest, to
garnish

**FOR THE LIME HOLLANDAISE
DRESSING:**

2 limes
15ml (3 tbsp) white wine vinegar
1 shallot, finely chopped
125g (4oz) butter, diced
2 egg yolks
salt and freshly ground black pepper

❶ Tie the asparagus into 2 equal bundles. Stand them tips upwards in a saucepan of boiling salted water, cover and simmer for 8-10 minutes.

❷ Meanwhile finely grate the rind from 1 lime. Cut both limes in half and using the Citrus Juicer, juice 1½ limes. Reserve the remaining half for garnish.

❸ Place the vinegar and shallot in a small saucepan and bring to the boil. Boil for a minute or so to reduce to 15ml (1 tbsp) then stir in the lime juice. At the same time place the butter in a saucepan and warm gently until the butter just begins to foam.

Illustrated opposite.

❹ Put the egg yolks and a little salt in the Liquidiser or Food Processing bowl fitted with the knife blade and with the motor running slowly pour in the lime and vinegar mixture. Slowly add the butter and continue blending for a few seconds or until the sauce is smooth and creamy.

❺ Drain the asparagus and arrange on warmed serving plates, drizzling over the lime dressing. Sprinkle with freshly ground black pepper and garnish with grated lime zest and pieces of lime.

Cook's Note If the sauce is too thin, place in a bowl over a pan of simmering water and whisk for 1-2 minutes, until slightly thickened.

CELERIAC SALAD WITH BRESAOLA

SERVES 4   PREPARATION TIME: 15 MINUTES   COOKING TIME: 2 MINUTES
TOOLS PRO SLICER/GRATER OR FOOD PROCESSING ATTACHMENT

INGREDIENTS

575g (1¼lb) celeriac
salt and freshly ground black pepper
45ml (3 tbsp) Greek style yogurt
30ml (2 tbsp) extra virgin olive oil
15ml (1 tbsp) grainy mustard
20 wafer thin slices bresaola (cured beef)
30ml (2 tbsp) snipped chives
30ml (2 tbsp) coarsely chopped walnuts

❶ Peel the celeriac and cut into 5cm (2 inch) pieces. Fit the Pro Slicer/Grater or Food Processing Attachment with the thin chipper plate and cut the celeriac into thin sticks.

❷ Place in a pan of lightly salted boiling water and boil for 2 minutes, to blanch. Drain and refresh under cold running water. Drain, pat dry with absorbent kitchen paper, place in a bowl and set aside.

❸ Mix the yogurt, oil and mustard together. Add to the celeriac and toss together.

❹ Arrange mounds of celeriac salad on individual serving plates, with slices of bresaola to one side and sprinkle with snipped chives, walnuts and freshly ground black pepper. Serve immediately with crusty bread, if wished.

COARSE COUNTRY PÂTÉ

SERVES 8-10   PREPARATION TIME: 20 MINUTES PLUS COOLING   COOKING TIME: 1¼ HOURS
TOOLS MULTI FOOD GRINDER / K BEATER

INGREDIENTS
450g (1lb) chicken livers
675g (1½lb) boneless belly of pork,
derinded and roughly chopped
1 lamb's kidney
225g (8oz) streaky bacon rashers
1 onion, finely chopped
2 cloves garlic, crushed
10ml (2 tsp) green peppercorns
30m (2 tbsp) sherry
1 egg
salt and freshly ground black pepper

1 Preheat the oven to 170°C/325°F/Gas 3. Using the Grinder, fitted with the coarse mincing screen, mince the chicken livers, pork and kidney into the Kenwood Bowl.

2 Using a rolling pin, flatten the bacon rashers, to make them thinner, then use to line a 1.1 litre (2 pint) ovenproof pâté dish, placing each rasher side by side, widthways across the dish, leaving the ends hanging over the side of the dish.

3 Using the K Beater at speed 1, mix the minced meats with the onion, garlic, green peppercorns, sherry and egg. Season with salt and freshly ground black pepper.

4 Spoon the mixture into the pâté dish. Fold over the bacon rashers, to cover the mixture. Cover with foil and bake for 1¼ hours. Leave to cool in the dish. Serve sliced with crusty bread or toast.

MELON, MANGO AND GRAPEFRUIT SALAD

SERVES 4   PREPARATION TIME: 20 MINUTES
TOOLS LIQUIDISER OR FOOD PROCESSING ATTACHMENT

INGREDIENTS
1 ripe galia melon, chilled
1 ripe mango, chilled
2 pink grapefruit, chilled
45ml (3 tbsp) lemon juice
mint sprigs, to garnish

1 Halve the melon and remove the seeds. Scoop out the flesh using a melon baller and place in a bowl. Scoop out the remaining flesh with a spoon and place in the Liquidiser or Food Processing Attachment fitted with the knife blade.

2 Cut through the mango lengthways 1cm (½ inch) from each side of the centre, to free the stone. Cut the flesh from around the stone. Peel the remaining pieces and then neatly cube all the flesh and add to the melon balls.

3 Using a sharp serrated knife cut all the peel and pith off the grapefruits. Holding each grapefruit over a bowl, to catch the juice, segment and discard the pith and membrane. Combine the segments with the melon and mango.

4 Add the grapefruit juice to the Liquidiser or Food Processing Attachment with the lemon juice and process to a purée. Divide between 4 serving dishes, top with fruits and serve garnished with mint.

SPICY WEDGES WITH SOURED CREAM AND CHIVE & TOMATO CHILLI DIPS

INGREDIENTS

1 orange, halved

1 lemon, halved

30ml (2 tbsp) Dijon mustard

5ml (1 tsp) salt

2.5ml (½ tsp) chilli powder

45ml (3 tbsp) sunflower oil

4 x 150g (5oz) potatoes, scrubbed
and cut into 6 lengthways

**FOR THE SOURED CREAM
AND CHIVE DIP:**

20-30 fresh chives, cut into 2.5cm
(1 inch) lengths

150ml (5fl oz) soured cream

FOR THE TOMATO CHILLI DIP:

2 spring onions, cut into 4

50g (2oz) sun dried tomatoes in oil

30ml (2 tbsp) olive oil

1 small chilli, finely chopped or
2.5ml (½ tsp) chilli powder

2 tomatoes, halved, seeded and
finely chopped

SERVES 4   PREPARATION TIME: 15 MINUTES   **COOKING TIME:** 30-35 MINUTES
TOOLS CITRUS JUICER / FOOD PROCESSING ATTACHMENT

1 Place a roasting tin in the oven and preheat to 220°C/425°F/Gas 7. Using the Citrus Juicer extract the juice from the orange and lemon. Mix with the mustard, salt and chilli powder.

2 Add the oil and potatoes to the hot roasting tin and toss to coat. Bake for 5 minutes. Add the citrus and mustard dressing and toss together. Bake for 25-30 minutes, or until cooked, stirring after 15 minutes.

3 Meanwhile make the dips. Using the Food Processing Attachment fitted with the knife blade roughly chop the chives. Stir into the soured cream and place in a small serving dish.

4 Using the Food Processing Attachment, roughly chop the spring onions. Remove and set aside. Add the sun dried tomatoes and olive oil and process to a coarse paste. Stir in the chopped chillies or chilli powder, onions and chopped tomatoes. Transfer to a serving dish.

5 Serve the hot potato wedges with the chive and tomato chilli dips.

CRISPY DUCK PARCELS WITH ORANGE SAUCE

SERVES 4   PREPARATION TIME: 30 MINUTES   COOKING TIME: 25 MINUTES
TOOLS MULTI FOOD GRINDER / K BEATER

INGREDIENTS

175g (6oz) duck breast fillets, skinned
1 clove garlic, crushed
2.5cm (1 inch) piece fresh root ginger, grated
2 spring onions, finely chopped
5ml (1 tsp) sesame oil
2.5ml (½ tsp) salt
2.5ml (½ tsp) Chinese five spice powder
8 sheets filo pastry measuring 15cm (6 inches) square
25g (1oz) butter, melted
coriander sprigs, to garnish

FOR THE ORANGE SAUCE:
5ml (1 tsp) butter
5ml (1 tsp) sugar
150ml (5fl oz) fresh orange juice
150ml (5fl oz) chicken stock
1.2cm (½ inch) piece fresh root ginger, grated
5ml (1 tsp) soy sauce
5ml (1 tsp) cornflour
salt and freshly ground black pepper

1 Preheat the oven to 180°C/350°F/Gas 4. Mince the duck, using the Grinder fitted with the fine mincing screen straight into the Kenwood Bowl. Add the garlic, ginger, spring onions, sesame oil, salt and Chinese five spice powder to the bowl and then mix together using the K Beater at minimum speed.

2 Lay out separately 4 sheets of filo pastry and brush with melted butter. Place another sheet on top, at an angle, so that it forms an 8-point star shape. Place a quarter of the duck filling in the centre of each pastry star.

3 Brush the exposed pastry with melted butter. Draw the pastry up around the filling, pinching to form a bag shape. Place on a greased baking sheet, brush with the remaining butter and bake for 25 minutes, or until golden.

4 Meanwhile make the sauce. Melt the butter in a small heavy based pan, add the sugar and fry until it caramelizes. Carefully add the orange juice, stock, ginger and soy sauce and simmer for 5 minutes. Mix the cornflour with 15ml (1 tbsp) cold water and pour into the sauce, stirring continuously, until the sauce thickens. Season with salt and pepper.

5 To serve, pour a little sauce on to warmed serving plates and place a duck parcel in the centre. Garnish with coriander sprigs and serve.

CHICKEN LIVER AND OLIVE PÂTÉ

SERVES 6-8   PREPARATION TIME: 10 MINUTES PLUS CHILLING   COOKING TIME: 20 MINUTES
TOOLS FOOD PROCESSING ATTACHMENT / LIQUIDISER

INGREDIENTS

1 large onion, peeled
2 cloves garlic, peeled
100g (4oz) butter
450g (1lb) chicken livers, trimmed
20 pitted green olives
30ml (2 tbsp) brandy
salt and freshly ground black pepper

1 Chop the onion and garlic using the Food Processing Attachment, fitted with the knife blade. Melt the butter in a frying pan, add the onion and garlic and sauté until softened.

2 Add the chicken livers and cook over a moderate heat, stirring occasionally, for about 10 minutes, or until just cooked. Remove from the heat and stir in the olives and brandy. Allow to cool slightly.

3 Transfer the mixture into the Food Processing Attachment or Liquidiser and blend until smooth. Season with salt and freshly ground black pepper. Transfer to a serving dish, cover and leave to cool. Chill in the fridge for 3-4 hours, until firm. Serve with toast or crusty bread.

Variation If wished reduce butter to 75g (3oz) and pour 50g (2oz) melted butter over the top of the finished pâté to prevent it drying out. Chill until set.

VEGETABLE SAMOSAS

SERVES 6-8 PREPARATION TIME: 30 MINUTES PLUS COOLING COOKING TIME: 35-45 MINUTES
TOOLS K BEATER/ MULTI-MILL

INGREDIENTS

225g (8oz) plain flour
2.5ml (½ tsp) salt
60ml (4 tbsp) vegetable oil

FOR THE FILLING:

400g (14oz) potatoes, unpeeled
1 onion, peeled and quartered
30ml (2 tbsp) vegetable oil
1 carrot, peeled and finely diced
2.5cm (1 inch) piece fresh root
ginger, peeled and sliced
1 green chilli, de-seeded
5ml (1 tsp) ground coriander
5ml (1 tsp) garam masala
50g (2oz) frozen peas
handful fresh coriander leaves
30ml (2 tbsp) lemon juice
salt and freshly ground black pepper
vegetable oil for deep-frying
lemon wedges and coriander leaves,
to garnish

❶ Place the flour and salt in the Kenwood Bowl. Using the K Beater on minimum speed gradually blend in the oil. Gradually add about 90ml (6 tbsp) water and mix to a firm dough. Mix for 2-3 minutes, until smooth. Knead into a ball, cover and set aside to rest, whilst preparing the filling.

❷ Boil the potatoes in lightly salted water for 15 minutes, until just tender. Drain, cool slightly, peel and cut into 5mm (¼ inch) dice.

❸ Using the Multi-Mill, finely chop the onion, in 2 batches, if necessary. Heat the oil in a frying pan, add the onion and fry for 2-3 minutes. Add the carrot and fry for a further 2 minutes.

❹ Using the Multi-Mill, finely chop the ginger and chilli, then add to the pan and cook for a further 2 minutes. Add the ground coriander, garam masala, potatoes and peas and cook for 2 minutes. Finely chop the coriander in the Multi-Mill and stir into the vegetable mix with the lemon juice. Season and set aside to cool.

❺ Divide the pastry into 8 balls. Keep covered until needed. On a lightly floured surface, roll one piece into an 18cm (7 inch) circle. Cut in half. Place a tablespoonful of filling on each semi-circle, dampen the edges with water and fold the pastry to form a cone. Press together the edges and crimp together to seal. Repeat with the remaining pastry and filling.

❻ Heat the oil in a wide deep pan to 180°C/350°F or until a cube of bread browns in 45 seconds. Fry 2-3 samosas at a time for 3 minutes, or until golden. Drain on absorbent kitchen paper, keep warm whilst frying the remainder. Serve garnished with lemon wedges and coriander leaves.

Fish is becoming evermore popular for everything from a simple supper to inspired entertaining. Use the Multi-Mill to quickly prepare a marinade or grind spices for a Goan style curry. The Food Processing Attachment will assist in making salsas to accompany fresh grilled or barbecued fish steaks, or for making a stuffing for whole fish.

Use the Liquidiser to make breadcrumbs for stuffings, crumb coatings or crusts for steaks and fillets. Fish soufflés and roulades make ideal summer lunch dishes and the Whisk will ensure perfect whipped egg whites resulting in light fluffy soufflés.

SALMON AND TROUT TERRINE

INGREDIENTS

350g (12oz) piece of skinless salmon
fillet, any bones removed
450ml (¾ pint) hot fish stock
250g (9oz) smoked salmon or trout
slices
10ml (2 tsp) powdered gelatine
30ml (2 tbsp) lemon juice
10 sprigs of parsley
small handful of dill sprigs
30ml (2 tbsp) snipped fresh chives
225g (8oz) hot smoked trout fillets, flaked
75g (3oz) crème fraîche
30ml (2 tbsp) hot horseradish sauce
225g (8oz) curd cheese
salt and freshly ground black pepper
fresh chives, to garnish

SERVES 4 PREPARATION TIME: 30 MINUTES PLUS COOLING AND CHILLING
COOKING TIME: 15 MINUTES TOOLS FOOD PROCESSING ATTACHMENT

1 Preheat the oven to 180°C/350°F/Gas 4. Cut the salmon into 3 lengthways about 1cm (½ inch) thick. Place in an ovenproof dish. Pour over the stock, cover with aluminium foil and poach in the oven for 8-10 minutes, until just cooked. Set aside to cool.

2 Oil a 1.1 litre (2 pint) terrine or loaf tin and line with clear film. Line the base and sides with slices of smoked salmon or trout, reserving some for the top.

3 Place the gelatine, lemon juice and 30ml (2 tbsp) of the fish poaching liquor in a small saucepan. Using the Food Processing Attachment fitted with the knife blade chop the parsley and dill. Reserve 30ml (2 tbsp) and mix the remainder with the chives.

4 Add the hot smoked trout, crème fraîche and horseradish to the Food Processing bowl and pulse to mix. Stir in the curd cheese, and season.

5 Place the remaining herbs on a sheet of greaseproof paper, drain the salmon strips and roll in the herbs, to coat. Heat the gelatine mixture over a low heat to dissolve. Stir into the trout mixture.

6 Place about half the trout mixture in the prepared tin. Add the salmon strips, slightly spaced apart and gently press into the trout mixture. Top with the remaining trout mixture. Cover with the remaining smoked salmon or trout slices, folding over any from the edges of the tin.

7 Chill in the fridge for at least 3 hours, or until firm to the touch. To serve, turn out onto a serving plate and remove the clear film. Garnish with fresh chives. Serve cut into slices.

Illustrated on page 42.

FISH BOULANGÈRE

INGREDIENTS

1 onion, halved
30ml (2 tbsp) sunflower oil
65g (2½oz) butter
675g (1½lb) potatoes, peeled
15ml (1 tbsp) fresh thyme leaves
salt and freshly ground black pepper
400ml (14fl oz) hot vegetable stock
675g (1½lb) thick cod or haddock
fillet, cut into 4 pieces
lemon wedges and dill sprigs, to
garnish

SERVES 4 PREPARATION TIME: 15 MINUTES COOKING TIME: 1 HOUR
TOOLS PRO SLICER/GRATER

1 Fit the thin slicing plate to the Pro Slicer/Grater and slice the onion. Heat half the oil in a frying pan and sauté the onion until pale golden.

2 Preheat the oven to 190°C/375°F/ Gas 5. Lightly grease a 1.7 litre (3 pint) ovenproof dish with a little of the butter. Using the Pro Slicer/Grater thinly slice the potatoes. Layer the potatoes and onions into the prepared dish, sprinkling each layer with thyme, salt and pepper.

3 Pour over the hot stock. Cut 25g (1oz) butter into small cubes and dot over the surface. Bake for 45 minutes.

4 Heat the remaining butter and oil in a frying pan and quickly sear the fish on both sides. Place on top of the potatoes and bake for 10 minutes. The fish should be cooked and the potatoes tender. Serve garnished with lemon wedges and sprigs of dill.

GOAN FISH CURRY

INGREDIENTS

5ml (1 tsp) turmeric
2.5ml (½ tsp) salt
10ml (2 tsp) plain flour
15ml (1 tbsp) lemon juice
4 x 175g (6oz) cod or haddock steaks
1 onion, halved lengthways
5ml (1 tsp) cumin seeds
10ml (2 tsp) coriander seeds
5ml (1 tsp) black peppercorns
2 cloves garlic, peeled
5cm (2 inch) piece fresh root ginger, chopped
1 small hot red chilli, seeded
45ml (3 tbsp) vegetable oil
3 mild green chillies, seeded and cut into thin strips
4 tomatoes, peeled, seeded and chopped
10ml (2 tsp) tomato purée
400ml (14fl oz) can coconut milk
coriander sprigs, to garnish
basmati rice, to serve

SERVES 4   PREPARATION TIME : 20 MINUTES   COOKING TIME : 30-35 MINUTES
TOOLS PRO SLICER/GRATER OR ROTO FOOD CUTTER / MULTI-MILL

❶ Mix the turmeric, salt and flour together. Sprinkle the lemon juice over the fish steaks and rub the turmeric mixture over the steaks to coat.

❷ Fit the Pro Slicer/Grater or Roto Food Cutter with the thick slicing plate or drum and slice the onion.

❸ Place the cumin seeds, coriander seeds and peppercorns in the Multi-Mill and mill to a powder. Add the garlic, ginger and red chilli and process for a few seconds.

❹ Heat 30ml (2 tbsp) vegetable oil in a large frying pan or flameproof casserole, then add the fish steaks and fry for 1-2 minutes per side to seal and brown. Remove on to a plate and set aside.

❺ Add the remaining oil and onions and cook for 5-6 minutes, to soften the onions. Add the green chillies and cook for 1-2 minutes. Add the ground spice paste, chopped tomatoes and tomato purée and fry for 1 minute.

❻ Add the coconut milk and stir to incorporate the spices, then bring to the boil and simmer gently for 10 minutes. Return the fish steaks to the pan and simmer for 6-8 minutes, or until the fish is cooked and opaque.

❼ Check the seasoning and adjust if necessary. Garnished with coriander sprigs and serve with basmati rice.

Cook's Note For a milder curry omit the red chilli in the spice paste in step 3.

STUFFED ROAST MONKFISH TAILS

SERVES 4-6   PREPARATION TIME: 25 MINUTES   COOKING TIME: 35 MINUTES
TOOLS FOOD PROCESSING ATTACHMENT

INGREDIENTS

25g (1oz) dried cep mushrooms
1 onion, quartered
1 clove garlic, peeled
15g (½oz) butter
60ml (4 tbsp) olive oil
50g (2oz) button mushrooms
25g (1oz) walnut halves
15ml (1 tbsp) fresh rosemary leaves
15ml (1 tbsp) fresh lemon thyme leaves
1kg (2¼lb) monkfish tail
2 red peppers, deseeded and
cut into 8 lengthways
1 onion, cut into 8 wedges
4 large cup mushrooms
6-8 baby corn cobs
30ml (2 tbsp) lemon juice
salt and freshly ground black pepper
few sprigs lemon thyme
fresh herb sprigs, to garnish, optional

❶ Place the ceps in a bowl, cover with hot water and leave to soak for 20 minutes. Meanwhile using the Food Processing Attachment fitted with the knife blade, chop the onion and garlic.

❷ Melt the butter with 15ml (1 tbsp) oil in a frying pan, add the onion and sauté for 5 minutes. Using the Food Processing Attachment, chop the button mushrooms, add to the onion and fry for 2-3 minutes. Remove from the heat.

❸ Drain the ceps and place in the Food Processing bowl with the walnuts and rosemary and chop. Add to the frying pan with the lemon thyme leaves, stir to combine and set aside to cool. Preheat the oven to 200°C/400°F/Gas 6.

Illustrated opposite.

❹ Remove any skin and membrane from the monkfish then fillet by cutting down either side of the bone. Place one fillet cut side up, spread with the mushroom stuffing and place the other fillet on top, cut side down. Tie with string. Heat 30ml (2 tbsp) oil in a heavy based frying pan and quickly sear the monkfish, for 2-3 minutes, to seal. Remove and set aside.

❺ Quickly brown the peppers, onion wedges and mushrooms. Transfer to a roasting tin with the corn cobs. Place the monkfish on top. Sprinkle with lemon juice, remaining oil, seasoning and lemon thyme sprigs. Bake for 20 minutes, or until fish turns opaque, basting after 10 minutes.

❻ To serve, remove string and lift monkfish on to a warmed serving platter with the roasted vegetables. Garnish with extra herbs, if wished.

PAN FRIED HALIBUT WITH TOMATO AND HERB SALSA

SERVES 4   PREPARATION TIME: 15 MINUTES PLUS INFUSING TIME
COOKING TIME: 6-8 MINUTES   TOOLS FOOD PROCESSING ATTACHMENT

INGREDIENTS

8 sprigs fresh basil
4 sprigs fresh tarragon
8 sprigs fresh coriander
1 small red onion, peeled and quartered
3 tomatoes, peeled, quartered and seeded
1 clove garlic, crushed
grated rind and juice 1 lemon
15ml (1 tbsp) capers
60ml (4 tbsp) olive oil
4 x 200g (7oz) halibut steaks
salt and freshly ground black pepper
fresh chives, to garnish

❶ Make the salsa. Using the Food Processing Attachment fitted with the knife blade, chop the basil, tarragon and coriander. Add the onion and coarsely chop. Add the tomatoes, and using the pulse action, coarsely chop. Transfer to a bowl.

❷ Add the garlic, lemon rind and juice, capers and half the olive oil. Mix together and set aside for 30 minutes to infuse.

❸ Season the halibut steaks with salt and freshly ground black pepper. Heat the remaining olive oil in a heavy based frying pan and cook the halibut steaks for 2-3 minutes, per side, or until just cooked through.

❹ Heat the salsa in a small pan, until just hot, and spoon over 4 warm serving plates. Place the halibut on the plates, garnish with chives, sprinkle with freshly ground black pepper and serve immediately.

HADDOCK AND PRAWN FISH PIE

SERVES 6   PREPARATION TIME: 20 MINUTES   COOKING TIME: 55-60 MINUTES
TOOLS ROTO FOOD CUTTER / K BEATER

INGREDIENTS

115g (4oz) mature Cheddar cheese
900g (2lb) floury potatoes, peeled
and cut into even sized chunks
450g (1lb) haddock fillet
225g (8oz) smoked haddock fillet
450ml (¾ pint) milk
75g (3oz) butter
40g (1½oz) plain flour
100ml (3½fl oz) single cream
salt and freshly ground black pepper
30ml (2 tbsp) chopped fresh parsley
115g (4oz) cooked shelled prawns

❶ Fit the Roto Food Cutter with the coarse shredding drum and grate the cheese. Set aside. Place the potatoes in a pan of boiling lightly salted water and cook for 12-15 minutes, or until tender, then drain.

❷ Meanwhile place the fish fillets in a frying pan or large saucepan. Reserve 30ml (2 tbsp) milk and pour the remainder over the fish. Slowly bring to the boil, cover, remove from the heat and leave to stand for 10 minutes. Strain the milk into a jug.

❸ Preheat the oven to 200°C/400°F/Gas 6. Melt 40g (1½oz) butter in a large saucepan and stir in the flour. Cook for 30 seconds, then gradually stir in the strained milk and cream.

❹ Bring to the boil, stirring continuously. Simmer for 2-3 minutes. Season with salt and freshly ground black pepper and stir in the parsley and half the grated cheese.

❺ Flake the fish and place in a 1.7-2 litre (3-3½ pint) ovenproof dish. Stir in the prawns and pour over the sauce.

❻ Place the potatoes with the remaining milk and butter in the Kenwood Bowl. Using the K Beater on speed 2, mash the potatoes and season to taste. Spoon over the fish and gently smooth over the top. Fork up and sprinkle with the remaining cheese.

❼ Bake for 35-40 minutes, or until the topping is golden and bubbling.

CHERMOULA CRUSTED FISH FILLETS

SERVES 4   PREPARATION TIME: 10 MINUTES   COOKING TIME: 10-15 MINUTES
TOOLS FOOD PROCESSING ATTACHMENT OR LIQUIDISER / MULTI-MILL

INGREDIENTS

115g (4oz) brown bread slices
2 cloves garlic, peeled
small bunch fresh coriander
12 large leaves fresh mint
10ml (2 tsp) ground cumin
2.5ml (½ tsp) paprika
salt and freshly ground black pepper
juice 1 lemon
30ml (2 tbsp) olive oil
4 x 175g (6oz) salmon or trout fillets
lemon slices and coriander, to garnish

❶ Preheat the oven to 200°C/400°F/Gas 6. Remove the crusts from the bread and tear into small pieces. Using the Food Processing Attachment fitted with the knife blade or the Liquidiser, process the bread to make breadcrumbs.

❷ Either add the coriander and mint leaves to the Food Processing Attachment or to the Multi-Mill and process until chopped.

❸ Mix the breadcrumbs, chopped herbs, ground cumin, paprika, a little salt and pepper, lemon juice and olive oil together and spread over the fish fillets.

❹ Place the fish fillets on a lightly oiled baking tray, and bake for 10-15 minutes, or until the fish is tender and cooked through. Serve garnished with lemon slices and sprigs of coriander.

CAJUN CRAB SOUFFLÉ

SERVES 4   PREPARATION TIME: 20 MINUTES   COOKING TIME: 35 MINUTES
TOOLS PRO SLICER/GRATER OR ROTO FOOD CUTTER OR FOOD PROCESSING ATTACHMENT / BALLOON WHISK

INGREDIENTS

15ml (1 tbsp) grated Parmesan cheese
50g (2oz) Cheddar cheese
25g (1oz) butter
25g (1oz) plain flour
225ml (8fl oz) milk
10ml (2 tsp) Cajun spices
10ml (2 tsp) anchovy essence
4 eggs separated, plus 1 egg white
75g (3oz) dressed crab
10ml (2 tsp) lime juice
salt and freshly ground black pepper

1 Butter a 1.3 litre (2¼ pint) soufflé dish and sprinkle the Parmesan cheese over the base and sides to coat evenly. Preheat the oven to 180°C/350°F/Gas 4.

2 Fit the coarse shredding plate to the Pro Slicer/Grater or Food Processing Attachment or the coarse shredding drum to the Roto Food Cutter and grate the Cheddar cheese. Melt the butter in a saucepan and stir in the flour to form a smooth paste.

3 Remove from the heat and gradually stir in the milk. Return to the heat and slowly bring to the boil, stirring continuously until the sauce thickens. Remove from the heat and stir in the Cajun spices, anchovy essence and grated Cheddar cheese.

4 Gradually beat in the egg yolks, and then add the crab, lime juice, salt and freshly ground black pepper, stirring to combine.

5 Using the Whisk at maximum speed, whisk the egg whites until they form soft peaks. Mix one large spoonful of egg white into the sauce, to lighten it. Using a metal spoon, gently fold in the remaining egg whites so as to retain as much air as possible.

6 Pour the soufflé mixture into the prepared dish; it should come about three-quarters of the way up the dish. Stand the dish on a baking sheet and bake for about 30 minutes, until brown, well risen and just firm to the touch. Serve immediately.

SMOKED HADDOCK ROULADE

SERVES 4 OR 8 AS A STARTER   PREPARATION TIME: 25 MINUTES
COOKING TIME: 27-30 MINUTES   TOOLS BALLOON WHISK / FOOD PROCESSING ATTACHMENT

INGREDIENTS

280g (10oz) smoked haddock fillet
300ml (½ pint) milk
25g (1oz) butter
25g (1oz) plain flour
4 eggs, separated
salt and freshly ground black pepper

FOR THE FILLING:

75g (3oz) watercress
15ml (1 tbsp) crème fraîche
75g (3oz) garlic and herb full fat
soft cheese
watercress or dill sprigs, to garnish

❶ Preheat the oven to 200°C/400°F/Gas 6. Line a 33 x 23cm (13 x 9 inch) Swiss roll tin with non-stick baking parchment. Place the haddock and milk in a shallow pan, bring to the boil, cover and simmer for 5 minutes or until fish is tender. Strain and reserve the liquor. Flake the fish, discarding any bone.

❷ Melt the butter in a saucepan, stir in the flour and cook for 30 seconds. Off the heat gradually stir in 250ml (8fl oz) of the reserved liquor. Bring to the boil, stirring continuously until thickened. Remove from the heat and stir in the haddock, egg yolks and season with salt and freshly ground black pepper.

❸ Place the egg whites in the Kenwood Bowl. Using the Whisk, whip the egg whites until stiff. Stir one spoonful into the haddock mixture, then lightly fold in the remainder.

❹ Spread the mixture evenly in the prepared tin and bake for 12-15 minutes, or until lightly browned and just firm to the touch.

❺ Meanwhile prepare the filling. Using the Food Processing Attachment fitted with the knife blade, chop the watercress. Add the crème fraîche and garlic and herb cheese and mix, using the pulse action, until just blended.

❻ Turn the roulade out onto a sheet of non-stick baking parchment. Remove the lining paper and spread over the filling, leaving a 1cm (½ inch) border. Roll up from a short side, using the paper to help. Serve cut into slices, garnished with watercress or dill sprigs.

PIQUANT GARLIC PRAWNS

SERVES 4-6   PREPARATION TIME: 20 MINUTES PLUS MARINATING
COOKING TIME: 4-5 MINUTES   TOOLS MULTI-MILL

INGREDIENTS

30 large raw prawn tails
2 cloves garlic, peeled
1 red chilli, seeds removed
30ml (2 tbsp) lemon juice
60ml (4 tbsp) olive oil
10 sprigs fresh parsley
crusty bread, to serve, optional

❶ Peel the prawns, leaving the tail end attached. Using a sharp knife, make a shallow cut along the outer curve from the tail to the head and remove the dark thread. Rinse under cold running water and dry with absorbent kitchen paper.

❷ Place the garlic, chilli and lemon juice in the Multi-Mill and process until the garlic and chilli are finely chopped. Transfer to a shallow dish. Add the olive oil and prawns and toss together to coat.

❸ Cover and leave to marinate in the fridge for 30 minutes, or longer, if time allows. Meanwhile place the parsley in the Multi-Mill and process to chop.

❹ Heat a heavy based frying pan until hot, add the prawns and marinade and cook very quickly, stirring all the time, for about 2-3 minutes, or until the prawns turn from grey to pink. Sprinkle over the parsley and serve immediately, with crusty bread, if wished.

GRIDDLED SWORDFISH WITH RED PESTO

INGREDIENTS

grated zest 1 lemon

60ml (4 tbsp) olive oil

15ml (1 tbsp) chopped flat leaf parsley

salt and freshly ground black pepper

4 x 175g (6oz) swordfish steaks

25g (1oz) pine nuts

1 clove garlic, chopped

25g (1oz) sun-dried tomatoes in oil, drained

30ml (2 tbsp) freshly grated Parmesan cheese

12 basil leaves

juice 1 lemon

15ml (1 tbsp) tomato purée

couscous, to serve

lime wedges and basil leaves, to garnish

SERVES 4 PREPARATION TIME: 10 MINUTES PLUS MARINATING
COOKING TIME: 8-10 MINUTES TOOLS MULTI-MILL

1 Mix the lemon zest, 30ml (2 tbsp) olive oil, flat leaf parsley and seasoning together in a shallow dish. Add the swordfish and spoon over the marinade. Cover and set aside for 30 minutes.

2 Place the pine nuts, garlic, sun-dried tomatoes, Parmesan cheese, basil leaves and the remaining olive oil in the Multi-Mill and process until finely chopped. Stir in the lemon juice and tomato purée.

3 Heat a griddle pan over a medium heat, until hot. Place the swordfish on the griddle and cook for 2-3 minutes, per side, until beginning to brown.

4 Place swordfish on individual warmed serving plates on a bed of couscous, topped with a little red pesto dressing. Garnish with lime wedges and basil leaves and serve immediately.

COD FISH CAKES

INGREDIENTS

75g (3oz) crustless white bread, cubed

8 sprigs fresh parsley

225g (8oz) potatoes, peeled and cut into even sized pieces

325g (12oz) cod fillets

15ml (1 tbsp) creamed horseradish

15ml (1 tbsp) lemon juice

salt and freshly ground black pepper

flour, for dusting

1 egg, beaten

sunflower oil, for shallow frying

lemon wedges, to garnish

tartare sauce, to serve, see page 102

SERVES 4 PREPARATION TIME: 20 MINUTES PLUS CHILLING COOKING TIME: 25 MINUTES
TOOLS LIQUIDISER / K BEATER / MULTI FOOD GRINDER

1 With the Liquidiser running add the bread and process to make breadcrumbs. Transfer to a plate. Add the parsley to the Liquidiser, chop and set aside.

2 Cook the potatoes in boiling water until tender. Drain and leave to cool for 10 minutes. Place in the Kenwood Bowl and using the K Beater on speed 2 mash the potatoes.

3 Using the Grinder, fitted with the fine screen, mince the fish straight into the Kenwood Bowl containing the mashed potatoes.

4 Add the parsley, horseradish, lemon juice and a little salt and pepper. Mix together, using the K Beater on minimum speed.

5 With floured hands divide the mixture into 8 and shape into cakes. Brush with beaten egg and coat in breadcrumbs. Chill in the fridge for 30 minutes.

6 Heat the oil in a large non-stick frying pan, add the fish cakes and fry for about 4-5 minutes, per side, until crisp and golden. Drain on absorbent kitchen paper and serve garnished with lemon wedges and parsley. Serve with tartare sauce, if wished.

The current interest in what we eat means it is important to know the quality of meat in sausages, burgers, meatballs and minced meat. By preparing your own you can choose the fat level and select the meat, organic meat, if preferred. The Multi Food Grinder will quickly prepare beef, lamb, pork or chicken for your favourite recipes, or by using the additional attachments make homemade sausages or kebbe.

Use the Pro Slicer/Grater or Food Processing Attachment to prepare vegetables for stir-fries, potatoes for meat bakes, hot pots and casseroles. The Liquidiser will quickly prepare smooth sauces to accompany pan fried, grilled or griddled steaks, burgers or kebabs.

HARISSA ROAST LAMB

INGREDIENTS

3 red peppers, halved and de-seeded

40g (1½oz) whole blanched almonds

2 red chillies, seeds removed

5ml (1 tsp) ground coriander

2.5ml (½ tsp) caraway seeds

3 cloves garlic, peeled

handful fresh coriander leaves

2.5ml (½ tsp) salt

15ml (1 tbsp) tomato purée

1 kg (2¼lb) boneless leg of lamb

1 aubergine, cut into large chunks

8 shallots, peeled with the root

left intact

45ml (3 tbsp) olive oil

30ml (2 tbsp) chopped fresh

coriander or parsley

SERVES 4   PREPARATION TIME: 20 MINUTES   COOKING TIME: 1 HOUR 20 MINUTES
TOOLS FOOD PROCESSING ATTACHMENT OR MULTI-MILL

❶ Place one pepper under a preheated grill until the skin is blackened and the flesh is soft. Leave to cool slightly, cover with clear film and leave until cold, then peel. Meanwhile place the almonds in the Food Processing Attachment fitted with the knife blade or the Multi-Mill and process until finely chopped. Set aside.

❷ Place the chillies, ground coriander, caraway seeds, garlic, fresh coriander and salt in the Food Processing Attachment or Multi-Mill and blend in batches if necessary. Add the cooked red pepper and tomato purée and blend to a coarse paste. Mix in the almonds.

❸ Preheat the oven to 190°C/375°F/Gas 5. Spread the harissa paste over the inside of the leg of lamb. Roll and secure with string or wooden cocktail sticks. Place on a wire rack in a roasting tin and roast for 1¼ hours, for medium lamb.

❹ After 30 minutes cut the remaining pepper halves into 3 lengthways, place in the roasting tin with the aubergine and shallots and drizzle over the olive oil. Stir the vegetables twice during cooking.

❺ Transfer the lamb to a warm serving dish. Drain off any excess fat and toss the vegetables with chopped coriander or parsley. Spoon around the lamb and serve immediately.

KASHMIRI ALMOND KOFTAS WITH YOGURT

INGREDIENTS

450g (1lb) lean lamb, cut into strips

2.5ml (1 inch) piece fresh ginger,

grated

1 fresh green chilli, seeded and

finely chopped

5ml (1 tsp) ground coriander

5ml (1 tsp) curry powder

salt and freshly ground black pepper

150g (5oz) natural yogurt

20ml (4 tsp) dried milk powder

75g (3oz) flaked almonds

5ml (1 tsp) sugar

15ml (1 tbsp) olive or sunflower oil

1.25ml (¼ tsp) chilli powder

SERVES 4   PREPARATION TIME: 15 MINUTES   COOKING TIME: 30 MINUTES
TOOLS MULTI FOOD GRINDER / K BEATER

❶ Preheat the oven to 190°C/375°F/Gas 5. Using the Grinder fitted with the fine screen, mince the lamb into the Kenwood Bowl.

❷ Add the ginger, green chilli, ground coriander, curry powder and season with salt and freshly ground black pepper.

❸ Add 15ml (1 tbsp) of yogurt and half the milk powder and using the K Beater, mix together on minimum speed.

❹ Divide into 12 and shape into balls. Roll in the flaked almonds and place on a baking tray, leaving sufficient space in between each one for them to expand during cooking.

❺ Stir together the remaining yogurt and milk powder, sugar, oil and chilli powder. Season with salt and spoon over the top of each kofta ball making sure they are well coated.

❻ Bake uncovered for 30 minutes, by which time the almonds should be golden and toasted.

LEBANESE LAMB KEBBE

SERVES 4   PREPARATION TIME: 30 MINUTES   COOKING TIME: 40 MINUTES
TOOLS MULTI FOOD GRINDER / K BEATER / KEBBE MAKER ADAPTOR

INGREDIENTS

115g (4oz) bulghur wheat
325g (12oz) lean boneless lamb, diced
15ml (1 tbsp) sunflower oil
1 small onion, finely diced
30ml (2 tbsp) pine nuts
2.5ml (½ tsp) ground allspice
salt and freshly ground black pepper
50g (2oz) plain flour
oil, for deep frying
spicy yogurt dressing, to serve

❶ Place the bulghur wheat in a saucepan, cover with water and bring to the boil. Simmer for 15 minutes, then drain and set aside.

❷ Meanwhile fit the Grinder and using the fine screen mince the lamb into the Kenwood Bowl. Set aside. Heat the oil in a frying pan, add the onion and sauté for 5-6 minutes until lightly golden.

❸ Add the pine nuts and cook for 30-60 seconds, until toasted. Stir in one-third of the minced lamb and fry for about 10 minutes. Season with half the allspice, salt and freshly ground black pepper.

❹ Add the drained bulghur wheat to the remaining minced lamb and season generously with salt, pepper and the remaining allspice. Using the K Beater at speed 1, mix together for 5 minutes. Add the flour and mix to incorporate thoroughly.

❺ Remove the screen and cutting blade from the Grinder and replace with the Kebbe Maker Adaptor. Pass the bulghur mixture through the Kebbe Adaptor, cutting the tubing at 7.5cm (3 inch) intervals. Lay the tubes on a tray.

❻ To make the Kebbe balls, close one end of each tube, squeezing tightly to seal. Press 15ml (1 tbsp) of the cooked meat mixture into each tube and seal the open end.

❼ Heat the oil for deep-frying, until moderately hot (160°C/325°F) and then fry the Kebbe balls, in batches, for 3-4 minutes, until golden. Keep warm in the oven until they are all cooked then serve immediately with a spicy yoghurt dressing and salad, if wished.

HERB CRUSTED RACK OF LAMB

SERVES 2   PREPARATION TIME: 10 MINUTES   COOKING TIME: 35-45 MINUTES
TOOLS LIQUIDISER OR FOOD PROCESSING ATTACHMENT

INGREDIENTS

50g (2oz) white bread with the crusts removed
handful fresh mixed herbs e.g. parsley, dill, basil
25g (1oz) butter, melted
salt and freshly ground black pepper
400-450g (14-16oz) rack of lamb, trimmed of excess fat

❶ Preheat the oven to 190°C/375°F/Gas 5. Tear the bread into small pieces and using the Liquidiser or Food Processing Attachment fitted with the knife blade process to make breadcrumbs. If using the Liquidiser, switch on first and add the bread through the filler cap. Add the herbs and chop.

❷ Transfer the breadcrumbs and herbs to a bowl, add the melted butter and mix together, seasoning with salt and freshly ground black pepper.

❸ Place the rack of lamb on a baking sheet and press the crumb mixture on to the top side of the lamb. Bake for 35 minutes, for pink lamb or 45 minutes if you prefer it to be well done.

❹ Serve the lamb, cut into double cutlets, with new potatoes and green salad, if wished.

STUFFED PORK FILLET WITH BAKED PLUMS

S E R V E S 4-6   P R E P A R A T I O N   T I M E : 25 MINUTES   C O O K I N G   T I M E : 65 MINUTES
T O O L S FOOD PROCESSING ATTACHMENT

INGREDIENTS

115g (4oz) white bread, crust removed
6 large sage leaves
6 sprigs of thyme
1 onion, quartered
50g (2oz) butter
grated rind and juice 1 lemon
salt and freshly ground black pepper
1 egg, lightly beaten
2 pork fillets about 350g (12oz) each
8 rashers streaky bacon
30ml (2 tbsp) vegetable oil
450g (1lb) small potatoes, halved
1 onion, cut into 8 wedges
6 plums, stoned and cut into wedges
10ml (2 tsp) wholegrain mustard
5ml (1 tsp) clear honey

❶ Break the bread into pieces, place in the Food Processing Attachment fitted with the knife blade, add the sage and thyme and process to make breadcrumbs and chop the herbs. Transfer to a bowl. Add the onion to the Food Processing Attachment and finely chop.

❷ Melt 25g (1oz) butter in a pan, add the onion and sauté until light golden. Stir into the breadcrumb mix with the lemon juice and rind, seasoning and beaten egg.

❸ Preheat the oven to 180°C/350°F/Gas 4. Split the pork fillets lengthways, without cutting right the way through. Spread the stuffing over one fillet, place the other fillet on top, cut side down to cover the stuffing.

❹ Stretch the bacon, using the back of a knife and then wrap it around the pork. Tie at 2.5cm (1 inch) intervals with string. Heat the oil and remaining butter in a roasting tin, in the oven, add the pork and baste. Cook for 20 minutes, then add the potatoes and baste again.

❺ Cook for 10 minutes then add the onion wedges. Cook for 30 minutes adding the plums for the last 5 minutes. Mix the mustard and honey together and drizzle over the meat when you add the plums. Serve thickly sliced with the roasted potatoes, onions and plums.

Illustrated opposite.

PORK, FENNEL AND PAPRIKA SAUSAGES

M A K E S 8 STANDARD OR 32 COCKTAIL SAUSAGES   P R E P A R A T I O N   T I M E : 20 MINUTES
C O O K I N G   T I M E : 15-20 MINUTES OR 10 MINUTES   T O O L S MULTI FOOD GRINDER / K BEATER / SAUSAGE FILLER

INGREDIENTS

450g (1lb) boneless, skinless belly of pork, cut into long thin strips
2.5ml (½ tsp) black peppercorns, coarsely crushed, not ground
2.5ml (½ tsp) fennel seeds
10ml (2 tsp) salt
freshly ground black pepper
15ml (1 tbsp) paprika
1 egg
25g (1oz) fresh breadcrumbs
length of sausage casing, standard or small, depending on size of sausage required

❶ Fit the coarse screen to the Grinder and mince the pork into the Kenwood Bowl. When all the pork has been minced, feed a little mince back through the Grinder to push through any remaining strips of meat left inside.

❷ Add the crushed peppercorns, fennel seeds, salt, pepper, paprika, egg and breadcrumbs to the Kenwood Bowl. Using the K Beater, mix together at minimum speed.

❸ Replace the screen and cutting blade with the Sausage Filler. Dampen the end of the nozzle and slip on the sausage casing. Feed the sausage filling into the Grinder and through the Filler. Once all the filling has been used, twist the casing to make individual sausages. See page 15 for further instructions.

❹ To cook the sausages, heat a little oil in a frying pan over a gentle heat. Fry slowly for 15-20 minutes, or 10 minutes for cocktail sausages, turning occasionally, until golden.

PORK STIR-FRY WITH NOODLES

INGREDIENTS

1 clove garlic
1 small red chilli
15ml (1 tbsp) hoisin sauce
15ml (1 tbsp) tomato purée
15ml (1 tbsp) rice vinegar
15ml (1 tbsp) soy sauce
325g (12oz) pork tenderloin, cut into strips
1 orange pepper, halved and seeds removed
2 carrots, peeled
45ml (3 tbsp) sunflower oil
115g (4oz) small broccoli florets
140g (5oz) sugar snap peas, topped and tailed
1 pak choi, quartered
2 spring onions, cut into long thin strips

FOR THE NOODLES:

250g (9oz) fresh egg noodles
15ml (1 tbsp) sesame oil
15ml (1 tbsp) chopped fresh coriander

SERVES 4 **PREPARATION TIME:** 15 MINUTES PLUS MARINATING
COOKING TIME: 8-10 MINUTES **TOOLS** MULTI-MILL / FOOD PROCESSING ATTACHMENT

1 Place the garlic, chilli, hoisin sauce, tomato purée, vinegar and soy sauce in the Multi-Mill or Food Processing Attachment fitted with the knife blade and blend together.

2 Place the meat in a non-metallic dish, add the marinade, toss together, cover and set aside in the fridge for 30 minutes or longer, if time allows.

3 Using the Food Processing Attachment fitted with the thick slicing plate, slice the pepper. Cut the carrots into ribbons, using a potato peeler.

4 Heat 30ml (2 tbsp) oil in a wok or large frying pan, add the pork strips and stir-fry for 3-4 minutes. Remove and set aside. Add the remaining oil and stir-fry the broccoli for 1 minute. Add the carrots, sugar snap peas and sliced pepper and stir-fry for 2 minutes.

5 Meanwhile place the noodles in a pan of boiling water and cook for 2 minutes, or according to the pack instructions.

6 Return the pork to the wok, add the pak choi and cook for 1-2 minutes, or until the pork is cooked and the vegetables are tender-crisp.

7 Drain the egg noodles and toss with the sesame oil and chopped coriander. Transfer the stir-fry to a warmed serving dish, sprinkle over the shredded spring onions to garnish and serve with the noodles.

AMERICAN MEAT LOAF WITH ONION GRAVY

SERVES 6-8   PREPARATION TIME: 35 MINUTES PLUS COOLING   COOKING TIME: 1½ HOURS
TOOLS MULTI FOOD GRINDER / K BEATER / PRO SLICER/GRATER OR FOOD PROCESSING ATTACHMENT

INGREDIENTS

900g (2lb) stewing steak, cut into strips

10ml (2 tsp) Worcestershire sauce

30ml (2 tbsp) chopped fresh basil

30ml (2 tbsp) chopped fresh parsley

15ml (1 tbsp) paprika

10ml (2 tsp) salt

10ml (2 tsp) hot chilli sauce

freshly ground black pepper

250g (9oz) puff pastry, see page 165

beaten egg, to glaze

FOR THE ONION GRAVY:

2 large onions, halved

30ml (2 tbsp) sunflower oil

20g (¾oz) plain flour

425ml (15fl oz) beef stock

left-over juices from baked meat loaf

5ml (1 tsp) soy sauce

salt and freshly ground black pepper

1 Oil a 1.1 litre (2 pint) loaf tin with base measurements of 19 x 9cm (7½ x 3½ inches) and set aside. Preheat the oven to 180°C/350°F/Gas 4. Using the Grinder fitted with the coarse screen, mince the beef into the Kenwood Bowl.

2 Add the Worcestershire sauce, basil, parsley, paprika, salt, chilli sauce and season with black pepper. Using the K Beater at minimum speed, mix all the ingredients together.

3 Press the mixture into the prepared loaf tin and bake for 1 hour. Leave to cool, then pour off the juices and set aside.

4 Roll out the puff pastry into a 35cm (14 inch) square and place the meat loaf in the middle. Cut out a square from each corner of the pastry up to about 1cm (½ inch) from the edge of the meat loaf. Reserve the pastry trimmings.

5 Brush each edge of the pastry with beaten egg. Bring the two pastry ends up and over the top of the loaf. Bring one of the pastry sides up and over so that the corners of the meat loaf are well sealed.

6 Brush the top with beaten egg and bring the remaining pastry side up, to meet it, allowing it to overlap a little.

7 Cut a few pastry leaves from the pastry trimmings and lay them on top to decorate. Place on a baking sheet and brush the complete loaf with egg glaze. Bake for 30 minutes, until golden.

8 Meanwhile make the onion gravy. Using the Pro Slicer/Grater or Food Processing Attachment fitted with the thick slicing plate, slice the onions.

9 Place the oil and onions in a frying pan and sauté over a gentle heat for about 20 minutes, or until a rich brown colour, stirring occasionally. It is important to develop the colour slowly as this is how the gravy develops its distinctive flavour.

10 Stir in the flour and let it cook for 1-2 minutes. Gradually stir in the stock and reserved meat loaf juices. Stir continuously until it boils and thickens. Simmer for 1 minute, then stir in the soy sauce and season to taste with salt and pepper.

11 Serve the meat loaf, cut into slices, with the onion gravy.

BEEFBURGERS

SERVES 4   PREPARATION TIME: 20 MINUTES   COOKING TIME: 10 MINUTES
TOOLS MULTI FOOD GRINDER / K BEATER

INGREDIENTS

675g (1½lb) beef sirloin or braising steak, cut into long thin strips
15ml (1 tbsp) chopped mixed fresh herbs e.g parsley, thyme, basil
juice and grated rind ½ lemon
freshly ground black pepper
flour, for dusting
vegetable oil for cooking

FOR THE ONION RINGS:
1 small onion sliced into rings
1 egg white, lightly beaten
30-45ml (2-3 tbsp) plain flour

TO SERVE:
toasted slices crusty bread
mixed salad leaves

❶ Fit the Grinder with the coarse screen and mince the beef into the Kenwood Bowl. For a finer texture pass through the screen again.

❷ Add the herbs, lemon juice and rind and a generous sprinkling of freshly ground black pepper. Using the K Beater at minimum speed, mix the ingredients together.

❸ Divide into 4 and with floured hands shape into thick burgers. Either brush with oil and place under a preheated grill for about 4 minutes on each side, or shallow fry over a medium heat.

❹ Meanwhile make the fried onion rings, dip the rings first into the egg white and then into the flour. Heat 2.5cm (1 inch) oil in a pan and fry for 1-2 minutes, until golden.

❺ Serve burgers garnished with onion rings accompanied by toasted crusty bread, mixed salad leaves and the remaining onion rings.

BEEF AND BLACK PEPPER SAUSAGES

MAKES 10 STANDARD OR 40 COCKTAIL SAUSAGES   PREPARATION TIME: 20 MINUTES
COOKING TIME: 15-20 OR 8-10 MINUTES   TOOLS MULTI FOOD GRINDER / K BEATER / SAUSAGE FILLER

INGREDIENTS

450g (1lb) boneless, shin of beef, cut into thin strips
5ml (1 tsp) salt
10ml (2 tsp) freshly ground black pepper
5ml (1 tsp) dried mixed herbs
1 egg
50g (2oz) fresh breadcrumbs
length of sausage casing, standard or small, depending on size of sausage required

❶ Fit the coarse screen to the Grinder and mince the beef into the Kenwood Bowl. When all the beef has been minced, feed a little back through the Grinder to push through any remaining strips of meat left inside.

❷ Add the salt, pepper, mixed herbs, egg and breadcrumbs to the Kenwood Bowl. Using the K Beater, mix together at minimum speed.

❸ Replace the screen and cutting blade with the Sausage Filler. Dampen the end of the nozzle and slip on the sausage casing.

❹ Feed the sausage filling into the Grinder and through the Filler. Once all the filling has been used, twist the casing to make individual sausages. See page 15 for further instructions.

❺ To cook the sausages, heat a little oil in a frying pan over a gentle heat. Fry slowly for 15-20 minutes, or 8-10 minutes for cocktail sausages, turning occasionally. These sausages are also particularly tasty when barbecued.

BEEF WELLINGTON

SERVES 4-6   PREPARATION TIME: 25 MINUTES   COOKING TIME: 45-50 MINUTES
TOOLS FOOD PROCESSING ATTACHMENT

INGREDIENTS

700g-900g (1½-2lb) fillet of beef
salt and freshly ground black pepper
50g (2oz) butter
15ml (1 tbsp) vegetable oil
2 onions, quartered
175g (6oz) mushrooms
280-325g (10-12oz) puff pastry, see page 165
75g (3oz) smooth chicken or duck pâté
beaten egg, to glaze
15ml (1 tbsp) plain flour
300ml (½ pint) beef stock
150ml (¼ pint) red wine

❶ Season the beef with pepper. Melt half the butter in a large frying pan, with the oil; add the beef and fry for 4-5 minutes, turning over to seal the meat. Transfer to a plate and leave to cool.

❷ Using the Food Processing Attachment, fitted with the knife blade, add the onions and process until finely chopped. Reserve a quarter of the onions and place the remainder in the frying pan and cook over a gentle heat for 10 minutes.

❸ Using the knife blade finely chop the mushrooms and add to the onions. Cook for 2-3 minutes, or until most of the liquid has evaporated. Season and set aside to cool.

❹ Preheat the oven to 220°C/425°F/Gas 7. On a lightly floured surface roll out the pastry into a rectangle, slightly longer than the beef and almost three times as wide. Mix the onions and mushrooms with the pâté and spread a layer along the top of the meat. Place the remainder in the centre along the length of the pastry to cover the same length as the beef.

❺ Place the meat on top. Trim away the corners of the pastry and then fold the ends and finally the sides to enclose the meat. Seal the edges and place join side down on a dampened baking sheet.

❻ Use the pastry trimmings to make leaves to decorate the top of the pastry. Brush with beaten egg and bake for 30 minutes, or until pastry is golden. Cook for a little longer if you prefer the meat less rare.

❼ Meanwhile melt the remaining butter, fry the remaining onions for 5-6 minutes, and then stir in the flour. Gradually stir in the stock and wine. Bring to the boil, stirring continuously.

POTATO TOPPED BEEF

SERVES 4   PREPARATION TIME: 20 MINUTES   COOKING TIME: 2½ HOURS
TOOLS PRO SLICER/GRATER OR FOOD PROCESSING ATTACHMENT / POTATO PREP ATTACHMENT

INGREDIENTS

2 onions, halved
2 carrots, peeled
550g (1¼lb) lean braising steak, cubed
30ml (2 tbsp) plain flour
salt and freshly ground black pepper
60ml (4 tbsp) vegetable oil
6 rashers streaky bacon, chopped
200ml (7fl oz) red wine
300ml (½ pint) beef stock
125g (4oz) button mushrooms, halved
550g (1¼lb) potatoes
15g (½oz) butter
chopped fresh parsley, to serve

① Using the Pro Slicer/Grater or Food Processing Attachment fitted with the coarse slicing plate, slice the onions, remove and set aside. Slice the carrots.

② Toss the beef in the flour and season with salt and pepper. Heat 30ml (2 tbsp) oil in a large flameproof casserole. Add the onions and sauté for 4-5 minutes; remove and set aside. Add the bacon and sauté for 3-4 minutes to brown. Set aside.

③ Add 15ml (1 tbsp) oil and the beef and brown over a high heat. Stir in the wine and stock and bring to the boil stirring. Add the onions, bacon and carrots, cover and simmer for 30 minutes. Add the mushrooms and simmer for 1 hour.

④ Preheat the oven to 190°C/375°F/Gas 5. Place the potatoes in the Potato Prep Attachment and use to clean the potatoes without peeling them completely.

⑤ Using the Pro Slicer/Grater or the Food Processing Attachment fitted with the coarse slicing plate, slice the potatoes and arrange in an overlapping layer on top of the meat and vegetables covering completely.

⑥ Brush with the remaining oil and dot with the butter. Season with salt and pepper. Bake for 40-45 minutes, until browned. Sprinkle with chopped parsley and serve, accompanied by a green vegetable such as sugar snap peas.

Cook's Note Depending on how much the sauce has reduced when it is time to top with the potatoes, you may wish to remove 200-300ml (7-10fl oz) so that it doesn't bubble over the potatoes. Re-heat and serve with the cooked potato topped beef.

LEMON PEPPER RUB STEAKS

SERVES 4   PREPARATION TIME: 10 MINUTES PLUS MARINATING
COOKING TIME: 4-6 MINUTES   TOOLS MULTI-MILL

INGREDIENTS

pared rind 1 lemon
5ml (1 tsp) black peppercorns
2 garlic cloves, peeled
2.5ml (½ tsp) coarse sea salt
8 sprigs fresh coriander or parsley
4 x 175g (6oz) rump, sirloin or fillet steaks
sunflower oil for cooking
fresh herb sprigs, to garnish

① Place the lemon rind in the Multi-Mill and chop until fairly small. Add the peppercorns and garlic and process until finely chopped.

② Add the sea salt and fresh herbs and process again until chopped and well blended. Rub the mixture over the steaks and set aside for 30 minutes, or longer if time allows, to marinate.

③ Brush a griddle pan with oil and heat. Cook the steaks for 2-3 minutes per side, or longer for less rare meat, according to your liking. If wished these steaks can be cooked on a barbecue. Serve garnished with fresh herb sprigs.

CHICKEN AND LEEK PANCAKES

SERVES 4 OR 8 FOR A STARTER **PREPARATION TIME:** 35 MINUTES
COOKING TIME: 30-35 MINUTES **TOOLS** PRO SLICER/GRATER / BALLOON WHISK

INGREDIENTS

1 large leek
225g (8oz) button mushrooms
30ml (2 tbsp) sunflower oil
325g (12oz) chicken breast fillets, cut into strips
2.5ml (½ tsp) grated nutmeg
salt and freshly ground black pepper
25g (1oz) butter
25g (1oz) plain flour
230ml (8fl oz) milk
8 pancakes, see page 166
115g (4oz) Gruyère cheese
60ml (4 tbsp) single cream

❶ Fit the Pro Slicer/Grater with the thick slicing plate and slice the leek and mushrooms into the Kenwood Bowl.

❷ Heat the oil in a heavy based frying pan until hot then stir-fry the chicken strips for 1-2 minutes. Add the leeks and mushrooms and stir fry for 5 minutes, or until the leeks are tender and the liquid from the mushrooms has evaporated.

❸ Season with nutmeg, salt and freshly ground black pepper. Remove from the heat and set aside to cool whilst making the sauce.

❹ Heat the butter in a saucepan, stir in the flour and cook, stirring for 1 minute. Remove from the heat and gradually stir in the milk. Return to the heat and bring to the boil, stirring continuously until the sauce thickens. Simmer for 2 minutes.

❺ Add to the chicken mixture and adjust the seasoning to taste. Set aside to cool before filling the pancakes.

❻ Preheat the oven to 200°C/400°F/Gas 6. Divide the chicken, leek and mushroom filling between the pancakes. Either spoon on to a flat pancake and tightly roll up, or place on one quarter, fold in half and then half again to form a pocket.

❼ Place the filled pancakes in a lightly greased ovenproof dish in a single layer. Fit the thin shredding plate to the Pro Slicer/Grater and grate the cheese. Sprinkle over the pancakes with the cream.

❽ Bake for 20-25 minutes, until the pancakes have heated through and the cheese is golden and bubbly. Serve immediately with a green salad.

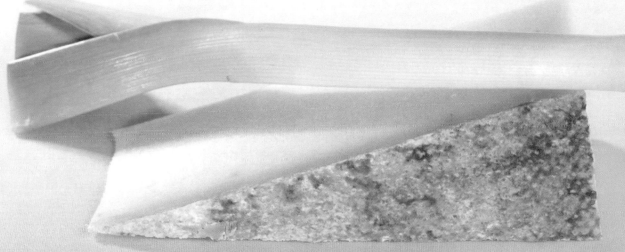

FRUIT GLAZED DUCK BREASTS

SERVES 4 **PREPARATION TIME:** 15 MINUTES **COOKING TIME:** 25-35 MINUTES
TOOLS MULTI-MILL / LIQUIDISER

INGREDIENTS

10 black peppercorns
5cm (2 inch) piece cinnamon stick, broken
10 cardamom pods
12 coriander seeds
2.5ml (½ tsp) sea salt crystals
4 x 175g (6oz) duck breast fillets
30ml (2 tbsp) sugar
grated rind and juice 2 oranges
150ml (¼ pint) red wine
225g (8oz) cranberries
30ml (2 tbsp) redcurrant jelly
15ml (1 tbsp) red wine vinegar
75g (2oz) redcurrants
sweet potato mash, to serve

❶ Place the peppercorns, cinnamon, cardamom pods, coriander seeds and sea salt in the Multi-Mill and process for 20-30 seconds until ground. Score the skin and fat of the duck breasts with a sharp knife and rub the spice blend over the skin.

❷ Place the sugar, orange juice, wine and cranberries in a pan and bring to the boil. Simmer for 5 minutes or until the cranberries are tender. Cool slightly, remove about a quarter of the cranberries and set aside. Place the remainder in the Liquidiser and blend to a purée. Pour back into the saucepan through a sieve.

❸ Cook the duck breasts on a ridged griddle pan. Place fat side down and cook over a low heat for 12-15 minutes, pouring off the fat as it is released.

Illustrated opposite.

❹ Turn over and cook for about 5 minutes. Alternatively cook in a preheated oven at 200°C/400°F/Gas 6 for 15-25 minutes, according to how well cooked you prefer duck.

❺ Meanwhile add the redcurrant jelly and vinegar to the sauce and bring to the boil. Let it bubble for 5 minutes, until syrupy. Add the reserved cranberries, orange rind and redcurrants and heat through.

❻ To serve, slice the duck and arrange on top of a bed of sweet potato mash, drizzle over a little fruit glaze and serve the remainder separately.

Cook's Note To make sweet mashed potato mix about 700g (1½lb) cooked mashed sweet potato with 50g (2oz) butter and 30ml (2 tbsp) mascarpone or single cream and season well.

TURKEY STEAKS WITH WATERCRESS SAUCE

SERVES 4 **PREPARATION TIME:** 15 MINUTES **COOKING TIME:** 25 MINUTES
TOOLS LIQUIDISER

INGREDIENTS

45ml (3 tbsp) plain flour
salt and freshly ground black pepper
2.5ml (½ tsp) freshly grated nutmeg
4 turkey breast steaks, total weight 500g (1¼lb)
30ml (2 tbsp) sunflower oil
15g (½oz) butter
1 onion, chopped
150ml (¼ pint) vegetable stock
150ml (¼ pint) dry white wine
1 bunch watercress
90ml (3fl oz) single cream
watercress sprigs, to garnish

❶ Mix 30ml (2 tbsp) flour, with a little salt and freshly ground black pepper and the nutmeg. Add the turkey and toss to coat, shaking off any excess.

❷ Heat the oil in a large frying pan and fry the turkey steaks for 5 minutes on each side, until golden and the juices run clear. Transfer to a plate.

❸ Add the butter and onions and cook for 4-5 minutes, or until the onions have softened.

❹ Stir in the remaining flour. Gradually add the stock and wine. Bring to the boil, stirring until thickened.

❺ Stir in the watercress and simmer for 5 minutes. Leave to cool slightly then transfer to the Liquidiser and blend until smooth. Return to the cleaned pan and stir in the cream. Season to taste.

❻ Add the turkey steaks and gently reheat. Arrange the turkey steaks on four serving plates, pour over the sauce, garnish with watercress sprigs and serve.

CAJUN STYLE CHICKEN MEATBALLS

SERVES 4 PREPARATION TIME: 20 MINUTES COOKING TIME: 15 MINUTES
TOOLS MULTI FOOD GRINDER / K BEATER / PRO SLICER/GRATER

INGREDIENTS

450g (1lb) boneless and skinless
chicken thigh meat

10ml (2 tsp) Cajun spice mix

10ml (2 tsp) hot chilli sauce

salt and freshly ground black pepper

15ml (1 tbsp) chopped fresh parsley

5ml (1 tsp) cornflour

30ml (2 tbsp) plain flour

30ml (2 tbsp) sunflower oil

1 small red pepper, halved
lengthways and deseeded

1 small yellow pepper, halved
lengthways and deseeded

60ml (4 tbsp) soured cream

boiled rice and salad leaves to serve,
optional

❶ Mince the chicken using the Grinder fitted with the fine screen, straight into the Kenwood Bowl.

❷ Add the Cajun spice mix, chilli sauce, a little salt, parsley and cornflour. Using the K Beater at minimum speed, mix together.

❸ Divide the mixture into 16, roll into balls and coat in flour to make them less sticky. Heat the oil in a large frying pan. Shallow fry over a gentle heat for about 10 minutes, turning occasionally until browned.

❹ Meanwhile fit the Pro Slicer/Grater with the thick slicing plate and slice the peppers into thin strips. Add the strips to the pan and increase the heat slightly. Fry for 5 minutes, or until the pepper is slightly burnt at the edges.

❺ Remove from the heat, pour in the soured cream and season well.

❻ Leave for 2-3 minutes and let the cream bubble whilst the pan is cooling. Serve on a bed of rice if wished, with a mixed leaf salad.

CHICKEN, LEMON AND CHIVE SAUSAGES

MAKES 8 STANDARD OR 32 COCKTAIL SAUSAGES PREPARATION TIME: 20 MINUTES COOKING TIME: 15-20 OR 10 MINUTES TOOLS MULTI FOOD GRINDER / K BEATER / SAUSAGE FILLER

INGREDIENTS

450g (1lb) boneless, skinless chicken,
preferably thigh meat, cut into strips

10ml (2 tsp) snipped fresh chives

5ml (1 tsp) salt

freshly ground black pepper

15ml (1 tbsp) lemon juice

5ml (1 tsp) finely grated lemon rind

1 egg

50g (2oz) fresh breadcrumbs

length of sausage casing, standard or
small, depending on size of sausage
required

❶ Fit the fine screen to the Grinder and mince the chicken into the Kenwood Bowl. Feed a little minced chicken back through the Mincer to push through any remaining strips of chicken.

❷ Add the chives, salt, pepper, lemon juice and rind, egg and breadcrumbs to the Kenwood Bowl. Using the K Beater, mix together at minimum speed.

❸ Replace the screen and cutting blade with the Sausage Filler. Dampen the end of the nozzle and slip on the sausage casing. Feed the chicken sausage filling into the Grinder and through the Filler.

❹ Once all the filling has been used, twist the casing to make individual standard or cocktail sausages. See page 15 for further instructions.

❺ To cook the sausages, heat a little oil in a frying pan over a gentle heat. Fry slowly for 15-20 minutes, or 10 minutes for cocktail sausages, turning occasionally. If preferred these sausages can be grilled.

Variation For skinless sausages omit the casings. Sprinkle 15ml (1 tbsp) each of flour and sesame seeds on a large tray. As the sausage mixture leaves the Filler lay it in straight lines on the tray. Roll in the flour mixture to coat then cut into individual sausages. Fry in a little oil, to cook.

CHICKEN TIKKA KEBABS

INGREDIENTS

450g (1lb) skinless chicken breast
fillets
10ml (2 tsp) ground coriander
10ml (2 tsp) ground cumin
½ small onion, peeled and roughly
chopped
1 clove garlic, peeled
2.5cm (1 inch) piece fresh root
ginger, peeled and roughly chopped
30ml (2 tbsp) lemon juice
10ml (2 tsp) paprika
2.5ml (½ tsp) chilli powder, optional
5ml (1 tsp) salt
few sprigs fresh coriander
45ml (3 tbsp) natural yogurt

SERVES 4 PREPARATION TIME: 15 MINUTES PLUS MARINATING
COOKING TIME: 10 MINUTES TOOLS MULTI-MILL

1 Cut the chicken into 2.5cm (1 inch) cubes and place in a shallow dish.

2 Place the ground coriander, cumin, onion, garlic, ginger, lemon juice, paprika, chilli powder, salt and fresh coriander in the Multi-Mill. Blend together until smooth.

3 Add to the chicken with the yogurt and stir well to make sure the chicken is well coated in the marinade. Cover and refrigerate for 1-2 hours, or overnight, if time allows.

4 Thread the chicken on to either 4 wooden or metal skewers. If using wooden skewers soak in water first to prevent them burning.

5 Place under a preheated hot grill and cook for 8-10 minutes, or until the juices run clear, turning occasionally. Serve with a mixed leaf salad and rice, if wished.

WEST INDIAN CHICKEN

INGREDIENTS

2 onions, peeled and quartered
3 large cloves garlic, peeled
5ml (1 inch) piece fresh root ginger,
chopped
45ml (3 tbsp) vegetable oil
45ml (3 tbsp) mild curry powder
5ml (1 tsp) chilli powder
3 tomatoes, quartered
8 chicken thighs, weighing 1.4-1.8kg
(3-4lb)
300ml (½ pint) chicken stock
115g (4oz) cashew nuts
30ml (2 tbsp) natural yogurt
10ml (2 tsp) ground coriander
salt and freshly ground black pepper

SERVES 4-6 PREPARATION TIME: 20 MINUTES COOKING TIME: 1 HOUR 10 MINUTES
TOOLS FOOD PROCESSING ATTACHMENT / MULTI-MILL

1 Place the onions, garlic and ginger in the Food Processing Attachment fitted with the knife blade and process until chopped.

2 Heat the oil in a large pan and sauté the onion mixture for 15-20 minutes, over a medium heat, until golden. Add the curry powder and chilli powder and fry for 1 minute.

3 Blend the tomatoes in the Multi-Mill, in batches if necessary, or in the Food Processing Attachment, until smooth. Add to the pan with the chicken thighs and stir to thoroughly coat the chicken.

4 Pour in the stock, bring to the boil, cover and simmer for 45 minutes. Stir occasionally to prevent the chicken from sticking to the base of the pan.

5 Using the Multi-Mill, chop the cashew nuts until they are very fine, almost to the point of becoming a nut butter.

6 Stir the cashew nuts, yogurt and coriander into the chicken and heat through. Season with salt and freshly ground black pepper and serve.

Eggs and cheese are probably the most versatile of foods, with endless culinary uses. Use the Whisk to help prepare fillings for tarts and quiches, mixing eggs for omelettes, whipping up egg whites for soufflés or batter for clafoutis.

The Pro Slicer/Grater and Roto Food Cutter or Food Processing Attachment will cope with all your needs for grating and shredding cheeses to use for filling omelettes, tortillas and frittatas, flavouring quiches and sauces, making cheese fondue or topping pizzas. The Roto Food Cutter is particularly useful for grating hard cheeses like Italian Parmesan and Pecorino.

TWICE BAKED SOUFFLÉS

SERVES 6   PREPARATION TIME: 25 MINUTES PLUS COOLING   COOKING TIME: 55-60 MINUTES
TOOLS ROTO FOOD CUTTER / LIQUIDISER / BALLOON WHISK

INGREDIENTS

50g (2oz) Parmesan cheese
75g (3oz) mature Cheddar cheese
115g (4oz) cauliflower florets
115g (4oz) broccoli florets
salt and freshly ground black pepper
150ml (¼ pint) milk
40g (1½oz) butter
40g (1½oz) plain flour
3 large eggs, separated
230ml (8fl oz) single cream
15ml (1 tbsp) wholegrain mustard
baby tomatoes, on the vine, to
garnish

❶ Fit the Roto Food Cutter with the fine shredding drum and grate the Parmesan cheese. Set aside 15ml (1 tbsp). Use the coarse drum to grate the Cheddar cheese.

❷ Grease and line the bases of six 200ml (7fl oz) ramekin dishes with non-stick baking parchment. Dust the sides with the reserved Parmesan cheese. Preheat the oven to 180°C/350°F/Gas 4.

❸ Place the cauliflower and broccoli florets in a saucepan pan of slightly salted boiling water and cook for 7-8 minutes, or until just tender. Drain, refresh under cold running water and drain well.

❹ Place the vegetables and milk in the Liquidiser and blend to a purée. Melt the butter in a saucepan, stir in the flour and cook for 30 seconds. Remove from the heat, stir in the vegetable purée and season with salt and freshly ground black pepper. Return to the heat and bring to the boil, stirring continuously until thickened.

Illustrated on page 68.

❺ Cool slightly then stir in the egg yolks, one at a time. Stir in the Cheddar cheese and remaining Parmesan cheese until well blended. Place the egg whites in the Kenwood Bowl. Using the Whisk, at maximum speed, whisk the egg whites, until stiff, and fold into the sauce.

❻ Divide between the dishes. Place in a roasting tin and add sufficient hot water to reach halfway up the sides of the dishes. Bake for 25-30 minutes, until risen, light golden and just firm to the touch.

❼ Remove from the tin and leave to cool. Using a round bladed knife, release the soufflés from the ramekins and turn out into individual gratin dishes.

❽ Preheat the oven to 200°C/400°F/Gas 6. Mix the cream and mustard together; pour over the soufflés to coat. Bake for 15 minutes, until golden. Serve garnished with baby tomatoes on the vine, roasted with the soufflés, if wished.

BRIE AND POTATO TORTILLA

SERVES 4 PREPARATION TIME: 15 MINUTES COOKING TIME: 27-30 MINUTES
TOOLS FOOD PROCESSING ATTACHMENT OR PRO SLICER/GRATER/BALLOON WHISK

1 Using the Food Processing Attachment or Pro Slicer/Grater fitted with the thick slicing plate, slice the onion and leek. Heat a large non-stick frying pan, add half the sunflower oil, onion and leek and cook gently for 8-10 minutes, or until soft.

2 Meanwhile slice the potatoes using the thick slicing plate. Remove the leek and onion, using a slotted spoon and set aside. Add the remaining oil and the potatoes to the pan and cook over a moderate heat, stirring frequently, for 10 minutes, or until potatoes are golden.

3 Using the Balloon Whisk, whisk the eggs and seasoning together, stir in the leek, onion and Brie. Pour over the potatoes and gently mix to combine with the potatoes. Sprinkle over the parsley.

4 Cook over a moderate heat for 6-8 minutes, or until set around the edges and the underneath is browned. Place under a preheated grill for about 3 minutes, or until just set and lightly browned. Serve hot or warm with salad.

INGREDIENTS
1 onion, peeled and halved lengthways
1 leek, topped, tailed and halved widthways
60ml (4 tbsp) sunflower oil
450g (1 lb) old potatoes, peeled
6 large eggs
salt and freshly ground black pepper
115g (4oz) Brie, cut into chunks
30ml (2 tbsp) freshly chopped parsley

SMOKED SALMON AND WATERCRESS QUICHE

SERVES 4-6 PREPARATION TIME: 15 MINUTES PLUS CHILLING COOKING TIME: 45-50 MINUTES
TOOLS FOOD PROCESSING ATTACHMENT

1 Roll out the pastry on a lightly floured surface and use to line a 20cm (8 inch) fluted flan ring or tin about 4cm (1½ inch) deep. Chill for 20 minutes.

2 Preheat the oven to 200°C/400°F/Gas 6. Prick the base of the pastry case and line with greaseproof paper and baking beans. Bake blind for 15-20 minutes, removing the paper and beans after 10-15 minutes. Reduce the oven to 180°C/350°F/Gas 4.

3 Meanwhile using the Food Processing Attachment, fitted with the knife blade, coarsely chop the watercress and set aside. Chop the onion and place in a frying pan with the sunflower oil. Sauté until soft and golden, then stir in the watercress and cook for 1 minute, until wilted.

4 Using the fine shredding plate, grate the cheese. Mix the eggs, milk, cream and seasoning together.

5 Sprinkle the onion and watercress mix over the base of the pastry case, sprinkle over half the cheese, top with the smoked salmon and remaining cheese. Pour over the egg mixture.

6 Bake for 30 minutes or until golden and set. Serve warm or cold.

Variation For a traditional Quiche Lorraine, replace the watercress and smoked salmon with 150g (5oz) lean streaky bacon chopped and fried until golden and double the quantity of cheese.

INGREDIENTS
1 quantity of oatmeal shortcrust pastry see page 165
50g (2oz) watercress
1 onion, quartered
15ml (1 tbsp) sunflower oil
50g (2oz) Cheddar cheese
3 eggs
150ml (5fl oz) milk
90ml (3fl oz) single cream
salt and freshly ground black pepper
100g (3½oz) smoked salmon trimmings, roughly chopped

POTATO GNOCCHI WITH GORGONZOLA

INGREDIENTS

700g (1¾lb) floury potatoes

salt and freshly ground black pepper

2 egg yolks

150-175g (5-6oz) plain flour, plus
extra for rolling

TO SERVE:

175g (6oz) Gorgonzola cheese,
crumbled

90ml (6 tbsp) double cream

15ml (1 tbsp) snipped fresh chives

fresh basil leaves

sea salt and freshly ground black
pepper

SERVES 4   PREPARATION TIME: 25 MINUTES   COOKING TIME: 30 MINUTES
TOOLS COLANDER AND SIEVE / K BEATER

❶ Cook the potatoes in their skins in lightly salted boiling water for about 20 minutes, or until soft. Drain well, leave until cool enough to handle and then peel. Using the Sieve fitted with the coarse screen, rough side up, sieve the potatoes into the Kenwood Bowl.

❷ Remove the Sieve and bowl carrier and using the K Beater on minimum speed add a little salt, the egg yolks and flour. Stop adding the flour when the mixture is smooth and slightly sticky. The moisture in the potatoes varies with variety.

❸ Turn on to a floured surface and roll the gnocchi into thick ropes about 2.5cm (1 inch) in diameter. Cut into 2cm (¾ inch) pieces. Place each piece on the end of your thumb and press the prongs of a fork lightly over the top to mark grooves.

❹ To cook drop 20-25 pieces at a time into a pan of boiling water and cook until they rise to the surface. Cook for 45-60 seconds more. Remove with a slotted spoon, into a large bowl whilst you cook the remainder.

❺ Place the Gorgonzola cheese and cream in a large saucepan and heat gently until the cheese melts. Add the drained gnocchi and toss to combine. Sprinkle with chives, basil, sea salt and black pepper and serve.

Illustrated opposite.

BACON, ONION AND TOMATO CLAFOUTIS

INGREDIENTS

6 rashers smoked back bacon

280g (10oz) baby plum tomatoes

75g (3oz) Pecorino cheese

2 eggs

1 egg yolk

25g (1oz) butter, melted

salt and freshly ground black pepper

50g (2oz) plain flour

300ml (½ pint) milk

6 spring onions, chopped

SERVES 4   PREPARATION TIME: 20 MINUTES   COOKING TIME: 30-40 MINUTES
TOOLS ROTO FOOD CUTTER / BALLOON WHISK

❶ Preheat the oven to 190°C/375°F/Gas 5. Lightly grease a 1.4 litre (2½ pint) shallow ovenproof dish. Grill the bacon until crisp, then cut into large pieces. Sprinkle over the base of the dish and top with the whole tomatoes.

❷ Using the Roto Food Cutter fitted with the fine shredding drum, grate the Pecorino cheese.

❸ Place the eggs, egg yolk, melted butter and seasoning in the Kenwood Bowl. Using the Whisk beat together. Add the flour and whisk to combine. Finally whisk in the milk until the batter is smooth.

❹ Stir in the spring onions and all but 30ml (2 tbsp) of the cheese. Pour over the bacon and tomatoes. Sprinkle over the remaining cheese and bake for 25-35 minutes, or until the batter is golden and lightly set. Serve warm.

CHEESE AND CHILLI STICKS

MAKES ABOUT 24   PREPARATION TIME: 15 MINUTES   COOKING TIME: 10-12 MINUTES
TOOLS K BEATER

INGREDIENTS
175g (6oz) plain flour
pinch of salt
75g (3oz) butter, cut into pieces
50g (2oz) Cheddar or Emmental
cheese, grated
5ml (1 tsp) mild chilli powder
1 egg
beaten egg, to glaze
sesame seeds and poppy seeds, to
sprinkle

1 Preheat the oven to 180°C/350°F/Gas 4. Lightly grease two baking sheets. Place the flour, salt and butter in the Kenwood Bowl and mix with the K Beater at minimum speed until the mixture resembles fine breadcrumbs.

2 Add the cheese and chilli powder and continue mixing until combined. Add the egg and mix to a smooth dough.

Illustrated on page 68.

3 On a lightly floured surface roll out the dough into an oblong 12.5cm (5 inches) wide and about 7mm (¼ inch) thick. Cut in half and brush with egg glaze. Sprinkle one half with sesame seeds and the other with poppy seeds.

4 Cut into sticks 1.2cm (½ inch) wide. Place on the prepared baking sheets and bake for 10-12 minutes, or until golden. Leave to cool slightly before transferring to a wire rack.

ASPARAGUS AND SPAGHETTI FRITTATA

SERVES 4   PREPARATION TIME: 20 MINUTES   COOKING TIME: 15-20 MINUTES
TOOLS FOOD PROCESSING ATTACHMENT / WHISK

INGREDIENTS
175g (6oz) asparagus, trimmed
115g (4oz) frozen broad beans,
thawed
50g (2oz) Parmesan cheese
handful of fresh herbs e.g. parsley,
oregano, basil
6 large eggs
30ml (2 tbsp) milk
salt and freshly ground black pepper
225g (8oz) cold, cooked spaghetti, or
any other leftover pasta

1 Cut the asparagus into 2.5cm (1 inch) lengths. Place in a pan of boiling water and cook for 5-6 minutes, or until just tender. Plunge in cold water, drain and pat dry on absorbent kitchen paper.

2 Slip the broad beans out of their waxy skins and mix with the asparagus.

3 Using the Food Processing Attachment fitted with the fine shredding plate, grate the Parmesan cheese and set aside. Use the knife blade to chop the herbs.

4 Place the eggs in the Kenwood Bowl and using the Whisk, blend the eggs, milk and seasoning together. Reserve 30ml (2 tbsp) cheese and add the remainder to the Bowl with the chopped herbs. Mix together on speed 1.

5 Stir the asparagus, broad beans and spaghetti into the egg mixture. Heat the oil in a 23cm (9 inch) non-stick frying pan. Pour in the egg mixture and cook over a moderate heat for 6-8 minutes or until the bottom is golden.

6 Sprinkle the reserved Parmesan cheese over the top and place under a preheated grill to lightly brown the cheese and just set the top. Slide on to a warmed serving plate and serve hot or warm, cut into wedges.

Cook's Note The traditional way to cook a frittata is to flip it over in the pan to cook the top, rather than under the grill. To try this, add all the cheese in step 3. To flip the frittata loosen the base, take a large plate and place it upside down over the frying pan. Using oven gloves hold it firmly and turn the pan over and the frittata on to the plate. Slide back into the pan and cook for 3-4 minutes.

MOZZARELLA, MUSHROOM AND TOMATO PIZZA

SERVES 4   PREPARATION TIME: 20 MINUTES PLUS RISING   COOKING TIME: 25-30 MINUTES
TOOLS DOUGH HOOK / PRO SLICER/GRATER OR FOOD PROCESSING ATTACHMENT

INGREDIENTS

225g (8oz) strong plain white flour
5ml (1 tsp) salt
5ml (1 tsp) fast action dried yeast
150ml (¼ pint) tepid water
15ml (1 tbsp) olive oil

FOR THE TOPPING:

1 onion, halved lengthways
75g (3oz) button mushrooms
1 yellow pepper, halved and seeded
150g (5oz) mozzarella cheese
45ml (3 tbsp) olive oil
45ml (3 tbsp) sun dried tomato paste
50g (2oz) feta cheese
4 tomatoes, roughly chopped
salt and freshly ground black pepper
basil leaves, to garnish

❶ Fit the Dough Hook. Place the flour, salt and yeast in the Kenwood Bowl. With the machine running at minimum gradually add the water and olive oil. Knead for 5 minutes, until smooth and elastic.

❷ Transfer the dough to a lightly floured surface and shape into a smooth ball. Roll out into a 30cm (12 inch) round and place in a lightly oiled pizza pan or on a baking sheet, pressing up the edges.

❸ Cover the dough with lightly oiled clear film and leave in a warm place for 30-40 minutes, or until slightly risen and puffy.

❹ Meanwhile prepare the topping. Fit the thick slicing plate to the Pro Slicer/Grater or Food Processing Attachment and slice the onion. Remove and set aside. Slice the mushrooms and pepper and set aside. Fit the coarse grating plate and grate the mozzarella.

❺ Heat 30ml (2 tbsp) olive oil in a frying pan, add the onions and cook gently for about 10 minutes, or until softened and light golden, stirring occasionally. Preheat the oven to 220°C/425°F/Gas 7.

❻ Spread the sun dried tomato paste over the pizza base. Mix the mozzarella and feta cheese together and sprinkle half over the pizza. Top with the tomatoes, onions, mushrooms and pepper. Sprinkle over the remaining cheese and season well.

❼ Drizzle over the remaining olive oil and bake for 25-30 minutes, or until golden and well risen. Serve garnished with fresh basil leaves.

CHEESE FONDUE

INGREDIENTS
1 clove garlic, cut in half

150g (5oz) Emmental cheese

175g (6oz) Gruyère cheese

150ml (5fl oz) dry white wine

30ml (2 tbsp) kirsch

10ml (2 tsp) cornflour

pinch of nutmeg

freshly ground black pepper

crusty bread cubes and raw
vegetables, to serve

SERVES 4   PREPARATION TIME: 10 MINUTES   COOKING TIME: 10 MINUTES

TOOLS ROTO FOOD CUTTER OR PRO SLICER/GRATER

❶ Rub the garlic round the inside of the fondue pot. Fit the fine shredding drum to the Roto Food Cutter or the fine plate to the Pro Slicer/Shredder and grate the cheeses.

❷ Place the wine in the fondue pot and heat slowly until hot. Meanwhile mix the kirsch and cornflour together.

❸ Slowly stir the Emmental and Gruyère cheeses into the hot wine with a wooden spoon. Add the kirsch mixture, nutmeg and black pepper and stir continuously until thick and smooth.

❹ Transfer to a spirit burner at the table and keep it slowly simmering. Serve with crusty bread and raw vegetables for skewering and dipping in the fondue sauce.

GOLDEN ONION TART

INGREDIENTS
1 quantity of shortcrust pastry, see
page 165

400g (14oz) onions, peeled and
halved lengthways

30ml (2 tbsp) vegetable oil

15ml (1 tbsp) balsamic vinegar

2 eggs

1 egg yolk

200ml (7fl oz) milk

100ml (3½fl oz) crème fraîche

salt and freshly ground black pepper

50g (2oz) Roquefort cheese

30ml (2 tbsp) freshly grated
Parmesan cheese

SERVES 4   PREPARATION TIME: 15 MINUTES PLUS CHILLING   COOKING TIME: 40-45 MINUTES

TOOLS PRO SLICER/GRATER / BALLOON WHISK

❶ Roll out the pastry on a lightly floured surface and use to line a loose-based 23cm (9 inch) fluted flan tin. Chill for 30 minutes.

❷ Preheat the oven to 200°C/400°F/Gas 6. Prick the base of the pastry case, line with greaseproof paper and baking beans. Bake blind for 15 minutes, remove the paper and beans and bake for a further 5 minutes. Reduce the oven to 190°C/375°F/Gas 5.

❸ Meanwhile using the Pro Slicer/Grater fitted with the thin slicing plate slice the onions.

❹ Heat the oil in a frying pan, add the onions and cook over a low heat, for about 20 minutes, until golden brown and caramelised. Stir in the balsamic vinegar and cook for 2 minutes.

❺ Using the Whisk mix the eggs, egg yolk, milk, crème fraîche and seasoning together in the Kenwood Bowl. Arrange the onion mixture in the pastry case, crumble over the Roquefort cheese then pour over the egg mixture. Sprinkle over the Parmesan cheese.

❻ Bake for 20-25 minutes or until just set and golden. Serve warm with salad leaves.

GOUGÈRE WITH WILD MUSHROOMS

SERVES 4 PREPARATION TIME: 20 MINUTES COOKING TIME: 30-40 MINUTES

TOOLS FOOD PROCESSING ATTACHMENT OR PRO SLICER/GRATER

INGREDIENTS

115g (4oz) Gruyère cheese

1 quantity choux pastry see page 164

salt and freshly ground black pepper

beaten egg, to glaze

FOR THE MUSHROOM FILLING:

1 onion, halved lengthways

25g (1oz) butter

15ml (1 tbsp) vegetable oil

1 clove garlic, crushed

450g (1lb) mixed mushrooms, e.g shittake, portabellini, chanterelle, chestnut, crimini

90ml (3fl oz) single cream

freshly grated nutmeg

10ml (2 tsp) meaux mustard

snipped chives, to garnish

❶ Preheat the oven to 220°C/425°F/Gas 7. Line a baking sheet with non-stick baking parchment and mark a 23cm (9 inch) circle.

❷ Fit the coarse grating plate to the Food Processing Attachment or Pro Slicer/Grater and grate the cheese. Reserve 25g (1oz) and beat the remainder into the choux pastry. Season with salt and freshly ground black pepper.

❸ Place spoonfuls of the cheese choux pastry around the inside edge of the marked circle on the baking parchment. Brush with a little beaten egg and sprinkle with the remaining cheese. Bake for 30-40 minutes, or until well risen, crisp and golden.

❹ Meanwhile make the filling. Fit the coarse slicing plate to either attachment and slice the onion. Melt the butter in a frying pan, add the oil and onion slices and cook for 5-6 minutes, until softened. Add the garlic and cook for a further 2 minutes.

❺ Slice any large mushrooms and halve smaller ones. Add the mushrooms to the onions and cook over a gentle heat for 10-15 minutes, depending on variety, until tender and most of the liquid has evaporated. Season to taste. Stir in the cream add a little freshly grated nutmeg and he mustard.

❻ To serve, transfer the gougère to a warmed serving plate. Pile the mushrooms in the centre, sprinkle over the snipped chives and serve immediately.

With two pasta machines to choose from you can make flat sheet pasta for lasagne or ravioli with the Italian Pasta Maker, or by using the Italian Pasta Maker Attachments make spaghetti or varieties of flat ribbon pasta such as Trenette, Tagliolini or Tagliatelle. Pasta Fresca will also produce spaghetti and tagliatelle and tubular shaped pasta such as macaroni and rigatoni.

Use the Pro Slicer/Grater and Roto Food Cutter attachments to prepare vegetables for sauces to accompany the pasta. These attachments are also ideal along with the Food Processing Attachment for preparing vegetables for risottos, fried rice, nut roast, lentil casseroles and stuffing for vegetables such as aubergines.

BASIC PASTA FOR PASTA FRESCA

SERVES 6   PREPARATION TIME: 10 MINUTES PLUS DRYING   COOKING TIME: 5 MINUTES
TOOLS K BEATER / PASTA FRESCA

1 Place the flour and salt in the Kenwood Bowl. Add the eggs and oil and using the K Beater, mix on minimum speed or speed 1 for 1-2 minutes, until the mixture resembles breadcrumbs, but is slightly moist.

2 Fit Pasta Fresca with the preferred screen and with the machine running on speed 2-3 drop small amounts of pasta dough mix into the feed tube. Leave to clear. Do not over-fill.

3 Cut pasta at preferred lengths and leave to dry for 30 minutes, before cooking, or allow to dry completely. Use as required in your chosen recipe. For general cooking instructions see below.

Cook's Note The moisture content of flour varies so if necessary adjust by adding a little extra if the mix is too wet and starts to form a dough, or add a little water if the mix is too dry. As a general guide allow 75-125g (3-4½oz) pasta per person. For 4 servings make a 3 egg mix and reduce the flour by 25%.

Variations Wholemeal pasta: replace plain flour with wholemeal flour. **Pasta Rossa:** replace 1 egg with 75g (3oz) tomato purée. **Pasta Verde:** replace 1 egg with 150g (5½oz) frozen chopped spinach, defrosted and squeezed dry to remove all excess moisture. Adjust the flour quantity if necessary. **Herb Pasta:** Add 60ml (4 tbsp) finely chopped fresh mixed herbs to the dry ingredients in step 1.

INGREDIENTS

500g (1lb 2oz) plain flour
2.5ml (½ tsp) salt
4 eggs, lightly beaten
2.5ml (½ tsp) sunflower or olive oil

BASIC PASTA FOR ITALIAN PASTA MAKER

SERVES 6   PREPARATION TIME: 10 MINUTES PLUS DRYING   COOKING TIME: 5 MINUTES
TOOLS DOUGH HOOK / ITALIAN PASTA MAKER

1 Place both flours and salt in the Kenwood Bowl. Add the eggs and using the Dough Hook, mix on speed 3-4 for about 3 minutes. The mixture should look crumbly, but moist. If necessary add a teaspoon of water if the mix is too dry.

2 Knead the crumbly mixture together by hand to form a dough. Knead until smooth, divide into two or three pieces and wrap in clear film. Leave to rest for 15 minutes, or up to 2 hours.

3 Fit the Italian Pasta Maker, shape one piece of dough into a long flat disc and feed through the rollers set on number 1. Sprinkle flour over the rollers as necessary.

4 Fold the dough in three, rotate and repeat several times. Pass through the rollers, gradually increasing the setting from 1 to 6 or 7, or your desired thickness. Use as flat pasta sheets or use one of the Cutting Attachments as required. Allow to dry for 30 minutes, then cook or cover and refrigerate for up to 24 hours.

Cooking Instructions Cook in a large pan of boiling salted water. The time will vary. Freshly made pasta can be cooked in as little as 15 seconds after the cooking water returns to the boil. Depending on the thickness, fresh pasta should be *al dente* within 2-4 minutes.

Variations Follow instructions as for Basic Pasta for Pasta Fresca above.

INGREDIENTS

350g (13oz) fine white flour, type 00
150g (5oz) strong plain white flour
2.5ml (½ tsp) salt
4 eggs, lightly beaten

PASTA RIBBONS WITH SHELLFISH AND RED PEPPER PURÉE

SERVES 4   PREPARATION TIME: 15 MINUTES PLUS MAKING PASTA
COOKING TIME: 16-18 MINUTES   TOOLS FOOD PROCESSING ATTACHMENT OR LIQUIDISER / PASTA FRESCA

INGREDIENTS

2 red peppers

2 cloves garlic

salt and freshly ground black pepper

1 small onion, quartered

15ml (1 tbsp) olive oil

175ml (6fl oz) dry white wine

12 large raw prawn tails in shells

24 mussels in shells, cleaned

2 small squid, cleaned and sliced

1 quantity plain or herb flavoured lasagne ribbons, see page 80

chopped parsley, to garnish

1 Place the peppers under a preheated grill with the unpeeled garlic cloves and cook until beginning to blacken, turning frequently. Leave to cool slightly then remove the pepper skins, deseed and roughly chop. Peel the garlic cloves.

2 Place the peppers and garlic in the Food Processing Attachment fitted with the knife blade or the Liquidiser and blend to a coarse purée, season and set aside. Using the knife blade with the Food Processing Attachment coarsely chop the onion, or chop by hand.

3 Place the onion and oil in a saucepan and cook for 4-5 minutes, until softened and pale golden. Add the wine.

4 Add the prawns and mussels and cook for 3-4 minutes, until the mussels have opened and the prawns changed colour. Remove and set aside. Add the squid and cook for 1 minute. Remove with a slotted spoon and allow the liquor to simmer and reduce to about a third.

5 Cook the lasagne ribbons in a pan of boiling salted water, until *al dente*, about 3 minutes, if fresh. Reheat the shellfish in the reduced wine liquor.

6 Drain the pasta, add the red pepper purée and toss to coat. Stir in the shellfish and serve garnished with chopped parsley.

Illustrated on page 78.

TAGLIATELLE WITH CHICKEN LIVERS AND SAGE

SERVES 4 PREPARATION TIME: 10 MINUTES, PLUS MAKING PASTA   COOKING TIME: 30-35 MINUTES
TOOLS FOOD PROCESSING ATTACHMENT / PASTA FRESCA OR ITALIAN PASTA MAKER

INGREDIENTS

1 onion, quartered

1 stick celery, cut into 5cm (2 inch) lengths

30ml (2 tbsp) vegetable oil

1 carrot, diced

225g (8oz) chicken livers, trimmed

400g (14oz) can chopped tomatoes

15ml (1 tbsp) tomato purée

5ml (1 tsp) sugar

5ml (1 tsp) white wine vinegar

salt and freshly ground black pepper

5ml (1 tsp) freshly chopped sage leaves

¾ quantity of fresh tagliatelle, plain or verde, see page 80

15ml (1 tbsp) capers, chopped

1 Fit the Food Processing Attachment with the knife blade and chop the onion and celery, or chop by hand. Heat the oil in a saucepan add the onion, celery and carrot and sauté for 6-8 minutes or until golden, stirring occasionally.

2 Using the knife blade chop the livers, or chop by hand. Add to the pan and sauté for 5 minutes. Add the chopped tomatoes, tomato purée, sugar and vinegar and stir to combine.

3 Season with salt and a generous sprinkling of black pepper and simmer gently for 15 minutes, adding the sage after 10 minutes.

4 Meanwhile cook the tagliatelle in a saucepan of slightly salted boiling water for 3 minutes or until *al dente*. Stir the capers into the sauce.

5 Drain the tagliatelle, add the sauce and toss together. Place in a warmed serving dish and serve immediately.

TOMATO AND FETA RIGATONI

SERVES 4   PREPARATION TIME: 5 MINUTES, PLUS MAKING PASTA
COOKING TIME: 25 MINUTES   TOOLS PASTA FRESCA

INGREDIENTS

1 onion, chopped

15ml (1 tbsp) olive oil

2 cloves garlic, crushed

400g (14oz) can chopped tomatoes

4 sun-dried tomatoes in oil, drained and finely chopped

¾ quantity of fresh rigatoni, see page 80

salt and freshly ground black pepper

150g (5oz) cherry tomatoes, halved

225g (8oz) Feta cheese, cubed

① Place the onion and oil in a saucepan and sauté the onion for about 5 minutes until softened. Add the garlic and cook for a further 2 minutes.

② Stir in the chopped tomatoes and sun-dried tomatoes and simmer gently for 10 minutes, stirring occasionally until the sauce thickens.

③ Meanwhile cook the rigatoni in a saucepan of lightly salted boiling water for about 5 minutes, or until al dente.

④ Stir the cherry tomato halves into the sauce, season with salt and pepper and simmer for 2 minutes. Drain the pasta and tip into a warmed serving bowl. Add the tomato sauce and feta cheese then stir gently to combine.

SPAGHETTI ALLA CARBONARA

SERVES 4   PREPARATION TIME: 10 MINUTES PLUS MAKING PASTA   COOKING TIME: 7-8 MINUTES   TOOLS PRO SLICER/GRATER / PASTA FRESCA OR ITALIAN PASTA MAKER

INGREDIENTS

75g (3oz) Parmesan cheese

3 eggs

salt and freshly ground black pepper

150g (5oz) smoked pancetta, sliced

15ml (1 tbsp) olive oil

1 clove garlic, halved

¾ quantity of fresh spaghetti, about 450g (1lb) see page 80

① Using the Pro Slicer/Grater fitted with the fine shredding plate, finely grate the Parmesan cheese. Beat the eggs together with a fork then mix in the cheese and season with salt and freshly ground black pepper.

② Cut the pancetta into thin strips. Heat the oil in a frying pan and sauté the pancetta and garlic for 4-5 minutes, or until the pancetta starts to brown. Remove from the heat and discard the garlic.

③ Meanwhile place the spaghetti in a pan of boiling lightly salted water and cook for 2-3 minutes, if fresh, until al dente. Allow 6-8 minutes if you have dried the pasta.

④ Drain the pasta and add the pancetta and egg mixture. Toss well to cook the eggs until they are creamy. Serve immediately, sprinkled with freshly ground black pepper.

Cook's Note If pancetta is unavailable replace with smoked streaky bacon rashers, increase to 200g (7oz).

RAVIOLI WITH SPINACH AND RICOTTA

SERVES4   PREPARATION TIME: 25 MINUTES PLUS RESTING   COOKING TIME: 15 MINUTES
TOOLS FOOD PROCESSING ATTACHMENT / PASTA FRESCA

INGREDIENTS

2 onions, quartered

25g (1oz) butter

200g (7oz) young spinach leaves

75g (3oz) ricotta cheese

2.5ml (½ tsp) freshly grated nutmeg

salt and freshly ground black pepper

½ quantity of plain or herb pasta, see page 80 basic pasta for Pasta Maker

about 15ml (1 tbsp) olive oil

flour, for dusting

1 egg white, lightly beaten

200ml (7fl oz) single cream

Parmesan shavings, to serve

chopped dill and snipped chives, to garnish

1 Fit the knife blade to the Food Processing Attachment and chop the onions, or finely chop by hand. Melt the butter in a saucepan, add the onions and sauté until softened and light golden. Remove half and set aside.

2 Add the spinach to the pan and cook for 2-3 minutes, until wilted. Leave to cool. Place in the Food Processing Attachment, fitted with the knife blade and process to chop. Add the ricotta, nutmeg, salt and freshly ground black pepper and pulse to mix.

3 Make the pasta following the instructions on page 80 adding a little extra oil, about 10ml (2 tsp) to mix to a soft dough. Cut in half, wrap one half in clear film and roll out the remaining half on a lightly floured surface into a rectangle measuring 20 x 40cm (8 x 16 inches). Cover and roll out the other half to the same size.

4 Place small spoonfuls of filling at 4cm (1½ inch) intervals across the uncovered dough. Brush the spaces between the filling with the egg white. Place the other sheet of pasta dough on top and press down firmly along the glazed lines.

5 Cut into squares using a sharp knife or pastry wheel. Transfer to a floured tray and leave to rest and dry for about 1 hour.

6 Bring a large pan of slightly salted water to the boil; add the ravioli and cook for 3-4 minutes or until *al dente*. Meanwhile place the reserved onion in a saucepan with the cream and season with salt and freshly ground black pepper and heat gently.

7 Drain the pasta and toss with the cream and onion mix. Season with a generous amount of freshly ground black pepper. Gently heat until sauce and pasta are hot.

8 Divide between four warmed serving plates and top with fresh Parmesan shavings and sprinkle with chopped fresh dill and chives. Serve immediately.

Cook's Note If you do not have a Food Processing Attachment, but would still like to make this recipe, chop the spinach before adding to the pan in step 2. Use the K Beater to mix the spinach, ricotta, nutmeg and seasoning together.

If you have an Italian Pasta Maker use this to roll out the dough. Use the basic pasta for Italian Pasta Maker recipe on page 80, and omit the extra oil in step 3 above.

BROWN RICE AND NUT ROAST

INGREDIENTS

115g (4oz) long grain brown rice
1 onion, quartered
1 clove garlic
25g (1oz) butter
115g (4oz) mushrooms
1 large carrot, peeled
15ml (1 tbsp) chopped thyme
salt and freshly ground black pepper
75g (3oz) mature Cheddar cheese
115g (4oz) wholemeal bread, crusts removed and cubed
100g (3½oz) almonds or unsalted peanuts
2 eggs, lightly beaten
2 tomatoes, sliced

SERVES 4-6   PREPARATION TIME: 25 MINUTES   COOKING TIME: 1¼ – 1½ HOURS
TOOLS FOOD PROCESSING ATTACHMENT OR PRO SLICER/GRATER / LIQUIDISER / K BEATER

❶ Cook the rice in lightly salted boiling water for 25-30 minutes, until tender then drain and set aside.

❷ Meanwhile fit the Food Processing Attachment with the knife blade and chop the onion and garlic or chop by hand. Melt the butter in a frying pan, add the onion and garlic and sauté for 3 minutes. Chop the mushrooms either with the knife blade or by hand.

❸ Fit the coarse shredding plate to the Food Processing Attachment or Pro Slicer/Grater and grate the carrot. Add to the frying pan with the mushrooms and cook for 3-4 minutes. Stir in the thyme and seasoning.

❹ Using the cleaned coarse shredding plate grate the cheese and set aside. Add the bread cubes and nuts to the Food Processing Attachment fitted with the knife blade or the Liquidiser and process to make breadcrumbs and chop the nuts. Process in batches if necessary, if using the Liquidiser.

❺ If using the Food Processing Attachment add the rice, cooked vegetables and eggs to the breadcrumb mixture and process on pulse to blend together. If using the Liquidiser, transfer the breadcrumb mixture to the Kenwood Bowl, add the rice, vegetables and eggs and mix together using the K Beater.

❻ Preheat the oven to 190°C/375°F/Gas 5. Grease a 900g (2lb) loaf tin and line the base with greaseproof paper. Pack half the mixture in the tin, sprinkle over the cheese, top with the tomato slices and remaining mixture.

❼ Bake for 50-60 minutes, or until the top is nicely browned and firm to the touch. Cool slightly for 5-10 minutes then turn out on to a serving plate. Serve sliced with fresh tomato sauce. See page 107.

EGG-FRIED RICE

INGREDIENTS

225g (8oz) long grain rice
3 eggs
2 spring onions, finely sliced diagonally
salt and freshly ground black pepper
2 carrots
30ml (2 tbsp) sunflower oil
1 clove garlic, crushed
1 chilli, finely chopped, optional
75g (3oz) cooked peeled prawns
75g (3oz) frozen peas, thawed
30ml (2 tbsp) soy sauce

SERVES 4   PREPARATION TIME: 10 MINUTES   COOKING TIME: 15 MINUTES
TOOLS BALLOON WHISK / PRO SLICER/GRATER OR ROTO FOOD CUTTER

❶ Cook the rice in slightly salted boiling water for about 9-10 minutes, or until almost tender. Drain, rinse with boiling water and drain well.

❷ Meanwhile, place the eggs, half the sliced spring onions and seasoning in the Kenwood Bowl. Fit the Whisk and whisk together. Using the Pro Slicer/Grater or Roto Food Cutter, fitted with the coarse shredding plate or drum, grate the carrots.

❸ Heat the oil in a wok or large frying pan, add the carrot, garlic and chilli, if using and stir-fry for 2 minutes. Add the egg mixture in a thin stream and stir to scramble and break up.

❹ Add the rice, prawns and peas and stir-fry for 2-3 minutes, until hot. Sprinkle over the soy sauce and remaining spring onions and serve at once.

PASTA, RICE & GRAINS

SQUASH RISOTTO

INGREDIENTS

15g (½oz) dried porcini mushrooms
900ml (1½ pints) hot vegetable stock
1 acorn or small kabocha squash,
skin and seeds removed
75g (3oz) Parmesan cheese
pinch of saffron
1 onion, quartered
25g (1oz) butter
15ml (1 tbsp) sunflower oil
280g (10oz) risotto rice
150ml (¼ pint) dry white wine
115g (4oz) asparagus tips, halved
widthways
salt and freshly ground black pepper

S E R V E S 4   **P R E P A R A T I O N   T I M E :** 15 MINUTES PLUS SOAKING   **C O O K I N G   T I M E :** 30 MINUTES

T O O L S FOOD PROCESSING ATTACHMENT OR PRO SLICER/GRATER

1 Put the dried porcini in a bowl, pour over 150ml (¼ pint) warm water and leave to soak for 20 minutes. Drain, straining the liquor into the hot vegetable stock. Chop the porcini coarsely.

2 Meanwhile cut the squash into 5cm (2 inch) lengths. Fit the Food Processing Attachment or Pro Slicer/Grater with the thin chipper plate and load the squash horizontally into the feed tube, and cut into fine strips. Set aside.

3 Fit the fine shredding plate, grate the Parmesan cheese and set aside. Soak the saffron in 15ml (1 tbsp) hot water. Fit the knife blade to the Food Processing Attachment and chop the onion, or chop by hand.

4 Heat the butter and oil in a large heavy based pan, preferably non-stick, add the onion and cook for 4 minutes. Add the porcini and cook for 2-3 minutes.

5 Add the rice and cook for 1 minute, stirring to coat the grains in oil. Pour in the wine and cook, stirring until the wine is absorbed.

6 Gradually add the stock allowing the rice to absorb the liquid before adding more. After about 15 minutes, stir in the squash and asparagus and cook for about 5 minutes, or until vegetables are softened all the stock has been absorbed and the rice is tender.

7 Stir in the saffron water and about half the Parmesan cheese. Season to taste with salt and freshly ground black pepper and serve, sprinkled with the remaining Parmesan cheese.

PUY LENTIL AND CAMARGUE RICE

INGREDIENTS

115g (4oz) Puy lentils
115g (4oz) red Camargue rice
1 onion, quartered
1 carrot, cut into four
1 stick celery, cut into four
30ml (2 tbsp) olive oil
175g (6oz) diced pancetta
4 tomatoes, skinned, quartered and
deseeded
1 clove garlic, halved
4 sprigs lemon thyme
150ml (¼ pint) red wine
115g (4oz) chorizo, skin removed
and cut into thick slices
45ml (3 tbsp) chopped flat leaf parsley
salt and freshly ground black pepper

SERVES 4   PREPARATION TIME: 15 MINUTES   COOKING TIME: 40-45 MINUTES
TOOLS FOOD PROCESSING ATTACHMENT OR PRO SLICER/GRATER

1 Place the lentils and rice in a saucepan, cover with boiling water and cook for 20-25 minutes, until tender. Drain, refresh under cold running water and drain thoroughly.

2 Fit the Food Processing Attachment with the knife blade, place the onion, carrot and celery in the bowl and using the pulse setting, chop the vegetables. If using the Pro Slicer/Grater fit the thick slicing disc and slice the vegetables.

3 Place in a heavy based saucepan with the olive oil and pancetta and cook for 8-10 minutes.

4 Place the tomatoes, garlic and thyme in the Food Processing Attachment and chop, or chop by hand. Add to the saucepan and cook for 3-4 minutes, stirring. Add the red wine and chorizo and simmer for 5 minutes.

5 Stir in the lentils and rice and heat through. Just before serving stir in the parsley and season to taste with salt and freshly ground black pepper.

POLENTA VERDE WITH MUSHROOM AND TOMATO SALSA

INGREDIENTS

75g (3oz) Parmesan cheese
6 sprigs flat leaf parsley
6 sage leaves
150ml (¼ pint) dry white wine
325ml (12fl oz) vegetable stock
115g (4oz) quick-cook polenta
75g (3oz) fresh young spinach leaves
1 egg yolk
salt and freshly ground black pepper
2.5 ml (½ tsp) grated nutmeg
25g (1oz) butter
1 clove garlic, crushed
75g (3oz) mixed mushrooms
75g (3oz) cherry tomatoes, halved
flat leaf parsley , to garnish

SERVES 4   PREPARATION TIME: 20 MINUTES PLUS COOLING   COOKING TIME: 12-15 MINUTES
TOOLS ROTO FOOD CUTTER / MULTI-MILL

1 Line a loose-bottomed 20cm (8 inch) cake tin with clear film. Fit the Roto Food Cutter with the fine shredding drum and grate the Parmesan cheese. Place the flat leaf parsley and sage in the Multi-Mill and chop.

2 Heat the wine and stock in a large saucepan, until boiling, sprinkle in the polenta, continually stirring for 1 minute. Stir in the spinach and cook for 1 minute or until thick.

3 Remove from the heat and stir in the herbs, 50g (2oz) grated Parmesan and egg yolk. Season well with salt, freshly ground black pepper and nutmeg.

4 Transfer to the prepared tin and spread it out, to cover evenly, using the Kenwood Spatula. Leave until cold and set and cut into 8 wedges.

5 Place on a lightly greased baking sheet and sprinkle with the remaining Parmesan cheese. Place under a preheated grill for 3-4 minutes, until golden.

6 Meanwhile heat the butter and garlic in a frying pan and sauté the mushrooms and cherry tomatoes for 2-3 minutes over a high heat. Arrange two polenta triangles on each plate and top with the mushrooms and tomatoes. Garnish with parsley and serve.

Illustrated opposite.

VEGETARIAN KEBBE

SERVES 4   PREPARATION TIME: 25 MINUTES   COOKING TIME: 45-50 MINUTES
TOOLS FOOD PROCESSING ATTACHMENT / K BEATER / KEBBE MAKER ADAPTOR AND MULTI FOOD GRINDER

INGREDIENTS
225g (8oz) fine bulghur wheat
900ml (1½ pints) water
1 small onion, quartered
175g (6oz) mushrooms, halved if large
15ml (1 tbsp) olive oil
25g (1oz) pine nuts
25g (1oz) mature Cheddar or Gouda cheese, grated
15ml (1 tbsp) freshly chopped parsley
salt and freshly ground black pepper
115g (4oz) plain flour
sunflower oil, for deep-frying
spicy yogurt dip, to serve, optional

❶ Place the bulghur wheat in a saucepan, pour over the water and bring to the boil. Simmer for 15 minutes then drain thoroughly and set aside.

❷ Fit the Food Processing Attachment with the knife blade; add the onion and process to roughly chop. Add the mushrooms and process until finely chopped or finely chop the onions and mushrooms by hand.

❸ Heat the olive oil in a frying pan, add the onions and mushrooms and sauté for 15-20 minutes, over a low heat until soft and the liquid has evaporated. Remove from the heat, stir in the pine nuts, cheese and parsley and season with salt and pepper.

❹ Place the bulghur wheat in the Kenwood Bowl. Add the flour and season liberally with salt and pepper. Using the K Beater at minimum speed mix for about 5 minutes, to form a stiff paste.

❺ Fit the Kebbe Maker to the Grinder Attachment. Pass the bulghur paste through the Adaptor, cutting the tube at 7.5cm (3 inch) intervals. Lay the tubes on a tray. Close one end of the tube, squeezing tightly to seal. Press 15ml (1 tbsp) mushroom stuffing into each shell and seal the open end.

❻ Heat a pan of oil until moderately hot (160°C/325°F) and then deep fry the kebbe balls, in batches, for 3-4 minutes, until golden. Serve with a spicy yogurt dip, if wished.

TABBOULEH

SERVES 4   PREPARATION TIME: 10 MINUTES PLUS SOAKING AND STANDING
TOOLS FOOD PROCESSING ATTACHMENT OR MULTI-MILL

INGREDIENTS
115g (4oz) bulghur wheat
30ml (2 tbsp) lemon juice
60ml (4 tbsp) olive oil
salt and freshly ground black pepper
40g (1½oz) flat leaf parsley
25g (1oz) fresh mint
3 plum tomatoes, diced
¼ cucumber, diced
6 spring onions, finely sliced

❶ Place the bulghur wheat in a bowl, cover with hot water and leave to soak for 1 hour, then drain and squeeze dry.

❷ Add the lemon juice and olive oil and season with salt and pepper. Place the parsley and mint in the Food Processing Attachment and chop. If using the Multi-Mill process in batches.

❸ Add the herbs to the bulghur wheat with the tomatoes, cucumber and spring onions and stir to blend. Serve immediately or leave to infuse, covered, for 2-3 hours or even overnight if time allows.

COUSCOUS STUFFED AUBERGINE

INGREDIENTS

2 aubergines, halved
45ml (3 tbsp) olive oil
salt and freshly ground black pepper
50g (2oz) couscous
75g (3oz) button mushrooms
50g (2oz) pine nuts, lightly toasted
8 sprigs basil
8 sprigs parsley
4 sun-dried tomatoes in oil, drained
and coarsely chopped
4 spring onions, chopped
50g (2oz) pitted black olives
1 clove garlic, crushed

FOR THE CRÈME FRAÎCHE DRESSING:
150g (6oz) crème fraîche
grated rind and juice 1 lime
30ml (2 tbsp) pesto sauce, see
page 106

SERVES 4 **PREPARATION TIME:** 20 MINUTES **COOKING TIME:** 30-35 MINUTES
TOOLS FOOD PROCESSING ATTACHMENT

1 Preheat the oven to 220°C/425°F/Gas 7. Cut the aubergines in half. Score the flesh and cut around the edges of each aubergine half, without damaging the skins.

2 Brush with half the olive oil, place on a baking sheet, sprinkle with salt and bake for 15-20 minutes, or until the flesh is soft and tender. Reduce the oven to 190°C/375°F/Gas 5.

3 Place the couscous in a bowl and pour over 150ml (¼ pint) boiling water. Set aside to puff up.

4 Using the Food Processing Attachment fitted with the thick slicing plate, slice the mushrooms. Fit the knife blade, add half the pine nuts with the basil and parsley and process until chopped.

5 Mix into the couscous with the sun-dried tomatoes, spring onions, pitted olives, whole pine nuts and garlic. Scoop the flesh out of the aubergines and chop finely using the knife blade. Stir into the couscous mixture and divide between the aubergine shells.

6 Place the aubergines in a shallow dish, sprinkle with the remaining oil and bake for 15 minutes.

7 Meanwhile mix the crème fraîche, grated lime rind and juice together. Swirl the pesto sauce through the crème fraîche mixture and serve as an accompaniment to the stuffed aubergines.

Never has the choice of vegetables and salads been so diverse. Whether you are a vegetarian, just enjoy including vegetable dishes for variety or need an accompaniment to a main meal, this chapter has lots of tasty ideas. Use either Pro Slicer/Grater or the Food Processing Attachment to help you prepare vegetables for salads, stir-fries and bakes.

The Potato Prep Attachment is a must for preparing potatoes for potato dishes as well as other root vegetables, like carrots, turnips, parsnips and swedes. The Colander and Sieve will purée these vegetables to perfection.

VEGETABLE TEMPURA

SERVES 4   PREPARATION TIME: 25 MINUTES   COOKING TIME: 15-20 MINUTES
TOOLS MULTI-MILL / BALLOON WHISK

INGREDIENTS

450g (1lb) vegetables e.g. selection of the following: broccoli, cauliflower, carrot, pepper, courgette, leek, green beans, sugar snap peas and mushrooms
200g (7oz) plain flour
25g (1oz) cornflour
15ml (1 tbsp) arrowroot
salt and freshly ground black pepper
2 eggs
1 egg white
300ml (½ pint) cold water
1 mild large red chilli, finely chopped
vegetable oil, for frying
FOR THE DIPPING SAUCE:
2.5cm (1 inch) piece fresh root ginger, sliced
60ml (4 tbsp) dry sherry
15ml (1 tbsp) soy sauce
30ml (2 tbsp) Thai sweet chilli sauce

❶ Place the ginger and sherry for the dipping sauce in the Multi-Mill and process until the ginger is finely chopped. Place in a bowl and pour over 150ml (¼ pint) boiling water. Leave for 5 minutes, then stir in the soy sauce, and Thai sweet chilli sauce.

❷ Prepare your chosen vegetables. Cut broccoli and cauliflower into florets; carrots and peppers into thin sticks, courgettes and leeks into slices and green beans in half.

❸ Sift the flour, cornflour and arrowroot into the Kenwood Bowl and season with salt and freshly ground black pepper. Using the Whisk, gradually whisk in one whole egg, one egg yolk and the cold water. Transfer to another bowl.

❹ Using a clean Kenwood Bowl whip the 2 egg whites using the Whisk, until they form soft peaks. Using a large metal spoon fold the egg whites and red chilli into the batter.

❺ Heat the oil in a wok or deep frying pan to 190°C/375°F - a cube of bread dropped in turns golden in 30 seconds. Cook the vegetables in batches. Dip a few at a time into the batter, then drop into the oil and cook for 3-4 minutes, or until crisp and golden.

❻ Drain on absorbent kitchen paper and keep warm until all the vegetables are cooked. Serve with the dipping sauce.

FLUFFY SPANISH POTATOES

SERVES 4-6   PREPARATION TIME: 10 MINUTES   COOKING TIME: 40 MINUTES
TOOLS POTATO PREP ATTACHMENT

INGREDIENTS

900g (2lb) potatoes
60ml (4 tbsp) olive oil
salt and freshly ground black pepper
2 cloves garlic, crushed

❶ Preheat the oven to 190°C/375°F/Gas 5. Cut the potatoes into 4cm (1½ inch) cubes and put them in the Potato Prep Attachment. Peel until the potatoes become rounded with a fluffy texture.

❷ Heat the olive oil in a roasting tin for 5 minutes in the oven. Rinse and dry the potato balls then spoon them into the roasting tin, tossing in the oil to coat completely.

❸ Season liberally with salt and freshly ground black pepper and bake for 30 minutes, until well cooked and golden. Sprinkle with garlic and cook for a further 5 minutes. Serve immediately.

CELERIAC PURÉE

SERVES 4   PREPARATION   TIME: 15 MINUTES   COOKING   TIME: 25-30 MINUTES
TOOLS COLANDER AND SIEVE

INGREDIENTS

450g (1lb) celeriac, peeled and cut into 2.5cm (1 inch) cubes

450g (1lb) potatoes, peeled and cut into 4cm (1½ inch) cubes

salt and freshly ground black pepper

15ml (1 tbsp) crème fraiche

❶ Preheat the oven to 190°C/375°F/Gas 5. Put the celeriac and potatoes cubes in a saucepan of lightly salted boiling water and cook for 10-15 minutes, or until tender.

❷ Drain and allow to cool slightly. Place in the Colander and Sieve fitted with the coarse screen, rough side uppermost and sieve the vegetables into the Kenwood Bowl.

❸ Stir in the crème fraîche and season with salt and freshly ground black pepper. Transfer to a baking dish, cover and place in the oven for 15 minutes, to re-heat, then serve immediately.

LIGHT VEGETABLE RÖSTI

SERVES 4   PREPARATION   TIME: 10 MINUTES   COOKING   TIME: 10 MINUTES
TOOLS NON-STOP CENTRIFUGAL JUICER

INGREDIENTS

450g (1lb) potatoes

15ml (1 tbsp) olive oil

5ml (1 tsp) lemon juice

salt and freshly ground black pepper

oil, for shallow frying

❶ Put the potatoes through the Non-Stop Centrifugal Juicer and collect the pulp in the Kenwood Bowl. Collect the juice in a jug and discard.

❷ Mix the pulp with the olive oil and lemon juice and season with salt and freshly ground black pepper.

❸ Pour a little oil in a large non-stick frying pan and place over a medium heat. Place spoonfuls of the potato mixture in the pan, to make four patty shapes and cook for 5 minutes on each side.

❹ Drain on absorbent kitchen paper and serve as an accompaniment to meat, fish or as part of a brunch.

LEEK AND POTATO BAKE

INGREDIENTS

2 large leeks, topped and tailed and
halved lengthways
675g (1½lb) potatoes, peeled
25g (1oz) plain flour
5ml (1 tsp) freshly grated nutmeg
5ml (1 tsp) salt
2.5ml (½ tsp) freshly ground black
pepper
50g (2oz) butter, cut into small
pieces
450ml (15fl oz) milk
50g (2oz) Gruyère cheese

SERVES 4-6   PREPARATION TIME: 15 MINUTES   COOKING TIME: 65-70 MINUTES
TOOLS PRO SLICER/GRATER

❶ Preheat the oven to 180°C/350°F/Gas 4. Fit the thick slicing plate to the Pro Slicer/Grater and slice the leeks into a bowl. Slice the potatoes into another bowl.

❷ Mix together the flour, nutmeg, salt and pepper. Place one third of the potatoes in a layer in a 1.8-2 litre (3-3½ pint) deep ovenproof baking dish. Sprinkle over half the leeks, half the seasoned flour and a third of the butter.

❸ Repeat with half the remaining potatoes, all the leeks and seasoned flour. Dot with half the remaining butter. Finish with a layer of potatoes and butter pieces.

❹ Heat the milk until almost boiling and pour over the potatoes and leeks. Cover with a layer of aluminium foil and bake for 45 minutes.

❺ Meanwhile fit the coarse shredding plate and grate the cheese. Remove the aluminium foil, sprinkle over the cheese and bake for 20-25 minutes, or until golden and the potatoes are tender.

Cook's Note Use the Potato Prep Attachment to peel the potatoes for this recipe.

VEGETABLE STIR-FRY

INGREDIENTS

175g (6oz) carrots, peeled and cut
into 5cm (2 inch) lengths
1 courgette, cut into 5cm (2 inch)
lengths
1 red pepper, halved, cored and
deseeded
75g (3oz) mushrooms
45ml (3 tbsp) sunflower oil
1 clove garlic, sliced
2.5cm (1 inch) piece fresh root
ginger, peeled and sliced
2.5cm (1 inch) piece lemon grass,
finely sliced
75g (3oz) French beans, halved
75g (3oz) baby corn, halved
30ml (2 tbsp) light soy sauce

SERVES 4   PREPARATION TIME: 15 MINUTES   COOKING TIME: 6-7 MINUTES
TOOLS FOOD PROCESSING ATTACHMENT OR PRO SLICER/GRATER / MULTI –MILL

❶ Using the Food Processing Attachment or Pro Slicer/Grater fitted with the thin chipper plate, place the carrots horizontally in the feed tube and cut into thin 'julienne style' strips. Repeat with the courgette.

❷ Fit the thick slicing plate and slice the pepper and mushrooms.

❸ Place 15ml (1 tbsp) oil in the Multi-Mill with the garlic, ginger and lemon grass and process until very finely chopped. Place in a wok or large frying pan with the remaining oil and heat until hot.

❹ Add the carrots and beans and stir-fry for 2 minutes, add the courgette, pepper, mushrooms and baby corn. Stir-fry for 2-3 minutes, or until just cooked but still crunchy. Sprinkle over the soy sauce and serve.

POTATO PURÉE WITH GARLIC AND OLIVE OIL

SERVES 4   PREPARATION TIME: 15 MINUTES   COOKING TIME: 37-42 MINUTES
TOOLS COLANDER AND SIEVE / K BEATER

INGREDIENTS

675g (1½lb) potatoes, peeled and
chopped
10ml (2 tsp) salt
30ml (2 tbsp) extra virgin olive oil
1 garlic clove, crushed
15ml (1 tbsp) crème fraîche or
double cream
15g (½oz) butter
salt and freshly ground black pepper

1 Preheat the oven to 200°C/400°F/Gas 6. Place the potatoes and salt in a pan of boiling water, cover and simmer for 10-15 minutes, or until just cooked. Drain and cool slightly.

2 Fit the Colander and Sieve with the coarse screen, rough side uppermost, and sieve the potatoes. Meanwhile place the olive oil and garlic in a small pan and heat gently for a couple of minutes, to infuse the flavours. Add to the potatoes.

3 Add the crème fraîche or cream, butter and season with salt and pepper. Using the K Beater at minimum speed, beat the potato until smooth. Transfer to an ovenproof dish and bake for 25 minutes or until golden.

GLAZED POTATO, TURNIP AND CARROT BALLS

SERVES 4   PREPARATION TIME: 15 MINUTES   COOKING TIME: 25 MINUTES
TOOLS POTATO PREP ATTACHMENT

INGREDIENTS

2 carrots
450g (1lb) potatoes
1 turnip
15g (½oz) butter
1 small onion, finely chopped
150ml (¼ pint) vegetable stock
2 bay leaves
salt and freshly ground black pepper

1 Cut the carrots into 4cm (1½ inch) lengths. Cut the potatoes and turnips into pieces roughly the same size as the carrots.

2 Cover the base plate of the Potato Prep Attachment with water. Add the vegetables and peel on speed 2-3 until they become rounded shapes.

3 Heat the butter in a saucepan and gently sauté the onion for 5 minutes, until soft, but not coloured. Remove the carrot balls from the peeler, rinse and add to the onions. Add the stock, bay leaves and seasoning. Cover and simmer for 5 minutes.

4 Rinse the potato and turnip balls and add to the pan. Cover and simmer for 10 minutes or until vegetables are almost cooked. Remove the lid and simmer for a further 5 minutes, to glaze. Transfer to a serving dish and serve immediately.

RUNNER BEAN SALAD

INGREDIENTS

275g (10oz) runner beans
175g (6oz) new potatoes, halved
30ml (2 tbsp) olive oil
15ml (1 tbsp) lemon juice
10ml (2 tsp) wholegrain mustard
8 baby plum tomatoes, halved
2 hard boiled eggs, quartered
115g (4oz) prosciutto, torn into
pieces
snipped chives, to garnish
FOR THE TAPENADE:
50g (2oz) pitted black olives
1 clove garlic, crushed
6 sprigs parsley
45ml (3 tbsp) olive oil
salt and freshly ground black pepper

SERVES 4   PREPARATION TIME: 20 MINUTES   COOKING TIME: 15-20 MINUTES
TOOLS FOOD PROCESSING ATTACHMENT OR MULTI-MILL / PRO SLICER/GRATER

1 Using the Food Processing Attachment or Multi-Mill make the tapenade. Process the olives, garlic and parsley together until fairly smooth. Add the olive oil and blend in. Season with salt and pepper and set aside.

2 Using the Pro Slicer/Grater fitted with the thick slicing plate, cut the beans into thin slivers. Feed the beans into Shredder via the bean slicing opening. Cook the potatoes in a pan of boiling lightly salted water until tender. Add the beans for the last 2-3 minutes and cook until tender-crisp.

3 Drain the potatoes and beans, refresh immediately under cold running water and drain again. Place in a serving bowl, with the olive oil, lemon juice and mustard and toss together. Add the tomatoes and eggs and toss gently.

4 Heat a non-stick frying pan, add the prosciutto and cook for a few seconds, until frazzled. Toss into the salad with spoonfuls of tapenade. Serve garnished with snipped chives.

Illustrated opposite.

SWEETCORN FRITTERS

SERVES 4   PREPARATION TIME: 5 MINUTES   COOKING TIME: 10 MINUTES
TOOLS LIQUIDISER / BALLOON WHISK

INGREDIENTS

200g (7oz) can sweetcorn kernels,
drained
150ml (5fl oz) milk
115g (4oz) plain flour
2.5ml (½ tsp) baking powder
salt and freshly ground black pepper
1 egg, separated
1 small chilli, de-seeded and finely
chopped
2 spring onions, finely chopped
oil, for frying

1 Place half the sweetcorn kernels in the Liquidiser with the milk and process to a purée.

2 Sift the flour, baking powder and a little salt into the Kenwood Bowl. Add the egg yolk and half the sweetcorn purée. Using the Whisk mix together, gradually adding the remaining purée, to form a thick batter.

3 On minimum speed mix in a sprinkling of pepper, the chilli, spring onions and remaining sweetcorn kernels.

4 Using the cleaned Whisk, whip the egg white until stiff and fold into the batter. Heat a little oil in a non-stick frying pan.

5 Drop spoonfuls of fritter mixture into the pan and cook for about 1½-2 minutes, or until golden underneath and bubbles appear on the surface of the sweetcorn fritters.

6 Turn over and cook for another minute, or until puffy and cooked through. Remove from the pan and keep warm whilst cooking the remainder.

FALAFEL SALAD WITH MINTED YOGURT DRESSING

SERVES 4 PREPARATION TIME: 15 MINUTES PLUS CHILLING COOKING TIME: 8-10 MINUTES
TOOLS FOOD PROCESSING ATTACHMENT

INGREDIENTS

1 onion, quartered

2 cloves garlic

410g (14oz) can chick peas, very well drained

8-10 sprigs fresh coriander

6 sprigs fresh parsley

5ml (1 tsp) ground coriander

5ml (1 tsp) ground cumin

2.5ml (½ tsp) chilli powder

2.5ml (½ tsp) salt

seasoned flour for shaping

30ml (2 tbsp) sunflower oil

225g (8oz) mixed salad leaves

45ml (3 tbsp) olive oil

15ml (1 tbsp) lemon juice

lemon wedges and coriander sprigs, to garnish

FOR THE MINTED YOGURT DRESSING:

30ml (2 tbsp) chopped fresh mint

1 clove garlic, crushed

150ml (¼ pint) natural yogurt

salt and freshly ground black pepper

❶ Using the Food Processing Attachment roughly chop the onion and garlic. Add the well drained chick peas, fresh coriander, parsley, ground coriander, cumin, chilli and salt and process to a fairly smooth but slightly grainy purée.

❷ Divide into 20 and using floured hands shape into balls and flatten slightly into patties. Dust with seasoned flour, cover and chill for 30 minutes, to allow flavours to develop.

❸ Meanwhile mix the mint, garlic and yogurt together for the dressing and season with salt and pepper. Set aside.

❹ Heat half the oil in a non-stick frying pan and fry half the patties, for 2-3 minutes, per side. Drain and keep warm whilst cooking the remaining patties in the remaining oil.

❺ Toss the salad leaves with the olive oil and lemon juice and arrange on four serving plates. Scatter over the falafel, garnish with lemon and coriander and serve with the minted yogurt dressing.

ORANGE AND FENNEL SALAD

SERVES 4-6 PREPARATION TIME: 15 MINUTES
TOOLS PRO SLICER/GRATER

INGREDIENTS

2 oranges

1 bunch radishes, trimmed

2 bulbs Florence fennel

olive oil, for drizzling

15ml (1 tbsp) snipped chives

freshly ground black pepper

❶ Peel the oranges and cut away any pith. Thinly slice and cut each slice in half or cut into segments, discarding the membrane. Place in a shallow bowl with any juice.

❷ Fit the Pro Slicer/Grater with the fine slicing plate and slice the radishes into the bowl. Cut the fronds from the fennel and reserve. Cut the fennel into pieces to fit the feed tube and slice into the bowl.

❸ Drizzle over the olive oil and toss together. Snip the fennel fronds over the salad, sprinkle over the chives and finish with a generous amount of freshly ground black pepper.

CRUNCHY COLESLAW

INGREDIENTS

325g (12oz) white cabbage, cored
1 onion, halved
2 carrots, peeled
150ml (¼ pint) mayonnaise see
page 102
15ml (1 tbsp) white wine vinegar
salt and freshly ground black pepper
30ml (2 tbsp) snipped chives
30ml (2 tbsp) chopped walnuts

SERVES 4   PREPARATION TIME: 10 MINUTES PLUS STANDING
TOOLS PRO SLICER/GRATER

❶ Fit the coarse shredding plate to the Pro Slicer/Grater. Cut the cabbage into large chunks to fit the feed tube and shred into the Kenwood Bowl.

❷ Shred the onion and carrots into the Bowl. Add the mayonnaise and vinegar and toss well to mix.

❸ Season generously with salt and freshly ground black pepper. Cover and leave to stand for an hour for the flavours to develop.

❹ Transfer to a serving dish. Sprinkle over the snipped chives and walnuts, to garnish.

POTATO SALAD

SERVES 4   PREPARATION TIME: 15 MINUTES   COOKING TIME: 15 MINUTES
TOOLS POTATO PREP ATTACHMENT / MULTI-MILL

INGREDIENTS

900g (2lb) new potatoes
salt and freshly ground black pepper
sprig of mint
6 sprigs fresh parsley
1 small onion, quartered
150ml (¼ pint) mayonnaise, see
page 102
5ml (1 tsp) Dijon mustard
30ml (2 tbsp) white wine vinegar

❶ Place the potatoes in the Potato Prep Attachment and use to just clean the potatoes, do not allow it to get to the peeling stage.

❷ Place the potatoes in a large pan, cover with cold salted water, add the sprig of mint, and bring to the boil. Cover and simmer for 10-12 minutes, or until tender.

❸ Place the parsley and onion in the Multi-Mill and process until chopped. Mix into the mayonnaise with the mustard and vinegar and then season with salt and freshly ground black pepper.

❹ Drain the potatoes and leave to cool slightly. Cut in half and toss with the mayonnaise dressing. Serve at room temperature.

A salad is rarely complete without a dressing. This chapter explains how to making the perfect mayonnaise every time, using the Whisk, Liquidiser or Food Processing Attachment, whilst the Multi-Mill is perfect for vinaigrette.

Use the Citrus Juicer for juicing citrus fruits for fruit curds, marmalades and sauces. An air of mystery seems to often surround sauce making, but all is required is a little time and attention and bit of help from the Liquidiser or Colander and Sieve. Both attachments are useful to ensure smooth sauces, purées and fruit or vegetable coulis.

MAYONNAISE

MAKES 300ML (½ PINT)   PREPARATION TIME: 10 MINUTES
TOOLS BALLOON WHISK OR FOOD PROCESSING ATTACHMENT OR LIQUIDISER

INGREDIENTS:

2 egg yolks

2.5ml (½ tsp) Dijon mustard

150ml (5fl oz) light olive oil

150ml (5fl oz) sunflower oil

15ml (1 tbsp) white wine vinegar or lemon juice

salt and freshly ground black pepper

① Place the egg yolks and mustard in the Kenwood Bowl. Mix the oils together in a jug.

② Using the Whisk at maximum speed start to whisk the egg yolks and mustard together. When they have combined add the oil, drop by drop to begin with and then in a slow steady stream, until half the oil is added.

③ Switch off the machine, add half the white wine vinegar or lemon juice and seasoning, then whisk slowly, to combine. The mayonnaise should now be quite thick and smooth.

④ Gradually add the remaining oil, whisking at maximum speed. Add the remaining vinegar or lemon juice. Store in a screw topped jar for up to 3 days in the fridge.

Using the Food Processing Attachment or Liquidiser
Place the egg yolks, mustard and half the vinegar or lemon juice in the Food Processing Bowl or Liquidiser jug and blend until pale and creamy. With the motor running gradually pour in the oil and blend until the mayonnaise is thick. Add the remaining vinegar and seasoning.

Cook's Note Mayonnaise is best made with ingredients at room temperature. If the eggs are straight from the fridge then the mayonnaise is liable to curdle.

Variations

CORIANDER AND LIME MAYONNAISE Replace the vinegar or lemon juice with lime juice and stir in 30ml (2 tbsp) finely chopped coriander and the finely grated rind of 2 limes.

AIOLI Add 4 crushed garlic cloves with the egg yolks and mustard in step 1.

CUCUMBER MAYONNAISE Finely chop 7.5cm (3 inch) piece of cucumber and pat dry on absorbent kitchen paper. Fold into the mayonnaise with 30ml (2 tbsp) chopped chervil or tarragon and a little extra salt. This mayonnaise makes a perfect accompaniment for fish.

TARTARE SAUCE Add 10ml (2 tsp) snipped chives and 15ml (1 tbsp) each of chopped gherkins, capers and parsley to the finished mayonnaise. Stir in 15-30ml (1-2 tbsp) lemon juice to thin the mayonnaise.

Illustrated on page 101.

VINAIGRETTE

MAKES 120ML (4FL OZ)   PREPARATION TIME: 5 MINUTES
TOOLS MULTI-MILL

❶ Place the oil, vinegar, mustard and seasoning in the Multi-Mill and blend briefly on speed 1 to combine. Do not over blend or the vinaigrette will become too thick. Adjust seasoning to taste.

Variations

HERB VINAIGRETTE Chop a handful of mixed herbs, such as parsley, marjoram and basil in the Multi-Mill. Add 30ml (2 tbsp) to the vinaigrette and blend briefly to combine.

BALSAMIC DRESSING Replace 15ml (1 tbsp) wine vinegar with balsamic vinegar and omit the mustard.

BLUE CHEESE DRESSING Add 25g (1oz) Gorgonzola or Roquefort and 15ml (1 tbsp) single cream or milk to the Multi-Mill and blend together with the vinaigrette until smooth.

MUSTARD VINAIGRETTE Replace Dijon mustard with 5ml (1 tsp) wholegrain mustard.

GARLIC VINAIGRETTE Add 1 crushed garlic clove to the Multi-Mill and blend with the vinaigrette ingredients.

INGREDIENTS
90ml (3fl oz) extra virgin olive oil
30ml (2 tbsp) white or red wine vinegar
2.5ml (½ tsp) Dijon mustard
salt and freshly ground black pepper

RED ONION MARMALADE

MAKES 1.4KG (3LB)   PREPARATION TIME: 10 MINUTES PLUS COOLING
COOKING TIME: 40-50 MINUTES
TOOLS PRO SLICER/GRATER OR FOOD PROCESSING ATTACHMENT

INGREDIENTS
900g (2lb) red onions, halved
60ml (4 tbsp) olive oil
7.5ml (1½ tsp) salt
75g (3oz) caster sugar
115g (4oz) redcurrant jelly
115g (4oz) redcurrants
75g (3oz) ready to eat dried apricots, finely chopped
5ml (1 tsp) fresh thyme leaves
125ml (4fl oz) red wine vinegar
125ml (4fl oz) red wine

❶ Fit the thick slicing plate to the Pro Slicer/Grater or Food Processing Attachment and slice the onions.

❷ Heat the olive oil in a heavy based saucepan and add the onions. Cook over a low heat for 10 minutes, stirring occasionally. Add the salt and cook for 5 minutes, then add the sugar and cook for a further 5 minutes.

❸ Stir in the redcurrant jelly, redcurrants and apricots, then add the thyme leaves, vinegar and red wine and bring to the boil. Cook over a low heat so the mixture is gently simmering and cook for 20-30 minutes, until the marmalade is thick. Stir regularly to prevent the marmalade burning.

❹ Cool slightly then transfer into sterilized jars. Leave to cool thoroughly and then store in the fridge for up to 1 month.

Illustrated on page 101.

LEMON AND LIME MARMALADE

INGREDIENTS
700g (1½lb) lemons and limes, washed and dried thoroughly, about 3 lemons and 6 limes
1.7 litres (3 pints) water
1.4kg (3lb) preserving sugar

MAKES ABOUT 2.2KG (5LB)   PREPARATION TIME: 30 MINUTES PLUS COOLING
COOKING TIME: 2-2½ HOURS   TOOLS CITRUS JUICER

❶ Wash the lemons and limes and dry thoroughly. Using a potato peeler, peel off the rind, cut into thin strips and set aside.

❷ Cut the lemons and limes in half. Using the Citrus Juicer extract the juice and save any pips. Chop the pith and any membrane from squeezing and tie in a large piece of muslin with the pips.

❸ Place the peel, muslin bag, lemon and lime juices and water in a preserving pan. Bring to the boil and then simmer gently, uncovered, for about 1½ – 2 hours or until the peel is quite soft and the liquid reduced by about half. Remove the muslin bag, squeezing the juices back into the pan.

❹ Add the sugar and stir until all the sugar has dissolved. Increase the heat and boil rapidly for 10-15 minutes or until it reaches setting point.

❺ To test for setting point, remove the pan from the heat, stir and then spoon a little marmalade on to a cold plate. Allow to cool for a few seconds. Push a finger across the marmalade; if the surface wrinkles setting point has been reached. If not boil for another 5 minutes and repeat the test again.

❻ Leave to settle for 15 minutes, remove any scum with a slotted spoon and pour into clean, sterilized, warm jars. Seal and label. Store in a cool dark place.

SEVILLE ORANGE MARMALADE

INGREDIENTS
1.4kg (3lb) Seville oranges, washed and dried throughly
2 lemons, washed and dried throughly
3.4 litres (6 pints) water
2.7kg (6lb) preserving sugar

MAKES 4.5KG (10LB)   PREPARATION TIME: 30 MINUTES PLUS COOLING
COOKING TIME: 2½ HOURS   TOOLS CITRUS JUICER

❶ Cut the oranges and lemons in half and using the Citrus Juicer extract the juice and save any pips. Discard the squeezed lemons.

❷ Cut the oranges in half again and using a metal spoon scrape the pith and any pips into the centre of a large piece of muslin. Add the reserved pips and tie to form a bag.

❸ Cut the orange peel into strips, chunky for coarse cut and thinner for fine shred.

❹ Place the peel, muslin bag, orange juice and water in a preserving pan. Bring to the boil and then simmer gently, uncovered, for about 2 hours or until

the peel is quite soft and the liquid reduced by about half. Remove the muslin bag, squeezing the juices back into the pan.

❺ Add the sugar and stir until all the sugar has dissolved. Increase the heat and boil rapidly for 10-15 minutes or until it reaches setting point. To test for setting point, follow the instructions in point 5 above.

❻ Leave to settle for 15 minutes, remove any scum with a slotted spoon and pour into clean, sterilized, warm jars. Seal and label. Store in a cool dark place.

RASPBERRY COULIS

SERVES 4   PREPARATION TIME: 10 MINUTES PLUS CHILLING
TOOLS COLANDER AND SIEVE

INGREDIENTS

250g (9oz) raspberries, fresh or frozen defrosted

15-30 ml (1-2 tbsp) icing sugar

dash of liqueur e.g. framboise, kirsch or cointreau, optional

① Place the fine screen from the Colander and Sieve rough side uppermost, in the bowl carrier and place in the Kenwood Bowl.

② Add the raspberries and icing sugar and sieve on speed 1-2. Remove the screens and stir in the liqueur, if using.

③ Serve cold with desserts, ice creams and gâteaux.

ORANGE AND LEMON CURD

550G (1LB 4OZ)   PREPARATION TIME: 15 MINUTES PLUS COOLING
ABOUT 25 MINUTES   TOOLS CITRUS JUICER

INGREDIENTS

2 lemons

1 orange

250g (9oz) caster sugar

3 eggs, beaten

100g (4oz) butter, cut into small pieces

① Finely grate the zest from one lemon nd the orange and place in a medium-sized heatproof bowl Add the sugar, eggs and butter.

② Halve the lemons and orange then extract the juice using the Citrus Juicer. Add to the owl and stir with a wooden spoon to combine.

③ Place the bowl over a pan of barely simmering water and stir for 15-20 minutes, or until the curd is thick enough to coat the back of the spoon. Do not allow to boil.

④ Pour into clean, sterilized warm jars and seal. Leave to cool then stor in the fridge and use within 2-3 weeks.

BREAD SAUCE

SERVES 4   PREPARATION TIME: 10 MINUTES PLUS INFUSING   COOKING TIME: 25 MINUTES
TOOLS LIQUIDISER OR FOOD PROCESSING ATTACHMENT

INGREDIENTS

1 small onion
4 whole cloves
1 small bay leaf
6 peppercorns
300ml (½ pint) milk
50g (2oz) crustless white bread, cubed
15g (½oz) butter
30ml (2 tbsp) single cream or crème fraîche
freshly grated nutmeg
salt and freshly ground black pepper

❶ Spike the onion with the whole cloves. Place in a small heavy saucepan with the bay leaf, peppercorns and milk.

❷ Slowly bring to the boil, and simmer for 10 minutes. Turn off the heat and leave uncovered, to infuse for 20 minutes.

❸ Meanwhile make the breadcrumbs using the Liquidiser or Food Processing Attachment fitted with the knife blade. If using the Liquidiser, switch on first and add the cubes through the filler cap.

❹ Strain the milk, then reheat it. Stir in the breadcrumbs and simmer gently for 10 minutes, stirring occasionally.

❺ Stir in the butter, cream or crème fraîche. Season with a little freshly grated nutmeg, salt and freshly ground black pepper. Transfer to a warmed bowl and serve immediately.

PESTO

SERVES 4   PREPARATION TIME: 5 MINUTES
TOOLS FOOD PROCESSING ATTACHMENT

INGREDIENTS

25g (1oz) fresh basil leaves, weighed without stalks
1 clove garlic, peeled
30ml (2 tbsp) pine nuts
100ml (3½fl oz) olive oil
25g (1oz) freshly grated Parmesan cheese
salt and freshly ground black pepper

❶ Place the basil leaves, garlic and pine nuts in the Food Processing bowl fitted with the knife blade and chop. Add the olive oil and blend until well chopped and creamy, using maximum speed.

❷ Add the Parmesan cheese and seasoning and briefly process to combine. Transfer to a screw topped jar if not using immediately. It is best used the same day, because the colour fades on keeping. It can however be kept in the fridge for up to 5 days. Serve with pasta, soups, fish or chicken.

Cook's Note For a smaller quantity of pesto, divide the quantities in half and process in the Multi-Mill.

Illustrated on page 101.

TOMATO COULIS

INGREDIENTS

6 tomatoes
30ml (2 tbsp) olive oil
1 clove garlic, crushed
10 basil leaves
2.5ml (½ tsp) sugar
salt and freshly ground black pepper

SERVES 2 **PREPARATION TIME:** 15 MINUTES **COOKING TIME:** 10 MINUTES
TOOLS COLANDER AND SIEVE

1 Place the tomatoes in a saucepan, cover with cold water and bring to the boil. Remove from the heat and leave in the hot water for 5 minutes.

2 Remove the tomatoes, using a slotted spoon and when cool enough, cut into quarters. Fit the Colander and Sieve with the fine screen, rough side uppermost and sieve the tomatoes.

3 Heat the olive oil and garlic over a very low heat, in order to infuse the flavours, rather than cook the garlic.

4 Finely shred the basil leaves and stir into the oil with the sieved tomatoes and sugar. Season to taste with salt and freshly ground black pepper.

5 Warm gently, just before serving, but do not overheat in order to preserve the beautiful fresh flavour. Serve as an accompaniment to stuffed vegetables, nut roasts, fish and chicken.

MEDITERRANEAN TOMATO SAUCE

INGREDIENTS

450g (1lb) plum tomatoes
2 cloves garlic, chopped
15 fresh basil leaves, torn
30ml (2 tbsp) olive oil
salt and freshly ground black pepper

SERVES 2 **PREPARATION TIME:** 15 MINUTES **COOKING TIME:** 35 MINUTES
TOOLS LIQUIDISER

1 Place the tomatoes in a large bowl, cover with boiling water and leave to stand for 1 minute. Remove with a slotted spoon and when cool enough to handle, remove the skins.

2 Cut in half and place in a clean bowl with the garlic, basil and olive oil. Toss together and season with salt and pepper. Transfer to a large frying pan and turn the tomatoes, cut side uppermost.

3 Heat until just starting to sizzle then cook over a low heat for 30 minutes. By now the tomatoes should have shrunk a little in size and be charred underneath. Remove from the heat.

4 Allow to cool slightly then transfer to the Liquidiser and blend until smooth. Serve with pasta, or as an accompaniment to meat dishes.

DRESSINGS, PRESERVES & SAUCES

This chapter includes just a selection of the many desserts you can make with the Kenwood Chef or Major. The K Beater will assist with making pastry for tarts, flans and pies, or mixing fruit sponge pudding or crumble toppings whilst the Whisk will whip up the frothiest mousse, fool, syllabub or lightest meringue.

Use either the Pro Slicer/Grater or Roto Food Cutter to prepare fruits for pies, tarts and crumbles and the Citrus Juicer for jellies and lemon or orange pie fillings. There is nothing quite like rich, creamy homemade ice cream or tangy fruit sorbet mixed and frozen to perfection with the Ice Cream Maker.

DESSERTS

APPLE AND PEAR CHARLOTTE

INGREDIENTS
500g (1¼lb) cooking apples
500g (1¼lb) ripe but firm pears
grated rind and juice of 1 lemon
150ml (¼ pint) dry white wine
75g (3oz) caster sugar
2.5ml (½ tsp) ground cinnamon
50-75g (2-3oz) butter
8-10 large slices close-textured white bread, 5mm (¼ inch) thick
caster sugar, for sprinkling

SERVES 6   PREPARATION TIME: 20 MINUTES PLUS STANDING   COOKING TIME: 40 MINUTES
TOOLS PRO SLICER/GRATER OR FOOD PROCESSING ATTACHMENT

1 Peel, core and quarter the apples and pears. Using the Pro Slicer/Grater or Food Processing Attachment fitted with the thick slicing plate, slice the fruit. Toss in the lemon juice.

2 Pour the wine into a frying pan, add the sugar, ground cinnamon and lemon rind and stir over a low heat, until the sugar has dissolved. Add the apples and pears, cover and cook over a low heat for about 5 minutes, until just tender, turning the fruit over 3-4 times to ensure it cooks evenly.

3 Lift the fruit out with a slotted spoon into a bowl and set aside. Boil the juices to reduce to about 45ml (3 tbsp) and pour over the fruit.

4 Preheat the oven to 200°C/400°F/Gas 6. Grease a 15cm (6 inch) Charlotte mould or deep cake tin. Lightly butter the bread slices and remove the crusts.

5 Cut a round of bread to fit the base of the mould or tin, filling any spaces if required and place butter side down. Cut the remaining slices of bread in half lengthwise.

6 Arrange sufficient bread slices around the sides of the mould so they fit neatly and tightly together, butter side out. Place the fruit slices in the mould, cover the top with the remaining bread slices, to fit.

7 Bake for 30 minutes, covering with foil after 20 minutes, if the top starts to over-brown. Leave to stand for 10 minutes, then turn out, dredge with caster sugar and serve.

Cook's Note If using the Food Processing Attachment slice the fruit in batches.

CRÊPES SUZETTE

INGREDIENTS
1 quantity crêpes see recipe page 166
8 sugar lumps
2 oranges
50g (2oz) caster sugar
1 lemon, halved
75g (3oz) butter
30ml (2 tbsp) Cointreau, Grand Marnier or other orange liqueur
30ml (2 tbsp) Cognac

SERVES 4   PREPARATION TIME: 20 MINUTES   COOKING TIME: 15 MINUTES
TOOLS BALLOON WHISK / CITRUS JUICER

1 Make the crêpes as page 166. Rub the sugar lumps over the oranges until they absorb the oil. Place in the frying pan with the caster sugar. Cut the oranges in half. Using the Citrus Juicer extract the juice from the oranges and lemon and set aside.

2 Gently heat the frying pan until the sugar begins to caramelise. Add the butter, then gradually stir in the citrus juices and bring to the boil.

3 Add a crêpe, place it in the sauce, baste with sauce then fold in half and then half again to form a triangle. Push to one side and repeat with the remaining crêpes.

4 Stir in the orange liqueur. Heat the Cognac in a ladle or separate small pan, pour over the crêpes and ignite. Serve immediately the flames die down.

MACARONI PUDDING

SERVES 6   PREPARATION TIME: 15 MINUTES   COOKING TIME: 45 MINUTES
TOOLS PASTA FRESCA

INGREDIENTS

¼ quantity fresh macaroni, see page 80
600ml (1 pint) milk
300ml (10fl oz) single cream
grated zest 1 lemon
40g (1½oz) caster or golden granulated sugar
115g (4oz) raisins
50g (2oz) ready to eat dried apricots, chopped
5ml (1 tsp) freshly grated nutmeg

❶ Lightly grease a 1.2 litre (2 pint) ovenproof dish. Place the macaroni, milk, cream and lemon zest in a large saucepan and bring to the boil, stirring. Preheat the oven to 180°C/350°F/Gas 4.

❷ Simmer the macaroni for 15 minutes, or until it is very soft. Remove from the heat and stir in the sugar, raisins and apricots. Transfer to the prepared dish and sprinkle with nutmeg.

❸ Bake, uncovered for 30 minutes, or until the top is golden. Serve hot or warm, according to taste.

PECAN PITHIVEIRS

SERVES 6-8   PREPARATION TIME: 25 MINUTES, PLUS CHILLING
COOKING TIME: 30-35 MINUTES   TOOLS FOOD PROCESSING ATTACHMENT / K BEATER

INGREDIENTS

115g (4oz) pecan nuts
100g (3½oz) whole blanched almonds
115g (4oz) butter
2 egg yolks
30ml (2 tbsp) rum
75g (3oz) caster sugar
15ml (1 tbsp) lemon juice
325g (12oz) puff pastry, see page 165
115g (4oz) ready to eat dried apricots, chopped
beaten egg, to glaze
15ml (1 tbsp) icing sugar, for dusting
single cream, to serve

❶ Place the pecan nuts and almonds in the Food Processing Attachment fitted with the knife blade and process until very finely chopped.

❷ Place the butter in the Kenwood Bowl. Fit the K Beater and cream the butter until very soft. Add the egg yolks, rum, caster sugar, lemon juice and ground nuts and mix to a paste.

❸ On a lightly floured surface roll out nearly half the pastry and cut a 25cm (10 inch) round. Place on a slightly dampened baking sheet. Roll out the remaining pastry and cut a 28cm (11 inch) round.

❹ Spread the nut mixture over the pastry on the baking sheet, to within 2.5cm (1 inch) of the edge. Sprinkle over the chopped apricots. Brush the edges with beaten egg.

❺ Place the second round of pastry on top and press together, around the edges, to seal. Press a 23cm (9 inch) plate or flan ring on top of the Pithivers to seal. Use a small sharp knife, to cut a scalloped edge.

❻ Remove the plate or flan ring and brush the pastry with egg glaze. Using the tip of a sharp knife mark feint curved lines, radiating out from the centre to the edge. Chill for 20 minutes.

❼ Meanwhile preheat oven to 200°C/400°F/Gas 6. Bake for 25-30 minutes, until golden. Sprinkle Pithiviers with icing sugar and increase the oven to 220°C/425°F /Gas 7. Bake for 4-5 minutes. Serve warm with single cream, if wished.

STICKY TOFFEE PUDDING

SERVES 4   PREPARATION TIME: 15 MINUTES   COOKING TIME: 1½ HOURS
TOOLS K BEATER

INGREDIENTS

150g (5oz) butter

150g (5oz) light muscovado sugar

2 large eggs

2.5ml (½ tsp) vanilla essence

175g (6oz) self-raising flour

50g (2oz) stoneless dates, roughly chopped

50g (2oz) sultanas or raisins

40g (1½oz) walnuts, chopped

FOR THE STICKY TOFFEE SAUCE:

50g (2oz) light brown muscovado sugar

50g (2oz) butter

100ml (3½fl oz) double cream

❶ Grease a 900ml (1½ pint) pudding basin. Place the butter and sugar in the Kenwood Bowl. Using the K Beater at speed 3, cream together until light and fluffy. Gradually beat in the eggs and vanilla.

❷ Using the K Beater at minimum speed, add the flour, dates, sultanas or raisins and walnuts and mix until just combined. Spoon into the prepared pudding basin.

❸ Cover with greased greaseproof paper or foil and secure with string. Sit the basin on a trivet in a large, deep saucepan.

❹ Add sufficient boiling water to come halfway up the side of the basin. Cover and steam for 2 hours, topping up with boiling water as necessary.

❺ Lift the pudding out of the pan and leave to rest whilst making the sauce. Place the sugar, butter and cream in a saucepan and heat gently, stirring until the butter has melted and the sugar dissolved. Bring to the boil and leave to gently bubble for 30 seconds to thicken.

❻ To serve, unmould the pudding on to a warmed serving plate and pour over the sauce.

Illustrated opposite.

CITRUS MERINGUE PIE

SERVES 6-8   PREPARATION TIME: 20 MINUTES PLUS PASTRY PLUS CHILLING
COOKING TIME: 30-35 MINUTES   TOOLS CITRUS JUICER / BALLOON WHISK

INGREDIENTS

1 quantity rich flan pastry, see page 165

1 lemon, halved

2 oranges, halved

2 limes, halved

65g (2½oz) cornflour

50g (2oz) caster sugar

3 egg yolks

FOR THE MERINGUE:

3 egg whites

150g (5oz) caster sugar

grated lime zest, to decorate

❶ Roll out the pastry and use to line a 23cm (9 inch) fluted flan ring or loose-bottomed flan tin. Prick the base with a fork and chill for 30 minutes. Preheat the oven to 190°C/375°F/Gas 5.

❷ Line the pastry case with greaseproof paper and baking beans and bake blind for 20 minutes, removing the paper and beans after 15 minutes.

❸ Meanwhile grate the zest from 1 lemon and 1 orange and set aside. Halve the citrus fruits and using the Citrus Juicer, squeeze the juice. Pour into a jug and make up to 450ml (¾ pint) with cold water.

❹ Mix the cornflour to a smooth paste with 120ml (4fl oz) cold water.

❺ Place the citrus juice mixture in a saucepan with the lemon and orange zest and sugar and bring to the boil. Stir in the cornflour mixture and cook, stirring until thickened. Beat in the egg yolks and pour into the pastry case.

❻ To make the meringue, place the egg whites in the Kenwood Bowl and using the Whisk, whisk the egg whites until stiff but not dry. Gradually whisk in the caster sugar until very stiff.

❼ Using a piping bag fitted with a star nozzle pipe the meringue over the citrus filling, or spoon over and swirl with a knife. Bake for 5-10 minutes, or until golden. Serve warm or cold decorated with the grated lime zest.

CREOLE COCONUT PIE

SERVES 6-8   PREPARATION TIME: 15 MINUTES PLUS COOLING
COOKING TIME: 65-70 MINUTES   TOOLS NON-STOP CENTRIFUGAL JUICER / K BEATER

INGREDIENTS
1 fresh coconut
150g (6oz) plain flour
75g (3oz) butter
3 eggs
30ml (2 tbsp) natural yogurt
30ml (2 tbsp) milk
2.5ml (1 tsp) vanilla essence
115g (4oz) caster sugar
fresh raspberries or physalis to decorate, optional

❶ Preheat the oven to 190°C/375°F/Gas 5. Pierce the eyes of the coconut, drain out the coconut milk and set aside. Break open the shell and break the flesh into pieces.

❷ Using the Non-Stop Centrifugal Juicer, process about 250g (9oz) of the coconut flesh, brown skin as well, and collect both the pulp and juice, if any. Shred the remaining coconut flesh, using a potato peeler to make long slivers and toast until golden. Set aside to use for decoration.

❸ Make the pastry case. Place the flour, butter and 15ml (1 tbsp) of the coconut pulp in the Kenwood Bowl. Using the K Beater at minimum speed mix together until the mixture resembles fine breadcrumbs. Add sufficient coconut milk, about 30-45ml (2-3 tbsp) to mix to a smooth dough.

❹ Roll out on a lightly floured surface and use to line a 23cm (9 inch) flan tin. Prick and bake blind for about 20 minutes, until pale golden. Reduce the oven to 180°C/350°F/Gas 4.

❺ Place the remaining coconut pulp, 75ml (3fl oz) coconut juice, if any and/or coconut milk, eggs, yogurt, milk, vanilla essence and sugar in the cleaned Kenwood Bowl and mix together using the K Beater. Pour into the pastry shell.

❻ Bake for 45-50 minutes, or until the filling is set. Serve warm or cold decorated with toasted coconut shreds. Top with a few fresh raspberries or physalis if wished.

MOCHA PROFITEROLES

SERVES 6   PREPARATION TIME: 25 MINUTES PLUS PASTRY PLUS COOLING
COOKING TIME: 30-35 MINUTES   TOOLS BALLOON WHISK

INGREDIENTS
1 quantity of choux pastry see page 164
150g (5oz) plain chocolate, broken into pieces
150ml (¼ pint) strong black coffee
15g (½oz) butter
15ml (1 tbsp) golden syrup
300ml (½ pint) double cream

❶ Preheat the oven to 220°C/425°F/Gas 7. Dampen 2 baking sheets. Either put the choux pastry in a piping bag fitted with a 1cm (½ inch) nozzle and pipe around 30 small bun shapes on to the baking sheets or use a teaspoon and place small mounds on the baking sheets.

❷ Bake for 20-25 minutes, until puffed up and golden. Reduce the oven to 190°C/375°F/Gas 5. Make a hole in the base of each bun and return to the oven for 5 minutes, to dry out. Transfer to a wire rack to cool.

❸ Place the chocolate, coffee, butter and syrup in a saucepan and heat gently, stirring until the chocolate has melted. Bring to the boil, then simmer for 10 minutes, or until rich and of a coating consistency. Leave to cool.

❹ Fit the Whisk, place the cream in the Kenwood Bowl and whip on speed 3 until it just holds its shape. Spoon into a piping bag fitted with a plain nozzle and fill the choux buns through the hole. Arrange in a pile on a serving dish and pour over the mocha sauce.

MANGO AND HAZELNUT MERINGUE

INGREDIENTS
150g (5oz) shelled hazelnuts
5ml (1 tsp) cornflour
5ml (1 tsp) white wine vinegar
5 egg whites
225g (8oz) caster sugar
2.5 ml (½ tsp) ground cinnamon
2 large mangoes
90ml (6 tbsp) orange juice
300ml (½ pint) crème fraîche
125g (4oz) redcurrants
few strands redcurrants, to decorate
icing sugar, to dust

SERVES 8   PREPARATION TIME: 30 MINUTES PLUS COOLING   **COOKING TIME:** 35-45 MINUTES
TOOLS FOOD PROCESSING ATTACHMENT OR LIQUIDISER / BALLOON WHISK

1 Preheat the oven to 180°C/350°F/Gas 4. Place the hazelnuts on a baking sheet and bake for 5-10 minutes, until lightly toasted. Cool slightly then transfer to the Food Processing Attachment or Liquidiser and process until finely chopped.

2 Line 2 baking sheets with non-stick baking parchment. Draw a 23cm (9 inch) circle on one sheet and an 18cm (7 inch) circle on the other sheet. Turn the paper over. Mix the cornflour and vinegar together.

3 Place the egg whites in the Kenwood Bowl and using the Whisk, whisk until stiff. Gradually whisk in the sugar, adding the cornflour mixture at the same time. Whisk in the cinnamon at the end.

4 Reserve 30ml (2 tbsp) of the finely chopped hazelnuts. Using a metal spoon, fold the remainder into the egg whites. Spoon on to the prepared baking sheets and spread to fill the marked circles. Sprinkle the reserved nuts over the top of the smaller meringue.

5 Bake for 30-35 minutes or until crisp, although still slightly soft inside. Transfer to wire racks to cool.

6 Halve the mangoes and remove the flesh and chop. Place about one third in the Food Processing Attachment or Liquidiser with the orange juice and process together to make a sauce.

7 Place the large meringue on a serving plate. Spread the crème fraîche over the meringue and scatter over the redcurrants and chopped mango.

8 Cover with the smaller meringue. Decorate with a few strands of redcurrants, dust with icing sugar and serve with the mango sauce.

TIRAMISU GÂTEAU

SERVES 8-10   PREPARATION TIME: 25 MINUTES PLUS CHILLING AND FREEZING
COOKING TIME: 20-25 MINUTES   TOOLS WHISK / ROTO FOOD CUTTER

INGREDIENTS

4 eggs

115g (4oz) caster sugar

100g (3½oz) plain flour

15g (½oz) cornflour

25g (1oz) butter, melted

FOR THE FILLING:

115g (4oz) plain chocolate

150ml (¼ pint) very strong black coffee

100ml (3½fl oz) Tia Maria or Kahlua

coffee liqueur

300ml (½ pint) double cream

2.5ml (½ tsp) vanilla essence

50g (2oz) caster sugar

3 x 250g (9oz) cartons mascarpone

cheese

chocolate shavings or grated

chocolate, to decorate

cocoa powder, for dusting

❶ Preheat the oven to 180°C/350°F/Gas 4. Grease and base line a 22cm (8½ inch) spring-form cake tin. Fit the Whisk. Place the eggs and sugar in the Kenwood Bowl and whisk until pale, thick and creamy. The mixture should be thick enough to hold a trail when the whisk is pulled from the surface.

❷ Sieve the flour and cornflour together and lightly fold in half using a metal spoon. Fold in half the melted butter, then repeat with the remaining flour and butter. Fold in lightly to avoid knocking the air from the mix.

❸ Pour into the prepared tin and bake for 20-25 minutes, or until golden. Turn out and leave to cool overnight if time allows. Fit the Roto Food Cutter and grate the plain chocolate. Mix the coffee and liqueur together. Cut the cake into three layers.

❹ Line the base and sides of the cake tin with clear film and the base with non-stick baking parchment. Place one sponge layer in the base. Sprinkle over about a third of the coffee mix.

❺ Using the Whisk, whip the cream, vanilla and sugar together until it forms soft peaks and fold into the cheese. Reserve 60ml (4 tbsp). Spread ⅓ of the mix over the sponge. Sprinkle over half the chocolate. Top with another layer of sponge. Drizzle over half the remaining coffee liqueur mix. Top with half the remaining cheese mixture and all the chocolate. Top with the last sponge and press down lightly. Finish with a final layer of cheese mixture. Chill for 2 hours.

❻ Release from the tin, peel off the clear film and transfer to a serving plate. Spread the reserved cheese mixture around the edges. Sprinkle with chocolate, dust with cocoa and serve.

Illustrated opposite.

VANILLA CHEESECAKE

SERVES 8-10   PREPARATION TIME: 20 MINUTES PLUS COOLING AND CHILLING
COOKING TIME: 30 MINUTES TOOLS K BEATER

INGREDIENTS

225g (8oz) digestive biscuits

75g (3oz) butter

450g (1lb) curd cheese

15ml (1 tbsp) cornflour

5ml (1 tsp) vanilla essence

3 eggs

150g (5oz) caster sugar

225ml (8fl oz) double cream or

Greek yogurt

450g (1lb) fresh soft fruits

❶ Preheat the oven to 180°C/350°F/Gas 4. Oil a 23cm (9 inch) spring-form cake tin and line the base with greaseproof paper. Place the biscuits in the Kenwood Bowl and use the K Beater on speed 2 to crush the biscuits into crumbs.

❷ Melt the butter and pour onto the crushed biscuits and mix together using the K Beater. Transfer to the prepared tin and press down over the base to form an even layer.

❸ In the cleaned Kenwood Bowl, using the K Beater, mix together the curd cheese, cornflour, vanilla essence, eggs and sugar. Add the double cream or yogurt and mix until smooth. Pour into the tin and bake for 30 minutes.

❹ Switch off the oven and leave the cheesecake inside to cool very slowly. Chill until required, then place on a serving plate and top with a mound of fresh fruits.

RASPBERRY AND LEMON SYLLABUB

INGREDIENTS

3 individual brioche, about 175g (6oz) or 275g (10oz) Madeira cake

90ml (3fl oz) sweet white wine or orange juice

450g (1lb) fresh raspberries

FOR THE SYLLABUB:

juice 1 lemon

125ml (4fl oz) sherry

30ml (2 tbsp) brandy

75g (3oz) caster sugar

450ml (¾ pint) double cream

TO DECORATE:

50g (2oz) caster sugar

45ml (3 tbsp) water

few fresh raspberries, to scatter

SERVES 6-8   **PREPARATION TIME:** 15 MINUTES PLUS CHILLING   **COOKING TIME:** 5 MINUTES
TOOLS BALLOON WHISK

❶ Slice the brioche into 5 or the Madeira cake into slices and place in a deep trifle bowl. Drizzle over the wine or orange juice. Scatter over the raspberries and chill for at least 1 hour.

❷ Make the caramel decoration. Line a baking sheet with non-stick baking parchment. Place the sugar and water in a pan and heat gently, stirring, to dissolve the sugar. Bring to the boil and boil without stirring until golden. Using a teaspoon drizzle threads of caramel in a criss-cross pattern to make decorations. Leave to cool then peel away the paper.

❸ Make the syllabub. Pour the lemon juice, sherry and brandy into the Kenwood Bowl. Stir in the sugar, until dissolved. Add the cream and using the Whisk, whip until the syllabub forms soft peaks. Do not over-whisk or the cream will split.

❹ Spoon the syllabub over the fruit, scatter with a few raspberries and decorate with the caramel shapes. Serve immediately.

SUMMER FRUIT FOOL

INGREDIENTS

450g (1lb) frozen, defrosted or fresh mixed summer fruits, e.g. strawberries, blackberries, redcurrants and raspberries

65g (2½oz) caster sugar

150ml (5fl oz) milk

15ml (1 tbsp) cornflour

2 egg yolks

200ml (7fl oz) double cream

mint or lemon geranium leaves, to decorate

SERVES 4   **PREPARATION TIME:** 15 MINUTES PLUS COOLING AND CHILLING
COOKING TIME: 10 MINUTES   **TOOLS** COLANDER AND SIEVE OR LIQUIDISER / BALLOON WHISK

❶ Place the fruits in a saucepan with 40g (1½oz) sugar. Bring to a gentle simmer and cook for 5 minutes, or until the fruit has softened.

❷ Cool slightly then using the Colander and Sieve fitted with the fine sieve, rough side uppermost, sieve the fruit into the Kenwood Bowl. Alternatively use the Liquidiser to purée the fruit then press through a nylon sieve to remove the pips.

❸ Place the milk in a saucepan and heat until boiling. Meanwhile mix the cornflour, egg yolks and remaining sugar together. Pour on the milk and stir to combine thoroughly.

❹ Return to the saucepan and heat until thickened, stirring continuously. Stir in the fruit purée and leave until cold.

❺ Using the Whisk, whip the cream until it forms soft peaks, then fold into the fruit purée mix to give a marbled effect. Spoon into individual glasses, chill for 30 minutes and then serve decorated with mint or geranium leaves.

OPEN FRUIT TART

SERVES 6-8   PREPARATION TIME: 25 MINUTES PLUS CHILLING AND COOLING
COOKING TIME: 30-35 MINUTES   TOOLS K BEATER

INGREDIENTS
1 quantity sweet rich flan pastry, see page 165

FOR THE FILLING:
115g (4oz) ground almonds
115g (4oz) icing sugar
2 eggs
2.5ml (½ tsp) almond essence
150ml (¼ pint) single cream
300ml (½ pint) crème fraîche
450g (1lb) mixed soft fruits e.g. strawberries, raspberries, redcurrants, blueberries

① Preheat the oven to 190°C/375°F/gas 5. Roll out the pastry on a lightly floured surface and use to line a 23cm (9 inch) fluted flan tin or a 33 x 11cm (13 x 4½ inch) fluted tranche tin. Chill for 30 minutes then bake blind for 15 minutes, or until barely coloured.

② Place the ground almonds, icing sugar, eggs, almond essence and cream in the Kenwood Bowl.

③ Using the K Beater at minimum speed, mix together until smooth. Pour into the pastry case and bake for 15-20 minutes or until set.

④ Transfer the tart to a cooling rack and leave until cold. Spread the crème fraîche over the top of the tart and pile the soft fruits on top.

Illustrated on page 108.

PAVLOVA

SERVES 6-8   PREPARATION TIME: 25 MINUTES PLUS COOLING   COOKING TIME: 1½ HOURS
TOOLS BALLOON WHISK

INGREDIENTS
4 egg whites
225g (8oz) caster sugar
5ml (1 tsp) cornflour
5ml (1 tsp) white wine vinegar
2.5ml (½ tsp) vanilla essence
300ml (½ pint) double cream
450g (1lb) fresh soft fruits e. g. strawberries, raspberries or peaches, plums and pineapple, sliced or chopped, as required

① Preheat the oven to 130°C/250°F/Gas ½. Line a baking sheet with non-stick baking parchment and draw a 23cm (9 inch) circle on the paper; turn the paper over.

② Place the egg whites in the Kenwood Bowl. Using the Whisk at speed 5, whisk the egg whites until they start to form soft peaks. Whilst the Whisk is still turning add the sugar, a spoonful at a time. The meringue should soon become stiff and shiny.

③ Mix the cornflour, white wine vinegar and vanilla essence together and fold in. Spoon half the meringue onto the prepared baking sheet to fill the marked circle, then add large spoonfuls of meringue around the edges to form a rim.

④ Bake for 1½ hours or until dry but still a little soft in the centre. Switch off the oven and leave the meringue to cool in the oven for at least 3 hours. Transfer to a wire rack and remove the non-stick baking parchment.

⑤ Using the Whisk, whip the cream until it forms soft peaks. Place the meringue on a serving plate, fill the centre with whipped cream and pile the fruits on top.

WHITE CHOCOLATE MOUSSE

SERVES 4   PREPARATION TIME: 15 MINUTES PLUS CHILLING   COOKING TIME: 5 MINUTES
TOOLS BALLOON WHISK

INGREDIENTS
175g (6oz) white chocolate, broken into pieces
90ml (3fl oz) milk
2 egg whites
1.25ml (¼ tsp) lemon juice
225ml (8fl oz) double cream
grated plain chocolate, to decorate

❶ Place the chocolate in a bowl over a pan of barely simmering water and stir until melted. Stir in the milk and set aside.

❷ Fit the Whisk and place the egg whites and lemon juice in the Kenwood Bowl. Whisk until the egg whites become stiff, then very gently fold into the chocolate mixture.

❸ Whip the double cream, using the Whisk, until it starts to form soft peaks. Gently fold into the chocolate mixture.

❹ Divide the mousse between four stemmed serving glasses and chill for at least 2 hours. Sprinkle with grated chocolate and serve.

FRESH ORANGE JELLY

SERVES 2-3   PREPARATION TIME: 10 MINUTES PLUS CHILLING   COOKING TIME: 3 MINUTES
TOOLS CITRUS JUICER

INGREDIENTS
5 oranges, halved
10ml (2 tsp) powdered gelatine
30ml (2 tbsp) caster sugar

❶ Using the Citrus Juicer, extract the juice from the oranges. Make up to 300ml (½ pint) with water if it is necessary.

❷ Place a quarter of the orange juice in a small pan, sprinkle over the gelatine and leave to stand for 5 minutes. Add the sugar and heat gently until the gelatine and sugar have dissolved.

❸ Stir in the remaining orange juice and pour into a jelly mould or serving dishes and leave to cool. Refrigerate to set.

Variation Use this orange jelly to make a fruit terrine. Layer fresh fruits such as raspberries, redcurrants and orange segments through the jelly. Just set each layer before adding the next so the fruits are suspended through the jelly.

STRAWBERRY ICE CREAM

INGREDIENTS
450ml (¾ pint) milk
5 egg yolks
175g (6oz) caster sugar
450g (1lb) strawberries, hulled
15ml (1 tbsp) lemon juice
450ml (¾ pint) double cream

SERVES 4 PREPARATION TIME: 30-40 MINUTES PLUS CHILLING AND FREEZING
COOKING TIME: 5 MINUTES TOOLS BALLOON WHISK / FOOD PROCESSING ATTACHMENT / ICE CREAM MAKER

❶ Heat the milk in a saucepan until almost boiling. Using the Whisk beat the egg yolks and sugar until light and thick then gradually mix in the milk on minimum speed.

❷ Strain back into the saucepan and cook over a low heat, stirring continuously until thickened, but do not boil. Leave to cool.

❸ Place half the strawberries in the Food Processing Attachment with the lemon juice and process to a purée. Sieve, if wished, to remove the seeds. Chop the remaining strawberries.

❹ Place the Ice Cream Maker with the frozen bowl in position and switch to minimum speed. Pour the custard mix, cream and strawberry purée through the feed tube and churn until it resembles freshly whipped cream.

❺ Add the chopped strawberries and churn for a couple of minutes, to distribute. Place in a plastic container and freeze until required. Soften slightly before serving.

CREAM OF COCONUT ICE CREAM

INGREDIENTS
115g (4oz) white chocolate, broken into pieces
75g (3oz) coconut milk powder
2 egg yolks
300ml (½ pint) milk
300ml (½ pint) double cream
15ml (1 tbsp) Malibu, coconut rum liqueur

SERVES 4-6 PREPARATION TIME: 30-40 MINUTES PLUS CHILLING AND FREEZING
COOKING TIME: 5 MINUTES TOOLS ICE CREAM MAKER

❶ Place the chocolate, coconut milk powder, egg yolks and milk in a saucepan, mix together and heat gently. Stir continuously, making sure it does not simmer, until thick and smooth. Do not boil.

❷ Stir in the double cream and coconut liqueur and leave to cool. Chill in the fridge.

❸ Place the Ice Cream Maker with the frozen bowl in position and switch to minimum speed. Pour the coconut mixture through the feed tube and churn until it resembles freshly whipped cream.

Serve immediately or transfer to plastic container and freeze until required. Soften slightly before serving.

VANILLA CREOLE ICE CREAM

SERVES 6-8 PREPARATION TIME: 30-40 MINUTES PLUS CHILLING AND FREEZING
COOKING TIME: 10 MINUTES TOOLS BALLOON WHISK / ICE CREAM MAKER

INGREDIENTS
600ml (1 pint) milk
1 vanilla pod, split or 5ml (1 tsp)
vanilla essence
4 egg yolks
150g (5oz) caster sugar
200g (7oz) crème fraîche

① Pour the milk into a heavy based saucepan, add the vanilla pod, if using and slowly bring almost to the boil. Remove from the heat and leave to infuse. If using vanilla essence just heat the milk then stir in the vanilla essence. Remove vanilla pod.

② Place the egg yolks and sugar in the Kenwood Bowl and using the Whisk, whisk together until thick and creamy. Gradually whisk in the milk on minimum speed. Strain back into the pan.

③ Cook over a low heat, stirring continuously, until thick enough to coat the back of a wooden spoon. Do not boil. Leave to cool then chill. Mix the vanilla custard and crème fraîche together.

④ Place the Ice Cream Maker with the frozen bowl in position and switch to minimum speed. Pour the liquid ice cream mix through the feed tube and churn until it resembles freshly whipped cream.

⑤ Serve immediately or place in a plastic container and keep frozen, until required. Soften slightly in the fridge or at room temperature, before serving.

Variations

CHOCOLATE CREOLE Omit vanilla and add 225g (8oz) melted plain chocolate to the cooked custard.

FUDGE CREOLE Reduce sugar to 50g (2oz). Melt 450g (1lb) fudge with 45ml (3 tbsp) milk over a low heat and add to the cooked custard.

BANOFFI ICE CREAM PIE

SERVES 6 PREPARATION TIME: 20 MINUTES PLUS COOLING AND CHILLING
COOKING TIME: 2 HOURS TOOLS COLANDER AND SIEVE / K BEATER

INGREDIENTS
400g (14oz) can sweetened
condensed milk
225g (8oz) digestive biscuits
115g (4oz) butter, melted
3 large bananas
about 9 scoops Vanilla Creole ice
cream, see above
or ready-made vanilla ice cream
cocoa powder, for dusting

① Place the unopened can of condensed milk in a saucepan, cover with water and bring to the boil. Cover, reduce the heat and simmer gently for 2 hours. Leave in the pan to cool.

② Fit the Colander and Sieve with the coarse screen, rough side uppermost and use to sieve the biscuits to make crumbs. Mix the crumbs and melted butter together and using a spoon press into the base and up the sides of a 20cm (8 inch) flan dish.

③ Shake out any remaining crumbs from the screen and sieve one of the bananas into the Kenwood Bowl.

④ Open the cooled can of milk, which will now have turned to soft toffee and empty into the Kenwood Bowl. Using the K Beater at minimum speed mix with the banana purée.

⑤ Peel and slice the remaining bananas and lay over the biscuit base. Spread the banana toffee over the bananas and chill for up to 2 hours. Serve topped with ice cream scoops, dusted with cocoa powder.

APPLE AND CINNAMON YOGURT ICE

SERVES 4-6   PREPARATION   TIME: 30-40 MINUTES PLUS CHILLING AND FREEZING
COOKING   TIME: 15 MINUTES   TOOLS PRO SLICER/GRATER / ICE CREAM MAKER

INGREDIENTS
325g (12oz) cooking apples, peeled, cored and quartered
2.5ml (½ tsp) ground cinnamon
3 strips of thinly pared lemon rind
150ml (¼ pint) cider or apple juice
50g (2oz) demerara sugar
60ml (4 tbsp) clear honey
90ml (6 tbsp) Greek yogurt

❶ Using the Pro Slicer/Grater slice the apples. Place in a saucepan with the cinnamon, lemon rind and cider or apple juice. Cover and simmer gently for 10 minutes, or until the apples turn to pulp.

❷ Discard the lemon rind, stir in the sugar, honey and yogurt and leave to cool. Chill.

❸ Place the Ice Cream Maker and frozen bowl in position and switch to minimum speed. Pour the mixture through the feed tube and churn for 20-30 minutes, until thickened and frozen.

❹ Serve immediately or place in a plastic container and keep frozen, until required. Soften slightly in the fridge for 30 minutes, before serving.

MANGO AND LIME SORBET

SERVES 4   PREPARATION   TIME: 25 MINUTES PLUS FREEZING
TOOLS LIQUIDISER / ICE CREAM MAKER

INGREDIENTS
2 ripe mangoes, chilled
60ml (4 tbsp) lime juice
50g (2oz) icing sugar

❶ Peel the mangoes and remove the flesh from the stone. Place the mango flesh in the Liquidiser with the lime juice and icing sugar and blend until completely smooth.

❷ Place the Ice Cream Maker with the frozen bowl, in position and switch to minimum speed. Pour the mango mixture through the feed tube and churn for 20 minutes, or until thickened.

❸ Serve immediately or place in a plastic container and keep frozen, until required. Soften slightly in the fridge for 30 minutes, before serving.

The aroma of freshly baked cakes and biscuits is hard to resist. From morning coffee cakes, muffins or tea bread to celebration fruits cakes, fresh strawberry sponge or a light fluffy roulade the K Beater and Whisk help to make home baking a pleasure. The K Beater also proves useful for mixing toppings and fillings whilst the Whisk is perfect for whipping fresh cream.

Homemade scones, strudel, doughnuts and brownies not to mention melt-in-the-mouth cookies, Viennese fingers and crisp golden biscotti biscuits are easy to make and offer a wide variety of recipes to serve for all occasions.

CELEBRATION FRUIT CAKE

INGREDIENTS

115g (4oz) glacé cherries
325g (12oz) currants
280g (10oz) raisins
325g (12oz) sultanas
115g (4oz) chopped candied peel
45ml (3 tbsp) brandy
250g (9oz) butter, softened
250g (9oz) light brown muscovado sugar
5 eggs, lightly beaten
300g (11oz) plain flour
5ml (1 tsp) ground mixed spice
2.5ml (½ tsp) ground cinnamon
2.5ml (½ tsp) ground nutmeg
finely grated rind 1 lemon
115g (4oz) whole blanched almonds, roughly chopped
60-90ml (2-3fl oz) barley wine, milk or orange juice

MAKES 1 X 20CM (8 INCH) ROUND OR 18CM (7 INCH) SQUARE CAKE
PREPARATION TIME: 40 MINUTES, PLUS SOAKING AND MATURING **COOKING TIME:** 3½ HOURS
TOOLS K BEATER

1 Grease and line a 20cm (8 inch) round cake tin. Tie a thick double band of brown paper around the outside of the tin. Stand the tin on a baking sheet, lined with a double thickness of brown paper.

2 Wash the glacé cherries to remove all the syrup, drain and pat dry with paper towel. Cut into quarters. Place in a large bowl with the currants, raisins, sultanas and candied peel. Pour over the brandy, toss together and leave to stand for 3-4 hours, or overnight, if time allows.

3 Preheat the oven to 150°C/300°F/Gas 2. Place the butter and sugar in the Kenwood Bowl and using the K Beater starting at speed 2, mix together until light and fluffy.

4 With the K Beater still turning, gradually add the beaten eggs, a little at a time and continue beating until smooth.

5 Sift the flour, mixed spice, cinnamon and nutmeg together. On minimum speed gradually add half the flour mixture. Stop mixing, add half the fruit and almonds. Mix on minimum until incorporated.

6 Add the remaining flour and fruit mixtures. Mix in sufficient barley wine, milk or orange juice to give a soft dropping consistency. Spoon into the prepared cake tin and level the surface with the back of a metal spoon. Make a slight depression in the centre. This will help to encourage a flat cake, when baked.

7 Bake in the centre of the oven for 2 hours. Reduce the oven to 140°C/275°F/Gas 1 for 1½ hours, or until cooked. Cover the top with greaseproof paper if it starts to over-brown.

8 Test the cake to see if it is cooked by inserting a fine skewer into the centre; it should come out clean. The cake should also feel firm to the touch.

9 Leave to cool in the tin until warm, then turn out onto a wire rack to cool. When completely cold, wrap in greaseproof paper, then in a double layer of aluminium foil. Leave in a cool dry place for 2 weeks to mature, or up to 2 months before applying almond paste and icing. Refer to pages 166-7 in the basic recipes chapter for recipes and quantities.

Cook's Note The 25cm (10 inch) round cake can only be made with the Kenwood Major. For the 30cm (12 inch) round cake and the 25cm (10 inch) round cake, if you only have a Kenwood Chef, use the mixer up to the end of step 4, then transfer the mix to a larger container, such as a clean washing-up bowl and mix the flour, fruit and nuts in by hand. Alternatively make the cake in 2 batches, using the machine and combine them by hand before transferring to the prepared tin.

QUANTITY GUIDE FOR VARIOUS DIFFERENT SIZES OF RICH FRUIT CAKE

FOR: 15CM (6 INCH) ROUND OR 12CM (5 INCH) SQUARE CAKE

INGREDIENTS
40g (1½oz) glacé cherries
200g (7oz) currants
150g (5oz) raisins
175g (6oz) sultanas
40g (1½oz) chopped candied peel
30ml (2 tbsp) brandy
150g (5oz) butter, softened
150g (5oz) light brown muscovado sugar
2 large eggs, lightly beaten
175g (6oz) plain flour
2.5ml (½ tsp) ground mixed spice
1.25ml (¼ tsp) ground cinnamon
1.25ml (¼ tsp) ground nutmeg
finely grated rind ½ lemon
40g (1½oz) whole blanched almonds, roughly chopped
30ml (2 tbsp) barley wine, milk or orange juice

Baking Time:
150°C/300°F/Gas 2 – 1½ hours then 140°C/275°F/ Gas 1 – 1-1½ hours

FOR: 18CM (7 INCH) ROUND OR 15CM (6 INCH) SQUARE CAKE

INGREDIENTS
65g (2½oz) glacé cherries
225g (8oz) currants
200g (7oz) raisins
225g (8oz) sultanas
65g (2½oz) chopped candied peel
30ml (2 tbsp) brandy
175g (6oz) butter, softened
175g (6oz) light brown muscovado sugar
3 eggs, lightly beaten
225g (8oz) plain flour
2.5ml (½ tsp) ground mixed spice
2.5ml (½ tsp) ground cinnamon
1.25ml (¼ tsp) ground nutmeg
finely grated rind ½ lemon
50g (2oz) whole blanched almonds, roughly chopped
45-60ml (3-4 tbsp) barley wine, milk or orange juice

Baking Time:
150°C/300°F/Gas 2 – 2 hours then 140°C/275°F/ Gas 1 – 1-1½ hours

FOR: 25CM (10 INCH) ROUND OR 23CM (9 INCH) SQUARE CAKE

INGREDIENTS
200g (7oz) glacé cherries
625g (1lb 6oz) currants
500g (1lb 2oz) raisins
625g (1lb 6oz) sultanas
200g (7oz) chopped candied peel
60ml (4 tbsp) brandy
500g (1lb 2oz) butter, softened
500g (1lb 2oz) light brown muscovado sugar
9 eggs, lightly beaten
600g (1lb 5oz) plain flour
10ml (2 tsp) ground mixed spice
5ml (1 tsp) ground cinnamon
5ml (1 tsp) ground nutmeg
finely grated rind 1½ lemons
175g (6oz) whole blanched almonds, roughly chopped
90ml (3fl oz) barley wine, milk or orange juice

Baking Time:
150°C/300°F/Gas 2 – 2¾ hours then 140°C/275°F/ Gas 1 – 1¾ hours

FOR: 30CM (12 INCH) ROUND OR 28CM (11 INCH) SQUARE CAKE

INGREDIENTS
275g (10oz) glacé cherries
1.0kg (2lb 4oz) currants
750g (1lb 11oz) raisins
1.0kg (2lb 4oz) sultanas
275g (10oz) chopped candied peel
90ml (6 tbsp) brandy
750g (1lb 11oz) butter, softened
750g (1lb 11oz) light brown muscovado sugar
14 eggs, lightly beaten
850g (1lb 14oz) plain flour
12.5ml (2½ tsp) ground mixed spice
7.5ml (1½ tsp) ground cinnamon
7.5ml (1½ tsp) ground nutmeg
finely grated rind 2 lemons
275g (10oz) whole blanched almonds, roughly chopped
120ml (4fl oz) barley wine, milk or orange juice

Baking Time:
150°C/300°F/Gas 2 – 4 hours then 140°C/275°F/ Gas 1 – 2-2½ hours

MORNING COFFEE CAKE

INGREDIENTS

115g (4oz) butter, melted
115g (4oz) caster sugar
2 eggs
5ml (1 tsp) almond essence
15ml (1 tbsp) lemon juice
150g (5oz) natural yogurt
225g (8oz) plain flour
2.5ml (½ tsp) salt
10ml (2 tsp) baking powder
50g (2oz) walnut pieces
45ml (3 tbsp) raspberry preserve
15ml (1 tbsp) demerara sugar
75g (3oz) walnut halves

MAKES 1 X 23CM (9 INCH) CAKE   PREPARATION TIME: 20 MINUTES
COOKING TIME: 30-40 MINUTES   TOOLS K BEATER

1 Grease and line the base of a 23cm (9 inch) loose-bottomed round cake tin. Preheat the oven to 180°C/350°F/Gas 4.

2 Place the melted butter and sugar in the Kenwood Bowl and using the K Beater on speed 2 beat the mixture until it is pale and fluffy.

3 Gradually beat in the eggs, almond essence, lemon juice and yogurt until thoroughly combined.

4 Using the K Beater at minimum speed mix in the flour, salt, baking powder and walnut pieces. Place half the cake mixture in the prepared tin. Spoon over the raspberry preserve and top with the remaining cake mix.

5 Sprinkle the demerara sugar over the top and decorate with the walnut halves. Bake for 30-40 minutes, until risen and firm to the touch. Leave in the tin for 5 minutes then turn out on to a wire rack to cool.

ALMOND ROULADE

INGREDIENTS

25g (1oz) flaked almonds, toasted
115g (4oz) whole blanched almonds
150g (5oz) caster sugar
5 eggs, separated
40g (1½oz) plain flour
1.25ml (¼ tsp) almond essence
150ml (¼ pint) double cream
150g (5oz) Greek yogurt
2 nectarine or 6 ripe apricots, sliced
caster sugar, for sprinkling

SERVES 8   PREPARATION TIME: 20 MINUTES, PLUS COOLING   COOKING TIME: 15-18 MINUTES
TOOLS FOOD PROCESSING ATTACHMENT OR ROTO FOOD CUTTER / BALLOON WHISK

1 Line a 33 x 23cm (13 x 9 inch) Swiss roll tin with non-stick baking parchment and sprinkle with flaked almonds. Preheat the oven to 180°C/350°F/Gas 4. Using the Food Processing Attachment fitted with the knife blade, or the Roto Food Cutter fitted with the fine shredding drum, very finely chop or grate the blanched almonds.

2 Place 125g (4oz) caster sugar and egg yolks in the Kenwood Bowl, and using the Whisk beat together until thick and creamy. Remove the bowl from the machine and fold in the grated almonds, flour and almond essence.

3 Using a clean Kenwood Bowl and Whisk, whip the egg whites with the remaining sugar, until they are stiff and form peaks. Carefully fold into the almond mixture, making sure not to knock the air out of the mixture.

4 Pour into the prepared tin and spread out evenly. Bake for 15-18 minutes, until well risen and firm to the touch. Remove from the oven and leave in the tin, Cover with non-stick baking parchment and a damp tea towel, until cold.

5 Invert on to a sheet of non-stick baking parchment, sprinkle another sheet with caster sugar and flip the roulade on to it. Using the Whisk, whip the cream until it just holds it shape. Fold in the Greek yogurt and spread over the roulade.

6 Sprinkle over the fruits, chopping the nectarine slices first, if large. Carefully roll up the roulade, using the paper to help. Dust with caster sugar and transfer to a serving plate.

Illustrated opposite.

TROPICAL FRUIT TEABREAD

SERVES 8-10   PREPARATION TIME: 15 MINUTES   COOKING TIME: 60-65 MINUTES
TOOLS K BEATER

INGREDIENTS

100g (3½oz) butter
115g (4oz) caster sugar
about 2 ripe bananas, 200g (7oz) peeled weight
3 eggs
200g (7oz) plain flour
5ml (1 tsp) baking powder
5ml (1 tsp) ground cinnamon
140g (5oz) ready to eat dried tropical fruits, coarsely chopped
50g (2oz) pecan nuts, chopped
10ml (2 tsp) demerara sugar

❶ Grease and line a 1.1 litre (2 pint) loaf tin. Preheat the oven to 170°C/325°F/Gas 3. Place the butter and sugar in the Kenwood Bowl. Fit the K Beater and cream together on speed 3, until pale and fluffy.

❷ Break the bananas into pieces, add to the butter and sugar mixture and beat in until smooth. Gradually beat in the eggs. Add the flour, baking powder, cinnamon, tropical fruits and pecan nuts and mix on minimum speed until incorporated. Transfer to the prepared tin and level the surface.

❸ Sprinkle with demerara sugar and bake for 60-65 minutes, or until well risen and firm to the touch. Leave to cool in the tin for 5 minutes, then turn out on to a wire rack to cool.

Cook's Note Ready to eat dried tropical fruits include such fruits as papaya, mango, melon and pineapple, but can be varied according to availability and your own preferred choice.

STRAWBERRIES AND CREAM SPONGE

SERVES 8-10   PREPARATION TIME: 25 MINUTES, PLUS COOLING
COOKING TIME: 25-30 MINUTES   TOOLS BALLOON WHISK

INGREDIENTS

150g (5oz) plain flour
25g (1oz) cornflour
6 eggs
175g (6oz) caster sugar
75g (3oz) butter, melted
300ml (½ pint) double cream
15ml (1 tbsp) caster sugar
juice and grated rind 1 orange
225g (8oz) strawberries
icing sugar, for dusting

❶ Preheat the oven to 180°C/350°F/Gas 4. Grease and base line a 23cm (9 inch) spring-form deep cake tin or 2 x 23cm (9 inch) sandwich tins. Sift the flour and cornflour together.

❷ Fit the Whisk, place the eggs and sugar in the Kenwood Bowl and whisk until pale and creamy and thick enough to leave a trail on the surface when the Whisk is lifted.

❸ Remove the Kenwood Bowl from the machine; gently fold in half the flour mixture using a large metal spoon. Pour half the butter around the edge of the bowl and lightly fold in. Gradually fold in the remaining flour mixture and butter.

❹ Pour into the prepared tin or tins and bake for 35-40 minutes, or 25-30 minutes for the sandwich tins, until risen, golden and beginning to shrink from the sides of the tin. Turn out on to a wire rack to cool.

❺ Using the Whisk, whip the cream, sugar and orange juice together until it forms soft peaks. Fold in the orange rind. Reserve 5 strawberries for decoration and slice the remainder.

❻ Split the deep cake in half and fill with the whipped cream and sliced strawberries or use to sandwich together the two separate sponges. Decorate the top with the reserved strawberries, dust with icing sugar and serve.

PASSION CAKE

INGREDIENTS

275g (10oz) carrots, peeled
225g (8oz) butter, softened
225g (8oz) light brown muscovado sugar
4 eggs, separated
15ml (1 tbsp) orange juice
grated rind 1 orange
175g (6oz) self-raising flour
5ml (1 tsp) baking powder
5ml (1 tsp) freshly grated nutmeg
50g (2oz) ground almonds
115g (4oz) walnut pieces, chopped

FOR THE ICING:

175g (6oz) mascarpone or full fat soft cheese
40g (1½oz) icing sugar
5ml (1 tsp) lemon juice
30-45ml (2-3 tbsp) walnut pieces, to decorate

❶ Grease and line a 20cm (8 inch) round cake tin. Preheat the oven to 180°C/350°F/Gas 4. Using the Pro Slicer/Grater or Roto Food Cutter fitted with the fine shredding plate or drum, grate the carrots.

❷ Place the butter and sugar in the Kenwood Bowl. Using the K Beater, at speed 3, cream together until light and fluffy. Beat in the egg yolks, orange juice and rind.

❸ Add the flour, baking powder, nutmeg, ground almonds and chopped walnuts and mix on speed 1, to combine. Add the carrots and mix in.

❹ Using a clean bowl and the Whisk, whip the egg whites until stiff. Using a large metal spoon fold into the cake mixture. Transfer to the prepared tin and bake for 1-1¼ hours until a skewer inserted in the cake comes out clean. Cover the top with greaseproof paper towards the end of baking, if the cake starts to over-brown.

❺ Leave to cool in the tin for 10 minutes, then transfer to a wire rack to cool completely. To finish place the cheese, icing sugar and lemon juice in the Kenwood Bowl. Using the K Beater on minimum speed, mix to a smooth icing.

❻ Spread over the top of the cake, sprinkle with walnuts pieces, and serve.

RICH CHOCOLATE CAKE

INGREDIENTS

200g (7oz) good quality plain chocolate, broken into pieces
175g (6oz) butter, softened
175g (6oz) caster sugar
4 eggs, separated
115g (4oz) ground almonds
75g (3oz) self-raising flour
15ml (1 tbsp) cocoa powder

FOR THE CHOCOLATE GANACHE:

400ml (14fl oz) double cream
225g (8oz) good quality plain chocolate, broken into pieces

❶ Grease and line the base of a 22cm (8½ inch) or a 23cm (9 inch) spring-form round cake tin. Preheat the oven to 180°C/350°F/Gas 4. Place the chocolate in a bowl and melt over a pan of simmering water.

❷ Place the butter and sugar in the Kenwood Bowl and using the K Beater on speed 4 cream together until pale and fluffy. Gradually beat in the egg yolks.

❸ On minimum speed mix in the ground almonds and melted chocolate. Mix in the flour and cocoa powder. Using the Whisk, whip the egg whites until stiff and gradually fold into the cake mixture.

❹ Transfer to the prepared tin and bake for 40 minutes or until just firm to the touch. Cool for 5 minutes, and then transfer to a wire rack to cool. Split the cake in half.

❺ Place the cream for the ganache in a saucepan and bring to the boil. Remove from the heat, add the chocolate pieces and stir until melted. Leave for 2-3 minutes, to cool. Transfer half to the Kenwood Bowl and using the Whisk, whip until it forms soft peaks. Use to sandwich the cakes together.

❻ Stir the remaining chocolate and cream mix, as soon as it starts to thicken pour over the cake, to cover and shake gently to spread the icing evenly. Leave to set in a cool place.

STICKY GINGERBREAD

MAKES 1 X 18CM (7 INCH) CAKE   PREPARATION TIME: 15 MINUTES
COOKING TIME: 1-1¼ HOURS   TOOLS K BEATER

INGREDIENTS
280g (10oz) plain flour
10ml (2 tsp) ground ginger
5ml (1 tsp) mixed spice
2.5ml (½ tsp) baking powder
7.5 ml (1½ tsp) bicarbonate of soda
115g (4oz) butter
50g (2oz) treacle
150g (5oz) golden syrup
115g (4oz) light brown muscovado sugar
150ml (¼ pint) milk
2 eggs
115g (4oz) drained, bottled stem ginger in syrup, thinly sliced
30ml (2 tbsp) stem ginger syrup or warmed golden syrup, to serve, optional

❶ Grease and line an 18cm (7 inch) square cake tin. Preheat the oven to 170°C/325°F/Gas 3. Sift the flour, ground ginger, mixed spice, baking powder and bicarbonate of soda into the Kenwood Bowl.

❷ Place the butter, treacle, golden syrup and sugar in a small saucepan and heat gently until the fat has melted, stirring occasionally.

❸ Using the K Beater on speed 1, mix the melted mixture, milk, eggs and 75g (3oz) of the stem ginger into the dry ingredients, until well combined. Pour into the prepared tin and sprinkle over the remaining stem ginger.

❹ Bake for 1-1¼ hours, or until risen and just firm to the touch. Leave to cool in the tin for 10 minutes, then turn out onto a wire rack. Serve cold. It is best left for a couple of days, to allow the sticky texture to develop. Store in an airtight container.

❺ Serve drizzled with a little of the stem ginger syrup or warmed golden syrup, if wished.

BLUEBERRY AND PECAN MUFFINS

MAKES 12   PREPARATION TIME: 10 MINUTES   COOKING TIME: 20-25 MINUTES
TOOLS K BEATER

INGREDIENTS
400g (14oz) plain flour
15ml (1 tbsp) baking powder
200g (7oz) caster sugar
2 eggs
280ml (½ pint) buttermilk
5ml (1 tsp) vanilla essence
75g (3oz) butter, melted
100g (3½oz) pecan nuts, roughly chopped
140g (5oz) blueberries

❶ Line a 12 hole muffin tin with paper cases. Preheat the oven to 200°C/400°F/Gas 6. Place the flour, baking powder and sugar in the Kenwood Bowl. Fit the K Beater.

❷ Mix the eggs, buttermilk, vanilla and melted butter together. Add to the Kenwood Bowl and mix on speed 1, until just combined, taking care not to over-mix.

❸ Add three-quarters of the pecan nuts and the blueberries and fold into the muffin mix. Divide between the muffin cases.

❹ Sprinkle over the remaining nuts and bake for 20-25 minutes, until risen and golden. Transfer to a wire rack to cool slightly and serve warm.

Variation Replace blueberries with raspberries, blackberries or rhubarb, cut into 5mm (¼ inch) pieces, to vary the flavour. If wished sprinkle 15ml (1 tbsp) demerara sugar over the top of the muffins before baking, for a crunchy finish.

Illustrated opposite.

PEACH AND CHERRY STREUSELKUCHEN

SERVES 8-10 PREPARATION TIME: 20 MINUTES COOKING TIME: 35-40 MINUTES TOOLS K BEATER

INGREDIENTS
250g (9oz) self-raising flour
5ml (1 tsp) ground cinnamon
175g (6oz) butter, cubed
115g (4oz) caster sugar
75g (3oz) ground almonds
1 egg
4 fresh peaches, halved, stoned and sliced
175g (6oz) fresh cherries, stoned, or fresh raspberries
10ml (2 tsp) cornflour

❶ Preheat the oven to 200°C/400°F/Gas 6. Grease a 23cm (9 inch) spring-form cake tin. Place the flour, cinnamon and butter in the Kenwood Bowl. Using the K Beater on minimum speed mix together until the mixture starts to stick together.

❷ Add the caster sugar and ground almonds and mix to a coarse, crumbly texture. Do not over-mix.

❸ Weigh 175g (6oz) of the mixture and set aside. Add the egg to the remainder and using the K Beater mix to a dough.

❹ Transfer to the prepared tin and using a metal spoon press over the base and about 2.5cm (1 inch) up the sides of the tin.

❺ Toss the peaches and cherries or raspberries with the cornflour and place in the tin.

❻ Sprinkle over the reserved crumble mixture and bake for 35-40 minutes, or until golden. Leave to cool for 30 minutes then remove from the tin and place on a wire rack to cool completely.

OAT, HONEY AND APPLE ROCK CAKES

MAKES 12 PREPARATION TIME: 15 MINUTES COOKING TIME: 20 MINUTES TOOLS GRAIN MILL / K BEATER

INGREDIENTS
150g (5oz) rolled oats
2.5ml (½ tsp) bicarbonate of soda
20ml (4 tsp) vegetable oil
50g (2oz) raisins
60ml (4 tbsp) clear honey
2 small eating apples, cored and finely chopped

❶ Place the oats in the Grain Mill and using setting 1, mill the oats into the Kenwood Bowl. Preheat the oven to 200°C/400°F/Gas 6. Lightly oil two non-stick baking sheets.

❷ Add the bicarbonate of soda, vegetable oil, raisins, honey and apples to the Kenwood Bowl. Using the K Beater on minimum speed mix all the ingredients together.

❸ Place 6 rough rocky-looking mounds on each baking sheet. Leave a space between each rock cake to allow room for spreading.

❹ Bake for 20 minutes, or until golden. The outside should be crispy, but the centre should be soft. Transfer to a wire rack to cool.

CAKES, PASTRIES & BISCUITS

RASPBERRY HAZELNUT MILLE FEUILLE

S E R V E S 8   P R E P A R A T I O N   T I M E : 30 MINUTES, PLUS COOLING   C O O K I N G   T I M E : 15-17 MINUTES
T O O L S FOOD PROCESSING ATTACHMENT / BALLOON WHISK

INGREDIENTS
175g (6oz) shelled hazelnuts
375g (13oz) puff pastry, see page 165
1 egg, lightly beaten
300ml (½ pint) double cream
25g (1oz) caster sugar
2.5ml (½ tsp) vanilla essence
225-275g (8-10oz) raspberries, hulled
icing sugar, to dust
Framboise or Cointreau liqueur, to drizzle, optional

❶ Preheat the oven to 190°C/375°F/Gas 5. Spread the hazelnuts on a baking tray and place in the oven for 5 minutes, or until pale golden, leave to cool for 5 minutes. Using the Food Processing Attachment fitted with the knife blade, chop the hazelnuts.

❷ Roll out the pastry into a rectangle measuring 30 x 28cm (12 x 11 inches) and place on a dampened baking sheet.

❸ Brush with beaten egg, prick well all over with a fork and scatter half the nuts over the pastry. Bake for 10-12 minutes, until risen and golden. Transfer to a wire rack to cool.

❹ Trim the edges and cut into 3 strips about 10cm (4 inches) wide and 23cm (10 inches) long. Using the Whisk, whip the cream, sugar and vanilla together on speed 1, until it forms soft peaks, then fold in the remaining hazelnuts with a metal spoon.

❺ Place one long layer of pastry on a serving plate, cover with half the cream and top with raspberries. Place a second layer of pastry, cream and raspberries on top and finish with the remaining pastry layer.

❻ Dust with icing sugar and serve. Use a serrated knife, to cut into slices. For a treat, serve slices, drizzled with Framboise – raspberry liqueur or orange liqueur, such as Cointreau.

LEMON CURD TARTLETS

M A K E S 8-10   P R E P A R A T I O N   T I M E : 20 MINUTES   C O O K I N G   T I M E : 30 MINUTES
T O O L S CITRUS JUICER / BALLOON WHISK

INGREDIENTS
1 quantity of shortcrust nut pastry, see page 165
FOR THE FILLING:
3 lemons, halved
115g (4oz) caster sugar
3 eggs
115g (4 oz) curd cheese
175ml (6fl oz) single cream
2.5ml (½ tsp) freshly grated nutmeg
raspberries or blueberries, to decorate
icing sugar, to dust

❶ Roll out the pastry and using a plain or fluted cutter cut out 10 x 11cm (4½ inch) rounds to line 10 deep muffin tins or 8 x 12cm (5 inch) rounds and use to line 8 x individual 10cm (4 inch) loose base tart tins.

❷ Prick the cases with a fork, line with non-stick baking parchment and fill with baking beans. Cover and chill for 20 minutes.

❸ Preheat the oven to 190°C/375°F/Gas 5 and bake the pastry cases for 10 minutes. Remove the baking beans.

❹ Meanwhile make the filling. Using the Citrus Juicer, juice the lemon halves. Place the juice in the Kenwood Bowl with the sugar, eggs and curd cheese and using the Whisk, mix together. Mix in the single cream.

❺ Reduce the oven to 180°C/350°F/Gas 4. Divide the lemon filling between the tartlet cases, sprinkle with grated nutmeg and bake for 20 minutes, or until filling is just set.

❻ Transfer the tartlets to a cooling rack and leave until cold. Top with a few raspberries or blueberries and sprinkle with icing sugar.

Illustrated on page 124.

DOUGHNUTS

INGREDIENTS

450g (1lb) strong plain white flour
5ml (1 tsp) salt
50g (2oz) butter
50g (2oz) caster sugar
7g sachet (1½ tsp) fast action dried yeast
1 egg
140ml (¼ pint) lukewarm milk
oil for deep frying
caster sugar for sprinkling
45ml (3 tbsp) seedless raspberry jam

MAKES 16 PREPARATION TIME: 30 MINUTES PLUS RISING COOKING TIME: 16-20 MINUTES
TOOLS K BEATER / DOUGH HOOK

❶ Lightly oil 2 baking sheets. Place the flour, salt and butter in the Kenwood Bowl. Fit the K Beater and mix on speed 1 to incorporate the butter into the flour. Mix in the sugar and yeast.

❷ Replace the K Beater with the Dough Hook. Add the egg, lukewarm milk and about 90ml (3fl oz) lukewarm water and mix on minimum speed to form a soft dough.

❸ Knead for 5-6 minutes on minimum speed, until the dough is smooth and elastic. Remove the Kenwood Bowl, cover with lightly oiled clear film and leave to rise in a warm place for about 1 hour, or until doubled in size.

❹ Using the Dough Hook on minimum speed for 30-60 seconds gently knead the dough to knock back. Transfer to a lightly floured surface and divide in half to make 8 ring and 8 jam doughnuts.

❺ Cover half the dough. Roll the remaining dough to a thickness of about 1.25cm (½ inch). Using a 7.5cm (3 inch) plain cutter, cut out 8 rounds. Remove the centre with a 4cm (1½ inch) cutter to make 8 ring doughnuts.

❻ Place on a prepared baking sheet and cover with oiled clear film. Divide the remaining dough into 8 and shape into round balls. Place on the other baking sheet and cover as before.

❼ Leave the doughnuts in a warm place to rise for about 30 minutes, until doubled in size. Heat the oil for deep-frying to 180°C/350°F or until a cube of stale bread when added to the oil, turns golden brown in 30-60 seconds.

❽ Cook the doughnuts, 3-4 at a time in the oil, for about 4-5 minutes, or until golden. Remove using a slotted spoon and transfer onto absorbent kitchen paper to drain.

❾ Toss in caster sugar and set aside to cool. For the jam doughnuts, heat the jam with 5ml (1 tsp) water in a small saucepan, until warm, stirring to combine. Cool and place in a piping bag fitted with a small plain nozzle.

❿ Using a skewer make a small hole in the side of each round doughnut to insert the jam. Place the piping nozzle in the hole and squeeze a little jam into each doughnut.

Illustrated opposite.

APPLE STRUDEL

SERVES 8   PREPARATION TIME: 25 MINUTES   COOKING TIME: 35-40 MINUTES
TOOLS PRO SLICER/GRATER

INGREDIENTS

grated rind and juice 1 lemon
5ml (1 tsp) mixed spice
115g (4oz) sultanas
25g (1oz) fresh breadcrumbs
15ml (1 tbsp) cornflour
75g (3oz) caster sugar
700g (1½lb) cooking apples
12 sheets filo pastry about 150g (5oz)
50g (2oz) butter, melted
50g (2oz) ground almonds
icing sugar, for dusting

① Preheat the oven to 190°C/375°F/Gas 5. Lightly grease a baking sheet. Mix the lemon rind, mixed spice, sultanas, breadcrumbs, cornflour and all but 15ml (1 tbsp) of the caster sugar together.

② Peel, quarter and core the apples. Fit the coarse slicing plate to the Pro Slicer/Grater and slice the apples. Toss in the lemon juice. Add the breadcrumb and sultana mixture and gently toss the mixture together.

③ Lay four sheets of filo pastry, side by side, overlapping the longest edges by about 2.5cm (1 inch). Brush between the overlap and the whole sheets of pastry with melted butter.

④ Cover with another four sheets and brush with butter. Repeat once more with the remaining filo sheets and more melted butter. Sprinkle with the ground almonds.

⑤ Place the apple filling on the pastry and spread to cover, leaving a 2.5cm (1 inch) gap around the edges. Fold the border over the filling and roll up, starting at one short side.

⑥ Place on the prepared baking sheet, brush with the remaining butter and sprinkle with the remaining sugar. Bake for 35-40 minutes, or until golden and the apples are tender.

⑦ Dust with icing sugar and serve warm or cold, cut into slices.

SCOTTISH DROP SCONES

MAKES 10   PREPARATION TIME: 15 MINUTES   COOKING TIME: 12-15 MINUTES
TOOLS CONTINUOUS JUICE EXTRACTOR / K BEATER

INGREDIENTS

325g (12oz) potatoes, peeled
15ml (1 tbsp) caster sugar
115g (4oz) self-raising flour
1 egg
90ml (3fl oz) milk
butter and maple syrup or honey, to serve

① Put the potatoes through the Continuous Juice Extractor and collect the juice and pulp. Collect the pulp in the Kenwood Bowl. Discard the juice as it is heavy in starch.

② Add the sugar, flour, egg and milk and using the K Beater, mix at minimum speed to a thick batter.

③ Pour a little oil into a heavy based frying pan and place over a medium heat. Cook the mixture in batches, dropping large spoonfuls of the mixture into the pan; flattening them slightly.

④ Fry for 2-3 minutes, or until bubbles rise to the surface, turn over and cook the other side for 2-3 minutes, or until golden. Place on a baking tray between sheets of greaseproof paper and keep warm in the oven whilst cooking the remainder.

⑤ Serve hot with butter and maple syrup or honey.

WHITE CHOCOLATE BROWNIES

MAKES 16   PREPARATION TIME: 20 MINUTES   COOKING TIME: 30-35 MINUTES
TOOLS FOOD PROCESSING ATTACHMENT / ROTO FOOD CUTTER / K BEATER

INGREDIENTS

100g (3½oz) hazelnuts or walnuts
250g (9oz) white chocolate
50g (2oz) butter
2 eggs
75g (3oz) caster sugar
5ml (1 tsp) vanilla essence
75g (3oz) self-raising flour

❶ Grease and line an 18cm (7 inch) square tin that is at least 5cm (2 inches) deep. Preheat the oven to 180°C/350°F/Gas 4. Using the Food Processing Attachment fitted with the knife blade roughly chop the nuts and set aside; or chop by hand.

❷ Using the Roto Food Cutter fitted with the coarse shredding drum, grate 175g (6oz) white chocolate and finely chop the remainder.

❸ Place 75g (3oz) grated white chocolate in a small saucepan with the butter and heat very gently until melted, stirring continuously. Leave to cool for 5 minutes.

❹ Place the eggs, sugar, vanilla and melted mixture in the Kenwood Bowl and using the K Beater, mix together on speed 1, mix until smooth. Add the nuts, remaining grated and chopped chocolate and flour. Mix to combine.

❺ Transfer to the prepared tin and bake for 30-35 minutes. Leave to cool in the tin then cut into small squares to serve.

Illustrated on page 124.

HONEY AND LEMON CREAMS

MAKES 18   PREPARATION TIME: 25 MINUTES PLUS COOLING   COOKING TIME: 5-7 MINUTES
TOOLS K BEATER

INGREDIENTS

225g (8oz) plain flour
50g (2oz) caster sugar
100g (3½oz) butter at room temperature, diced
100g (3½oz) clear honey

FOR THE FILLING:

50g (2oz) butter
100g (3½oz) icing sugar
finely grated rind 1 lemon
15ml (1 tbsp) lemon juice

❶ Lightly grease 2 baking sheets. Preheat the oven to 190°C/375°F/Gas 5. Place the flour, sugar and butter in the Kenwood Bowl.

❷ Using the K Beater, mix together on speed 1, until the mixture resembles fine breadcrumbs. Add the honey and mix to a smooth dough.

❸ On a lightly floured surface roll out the biscuit dough to 3mm (⅛ inch) thickness and using a 5cm (2 inch) fluted pastry cutter cut out 36 rounds, re-rolling the trimmings as necessary.

❹ Remove the centres from 18 rounds using a small round or heart shaped pastry cutter. Transfer to the prepared baking sheets and bake for 5-7 minutes, or until pale golden. Transfer to a wire rack to cool.

❺ To make the lemon filling. Place the butter, icing sugar, lemon rind and juice in the Kenwood Bowl. Using the K Beater on speed 1, beat together until light and creamy.

❻ Sandwich the biscuits together, with the lemon cream, placing the open centre biscuits on top.

BUTTERSCOTCH AND CHOCOLATE CHIP COOKIES

MAKES 18 PREPARATION TIME: 15 MINUTES COOKING TIME: 12-15 MINUTES
TOOLS K BEATER

INGREDIENTS
125g (4oz) butter, softened
150g (5oz) light brown sugar
1 egg
2.5ml (½ tsp) vanilla essence
175g (6oz) plain flour
2.5ml (½ tsp) baking powder
pinch of salt
175g (6oz) plain chocolate chips or
plain chocolate, finely chopped

① Lightly grease 2 baking sheets. Preheat the oven to 190°C/375°F/Gas 5. Place the butter and sugar in the Kenwood Bowl and using the K Beater, beat together on speed 2, until light and fluffy.

② Beat in the egg and vanilla. Sift the flour, baking powder and salt together and add on minimum speed with the chocolate chips, until incorporated.

③ Place large teaspoonfuls of the mixture onto the baking sheets, spaced apart to leave room for spreading.

④ Bake for 12-15 minutes, or until pale golden, Allow to cool slightly before transferring to a wire rack to cool completely.

BISCOTTI

MAKES 24 PREPARATION TIME: 15 MINUTES PLUS COOLING
COOKING TIME: 45-50 MINUTES   TOOLS K BEATER

INGREDIENTS
50g (2oz) whole blanched almonds
50g (2oz) butter, softened
115g (4oz) caster sugar
1 egg
15ml (1 tbsp) orange liqueur e.g.
Grand Marnier
finely grated rind 1 small orange
175g (6oz) plain flour
10ml (2 tsp) baking powder
5ml (1 tsp) ground coriander
40g (1½oz) polenta
50g (2oz) pistachio nuts

① Preheat the oven to 170°C/325°F/Gas 3. Lightly grease a baking sheet. Spread the almonds on a second baking sheet and roast in the oven for 5-10 minutes, or until golden. Cool and very coarsely chop.

② Place the butter and sugar in the Kenwood Bowl. Using the K Beater at speed 3, cream together, until smooth. Beat in the egg, liqueur and orange rind. Add the flour, baking powder, ground coriander and polenta to the Kenwood Bowl and mix at speed 1, to make a soft dough.

③ Turn out on to a floured surface, sprinkle with almonds and pistachio nuts and knead, to distribute them through the dough. Halve the mixture and shape each half into a 5cm (2 inch) wide, 2cm (¾ inch) deep sausage.

④ Place on the prepared baking sheet and bake for about 30 minutes, until just firm. Transfer to a wire rack to cool for about 10 minutes, then cut diagonally into 1cm (½ inch) wide slices.

⑤ Place the Biscotti cut side down on the baking sheet and bake for 10 minutes, until crisp. Cool on a wire rack and store in an airtight container.

FUDGE-NUT CRUMBLES

MAKES 24 PREPARATION TIME: 20 MINUTES COOKING TIME: 12-15 MINUTES
TOOLS ROTO FOOD CUTTER / K BEATER

INGREDIENTS
75g (3oz) whole blanched almonds
75g (3oz) vanilla fudge pieces
200g (7oz) plain flour
2.5ml (½ tsp) bicarbonate of soda
115g (4oz) butter, at room temperature, cut into pieces
115g (4oz) caster or light brown muscovado sugar
1 egg
2.5ml (½ tsp) almond essence
25g (1oz) flaked almonds

❶ Lightly grease 2 baking sheets. Preheat the oven to 190°C/375°F/Gas 5. Fit the Roto Food Cutter with the fine shredding drum.

❷ On minimum speed grate the almonds and fudge alternately so that the almonds help to push the fudge through the attachment.

❸ Place the flour, bicarbonate of soda and butter in the Kenwood Bowl and using the K Beater, mix together on speed 1, until the mixture resembles breadcrumbs.

❹ Add the sugar, egg, almond essence, grated almonds and fudge and mix to form a dough.

❺ Shape into a log about 25cm (10 inches) long and cut into 24 slices. Place on the baking sheets, spaced apart to leave room for spreading.

❻ Sprinkle with the flaked almonds and bake for 12-15 minutes, or until golden, Allow to cool for 4-5 minutes before transferring to a wire rack to finish cooling.

VIENNESE FINGERS

MAKES 24 PREPARATION TIME: 15 MINUTES COOKING TIME: 10 MINUTES
TOOLS K BEATER

INGREDIENTS
225g (8oz) butter
50g (2oz) icing sugar
2.5ml (½ tsp) vanilla essence
225g (8oz) plain flour
75g (3oz) plain chocolate, broken into pieces
40g (1½ oz) pistachio nuts, skinned and chopped

❶ Lightly grease 2 baking sheets. Preheat the oven to 180°C/350°F/Gas 4. Place the butter and sugar in the Kenwood Bowl and using the K Beater, beat together on speed 1, until light and fluffy.

❷ Beat in the vanilla essence. Add the flour and continue mixing on minimum speed until a dough is formed. Put the mixture in to a piping bag fitted with a 1cm (½ inch) star nozzle.

❸ Pipe the mixture into 6cm (2½ inch) lengths onto the prepared baking sheets, spaced apart to leave room for spreading. Bake for 10 minutes, or until pale golden. Transfer to a wire rack to cool

❹ Put the chocolate in a small bowl over a pan of simmering water and stir until melted. Dip the ends of the fingers into the melted chocolate, sprinkle with pistachio nuts and place on a wire rack until the chocolate sets.

Variation Pipe mixture into 6cm (2½ inch) diameter rings instead of fingers. Either dip or drizzle tops with chocolate and sprinkle with chopped pistachio nuts.

Bread making is one of those tasks, which is often considered difficult, but with the Dough Hook it couldn't be easier. Just add the ingredients to the Kenwood Bowl and the Dough Hook will mix and knead the dough, just leaving you the pleasurable tasks of shaping and baking.

This chapter contains basics such as white rolls, wholemeal, granary and rye bread; easy to make breads from around the world like Irish Soda bread, Indian Naan, Italian breadsticks and Focaccia and Swiss Zopf; and tasty sweet breads like stollen, Chelsea buns and cranberry, honey and oat bread.

BREAD

WHOLEMEAL BREAD

MAKES 1 LOAF   PREPARATION TIME: 20 MINUTES PLUS RISING   COOKING TIME: 30 MINUTES   TOOLS DOUGH HOOK

INGREDIENTS

375g (13oz) strong plain wholemeal flour

75g (3oz) strong plain white flour

10ml (2 tsp) salt

7g sachet (1½ tsp) fast action dried yeast

300ml (½ pint) lukewarm water

FOR THE TOPPING:

30ml (2 tbsp) water

2.5ml (½ tsp) salt

wholemeal flour, to sprinkle

Illustrated on page 142.

❶ Place the wholemeal and white flours, salt and yeast in the Kenwood Bowl. Using the Dough Hook on minimum speed, gradually mix in the lukewarm water to form a soft dough.

❷ Knead for 1 minute on minimum and 4 minutes on speed 1, until smooth and elastic. Remove the Kenwood Bowl, cover with oiled clear film and leave to rise in a warm place for about 1 hour, or until doubled in size.

❸ Using the Dough Hook on minimum speed for 30-60 seconds gently knead the dough to knock back. Transfer to a floured surface and shape into a ball. Knead from the sides to the centre, then turn over and place on a floured baking sheet.

❹ Cover with oiled clear film and leave to rise for about 30 minutes, until doubled in size. Meanwhile preheat the oven to 230°C/450°F /Gas 8. Mix the water and salt together and brush over the bread. Sprinkle with flour.

❺ Using a sharp knife make 3 or 4 slashes across the loaf, then again at right angles. Bake for 10 minutes, then reduce the oven to 200°C/400°F/Gas 6 for 20 minutes, or until the bread sounds hollow when tapped on the base. Cool on a wire rack.

Variation For Granary bread replace the wholemeal and white flours with Granary flour and proceed as above. Sprinkle with rye or wheat flakes instead of sprinkling with flour and slashing the top.

RYE BREAD

MAKES 1 SMALL LOAF   PREPARATION TIME: 20 MINUTES PLUS RISING   COOKING TIME: 30-35 MINUTES   TOOLS DOUGH HOOK

INGREDIENTS

225g (8oz) rye flour

75g (3oz) strong plain wholemeal flour

75g (3oz) strong plain white flour

50g (2oz) coarse cornmeal

5ml (1 tsp) caraway seeds

10ml (2 tsp) salt

7g sachet (1½ tsp) fast action dried yeast or 20g (¾oz) fresh yeast

5ml (1 tsp) clear honey

140ml (¼ pint) lukewarm water

140ml (¼ pint) lukewarm milk

wholemeal flour, for dusting

❶ Lightly oil a baking sheet. Place the rye, wholemeal and white flours, cornmeal, caraway seeds, salt and dried yeast in the Kenwood Bowl. If using fresh yeast mix with the honey and water. Leave to stand for 15 minutes.

❷ Using the Dough Hook on minimum speed, gradually mix in the honey, water and milk or yeast mixture and milk to form a soft dough.

❸ Knead for 1 minute on minimum and 4 minutes on speed 1, until smooth and elastic. Remove the Bowl, cover with lightly oiled clear film and leave to rise in a warm place for 1½-2 hours, or until doubled in size.

❹ Using the Dough Hook on minimum speed for 30-60 seconds gently knead the dough to knock back. Transfer to a lightly floured surface and shape into an oval loaf. Place on the prepared baking sheet.

❺ Dust with wholemeal flour, cover with lightly oiled clear film and leave to rise for about 60 minutes, until doubled in size. Meanwhile preheat the oven to 220°C/425°F/Gas 7.

❻ Bake for 30-35 minutes, or until the bread sounds hollow when tapped on the base. Cool on a wire rack.

CIABATTA

MAKES 2 LOAVES   PREPARATION TIME: 35 MINUTES PLUS RISING
COOKING TIME: 25-30 MINUTES   TOOLS K BEATER / DOUGH HOOK

INGREDIENTS

FOR THE STARTER:

7g (¼oz) fresh yeast

200ml (7fl oz) lukewarm water

175g (6oz) strong plain white flour

FOR THE DOUGH:

7g (¼oz) fresh yeast

30ml (2 tbsp) milk

200ml (7fl oz) lukewarm water

30ml (2 tbsp) olive oil

325-340g (11½-12oz) strong plain white flour

7.5ml (1½ tsp) salt

flour, to sprinkle

1 Cream the yeast for the starter with a little of the water. Place the flour in the Kenwood Bowl. Add the yeast mixture and remaining water. Using the K Beater on minimum speed, gradually mix to form a thick batter.

2 Remove the Kenwood Bowl from the machine, cover with lightly oiled clear film and leave to rise in a warm place for about 12 hours or overnight, or until dough has risen and is just starting to collapse.

3 Mix the yeast for the dough with the milk. Using the Dough Hook on minimum speed mix into the starter with the water and olive oil. Increase to speed 1.

4 Gradually add 325g (11½oz) flour and salt and continue mixing to form a very soft dough, impossible to knead on a work surface. Knead for 5-6 minutes or more until the dough becomes springy and starts to pull away from the sides of the bowl. Add the remaining flour if necessary.

5 Cover the dough with lightly oiled clear film and leave to rise for 1½-2 hours, or until almost trebled in size. Sprinkle two baking sheets with flour

6 Using a dough scraper or spoon, divide the dough in half and tip one portion on to a prepared baking sheet, trying to avoid knocking the air out of the dough in the process. Using floured hands shape into a roughly rectangular loaf about 2.5cm (1 inch) thick, pulling and stretching as required. Neaten the loaf by running floured fingers down each side and gently tucking any mis-shapen dough underneath.

7 Repeat with the remaining dough. Sprinkle both loaves with flour and leave to rise in a warm place for about 20 minutes. The loaves will spread as well as rise. Meanwhile preheat the oven to 220°C/425°F/Gas 7.

8 Bake for 25-30 minutes, or until risen and light golden and the bread sounds hollow when tapped on the base. Cool on a wire rack. Serve warm, with olive oil for dipping.

Cook's Note The dough for this bread is extremely wet; do not be tempted to add extra flour to make the dough more manageable. It is the starter dough, slow rise and high liquid content, which produce this unique open, holey, textured light bread.

FOCACCIA

MAKES 1 LOAF   PREPARATION TIME: 25 MINUTES PLUS RISING
COOKING TIME: 20-25 MINUTES   TOOLS DOUGH HOOK

INGREDIENTS

350g (12oz) strong plain white flour
2.5ml (½ tsp) salt
7g sachet (1½ tsp) fast action dried yeast
210ml (7½fl oz) lukewarm water
15ml (1 tbsp) olive oil

FOR THE TOPPING

6 fresh sage leaves
½ red onion, thinly sliced
coarse sea salt or crystal salt
coarsely ground black pepper
30ml (2 tbsp) olive oil

1 Lightly oil a 25cm (10 inch) shallow round cake tin or pizza pan. Place the flour, salt and yeast in the Kenwood Bowl. Using the Dough Hook on minimum speed, gradually mix in the lukewarm water and olive oil to form a soft dough.

2 Knead for 1 minute on minimum and 4 minutes on speed 1, until smooth and elastic. Remove the Kenwood Bowl, cover with lightly oiled clear film and leave to rise in a warm place for about 1 hour, or until the dough has doubled in size.

3 Using the Dough Hook on minimum speed for 30-60 seconds knead the dough to knock back.

4 Transfer to a lightly floured surface and shape into a ball. Roll out into a 25cm (10 inch) circle and place in the prepared tin.

5 Cover with oiled clear film and leave to rise, in a warm place, for about 20 minutes or until almost doubled in size. Using your fingertips make deep dimples over the surface of the dough. Cover and leave to rise for about 10 minutes.

6 Meanwhile preheat the oven to 200°C/400°F/Gas 6. Uncover and sprinkle over the sage leaves, red onion, salt and pepper. Drizzle with the olive oil and bake for 20-25 minutes, or until golden. Cool on a wire rack and serve warm.

PROSCIUTTO AND PARMESAN BREAD

MAKES 2 SMALL LOAVES   PREPARATION TIME: 20 MINUTES PLUS RISING
COOKING TIME: 25 MINUTES   TOOLS DOUGH HOOK

INGREDIENTS

450g (1lb) strong plain white flour
50g (2oz) freshly grated Parmesan cheese
7.5ml (1½ tsp) salt
2.5ml (½ tsp) freshly ground black pepper
7g sachet (1½ tsp) fast action dried yeast
15ml (1 tbsp) olive oil
1 egg, lightly beaten
250ml (8fl oz) lukewarm water
50g (2oz) prosciutto, torn into small pieces
cornmeal, for dusting

1 Place the flour, Parmesan cheese, salt, pepper and yeast in the Kenwood Bowl. Using the Dough Hook on minimum speed, gradually mix in the olive oil, egg and lukewarm water to form a soft dough.

2 Knead for 1 minute on minimum and 4 minutes on speed 1, until smooth and elastic. Remove the Bowl, cover with lightly oiled clear film and leave to rise in a warm place for about 1 hour, or until doubled in size.

3 Using the Dough Hook on minimum speed for 30-60 seconds gently knead the dough to knock back. Transfer to a lightly floured surface and divide in two. Flatten each half into a round and sprinkle over half the prosciutto ham.

4 Fold each piece of dough in half, flatten slightly and sprinkle with the remaining ham. Roll up, tuck in the sides, and roll into stubby long loaves. Transfer to a baking sheet dusted with cornmeal, leaving a space between the loaves. Cover with lightly oiled clear film and leave to rise for about 30 minutes, or until nearly doubled in size.

5 Meanwhile preheat the oven to 200°C/400°F/Gas 6. Brush the top with water and dust with cornmeal. Slash the top of the loaves diagonally 5 or 6 times. Bake for 20 minutes, or until the bread is golden and sounds hollow when tapped on the base. Cool on a wire rack.

Both breads illustrated opposite.

NAAN BREADS

MAKES 6 PREPARATION TIME: 25 MINUTES PLUS RISING   COOKING TIME: 15 MINUTES
TOOLS DOUGH HOOK

INGREDIENTS

450g (1lb) strong plain white flour

5ml (1 tsp) salt

7g sachet (1½ tsp) fast action dried yeast

75ml (5 tbsp) natural yogurt

15ml (1 tbsp) melted ghee or butter

200-225ml (7-8fl oz) lukewarm water

45ml (3 tbsp) melted ghee or butter, for brushing

❶ Place the flour, salt and yeast in the Kenwood Bowl. Add the yogurt and melted ghee or butter. Using the Dough Hook on minimum speed, gradually mix in sufficient water to form a soft dough.

❷ Knead for 1 minute on minimum and 4 minutes on speed 1, until smooth and elastic. Remove the Bowl, cover with lightly oiled clear film and leave to rise in a warm place for 1 hour, or until doubled in size.

❸ Using the Dough Hook on minimum speed for 30-60 seconds gently knead the dough to knock back. Preheat the oven to 230°C/450°F/Gas 8. Place 3 heavy baking sheets in the oven to heat. Transfer the dough to a lightly floured surface and shape into six balls.

❹ Cover 5 balls with oiled clear film. Roll out the remaining ball into a teardrop shape 25cm (10 inches) long and about 5-8cm (¼ –⅓ inch) thick. Cover with oiled clear film whilst shaping two more naan breads.

❺ Place the 3 naan on the preheated baking sheets and bake for 4-5 minutes until puffed up. Meanwhile preheat the grill on its highest setting.

❻ Remove each baking sheet from the oven and place under the hot grill for a few seconds, until the top of the naan starts to brown. Wrap in a clean dish towel and keep warm whilst rolling out and cooking the remaining 3 naan. Brush with melted ghee or butter and serve warm.

ITALIAN BREADSTICKS

MAKES: ABOUT 30 PREPARATION TIME: 35 MINUTES PLUS RISING
COOKING TIME: 15-20 MINUTES   TOOLS DOUGH HOOK

INGREDIENTS

350g (12oz) strong plain white flour

7.5ml (1½ tsp) salt

7g sachet (1½ tsp) fast action dried yeast

200ml (7fl oz) lukewarm water

45ml (3 tbsp) olive oil

extra olive oil for brushing

sesame seeds, poppy seeds or coarse sea salt, for coating, optional

❶ Lightly oil 2 baking sheets. Place the flour, salt and yeast in the Kenwood Bowl. Using the Dough Hook on minimum speed, gradually mix in the lukewarm water and olive oil to form a soft dough.

❷ Knead for 1 minute on minimum and 4 minutes on speed 1, until smooth and elastic. Remove the Bowl, cover with oiled clear film and leave to rise in a warm place for about 1 hour, or until doubled in size.

❸ Using the Dough Hook on minimum speed for 30-60 seconds gently knead the dough to knock back. Transfer to a lightly floured surface and roll into a 20 x 23cm (8 x 9 inch) rectangle.

❹ Cut into 3 rectangles measuring 20 x 7.5cm (8 x 3 inches) Cut each piece into 10 strips each 7.5cm (3 inches) long. Roll and stretch each strip gently until it is about 25-30cm (10-12 inches) long.

❺ Brush with olive oil and roll in or sprinkle with sesame or poppy seeds, sea salt or leave plain. Place spaced apart on the baking sheets, cover with oiled clear film and leave to rise for about 10-15 minutes, to puff up.

❻ Meanwhile preheat the oven to 200°C/400°F/Gas 6. Bake for 15-20 minutes, or until golden. Transfer to a wire rack to cool.

WHITE ROLLS

MAKES 12   PREPARATION TIME: 30 MINUTES PLUS RISING   COOKING TIME: 15-18 MINUTES
TOOLS DOUGH HOOK

INGREDIENTS

1 quantity of basic white bread dough, made with 300ml (½ pint) lukewarm milk in place of the water, see page 164

FOR THE TOPPING:

1 egg yolk

15ml (1 tbsp) water

sesame seed or poppy seeds, to sprinkle

❶ Lightly oil 2 baking sheets. Make the dough using milk instead or water, following the instructions on page 164, up to the end of step 4, then divide the dough into 12 equal pieces.

❷ Shape into batons, knots, plaits or cottage rolls.
For Batons: Shape the dough into oblongs and cut 2-3 diagonal slashes just before baking.
For Knots: Shape the dough into a long rope and tie in a knot.
For Plaits: Divide the dough into three and roll into long ropes. Pinch the ends together and loosely plait, pinching and tucking the ends under.
For Cottage Rolls: Divide the dough into two-thirds and one-third and shape into round balls. Place the smaller one on top of the larger one and make a hole through the centre with a floured finger.

❸ Place on the prepared baking sheets. Cover the shaped dough with oiled clear film and leave to rise for about 30 minutes, until doubled in size. Meanwhile preheat the oven to 220°C/425°F/Gas 7.

❹ Mix the egg yolk and water together and brush over the rolls. Sprinkle with seeds or leave plain. Bake for 15-18 minutes, or until the rolls are golden. Cool on a wire rack.

Variation For soft baps use 150ml (¼ pint) each of milk and water to make the dough. Divide into 10 and shape into flat 9cm (3½ inch) rounds. After proving, press down gently on the tops to flatten slightly, using the three middle fingers. Brush with milk and dust with flour. Bake for 15-20 minutes at 200°C/400°F/Gas 6.

SPELT FLOUR BREAD

MAKES 1 LOAF PREPARATION TIME: 20 MINUTES PLUS RISING   COOKING TIME: 35 MINUTES
TOOLS GRAIN MILL / DOUGH HOOK

INGREDIENTS

450g (1lb) spelt grain

7.5ml (1½ tsp) salt

7g sachet (1½ tsp) fast action dried yeast

30ml (2 tbsp) sunflower oil

5ml (1 tsp) clear honey

400ml (14fl oz) lukewarm water

❶ Using the Grain Mill on the finest setting, mill the spelt grain straight into the Kenwood Bowl. Oil a 900g (2lb) loaf tin.

❷ Add the salt, yeast, sunflower oil, honey and water to the Kenwood Bowl. Using the Dough Hook on minimum speed, gradually mix to form a very soft, sticky dough.

❸ Knead for 4 minutes on speed 1. Remove the Kenwood Bowl, cover with lightly oiled clear film and leave to rise in a warm place for about 1 hour, or until doubled in size.

❹ Using the Dough Hook on minimum speed for 30-60 seconds gently knead the dough to knock back. Transfer to the prepared loaf tin using the spatula. It will be sticky so pat it down with the spatula and a little spelt flour if necessary.

❺ Cover the shaped dough with oiled clear film and leave to rise for about 30 minutes, until puffed up. Meanwhile preheat the oven to 190°C/375°F/Gas 5. Bake for 35 minutes, or until the bread is firm to the touch and the bread sounds hollow when tapped on the base. Cool on a wire rack.

FESTIVE STOLLEN

INGREDIENTS

75g (3oz) sultanas
75g (3oz) currants
50g (2oz) mixed chopped peel
60ml (4 tbsp) dark rum
400g (14oz) unbleached white bread flour
2.5ml (½ tsp) salt
50g (2oz) caster sugar
2.5ml (½ tsp) ground cinnamon
7g sachet (1½ tsp) fast action dried yeast
1 egg, lightly beaten
140ml (5fl oz) lukewarm milk
50g (2oz) butter, melted
50g (2oz) whole blanched almonds, chopped
50g (2oz) glacé cherries
225g (8oz) almond paste, see page 166
melted butter, for brushing
icing sugar, for dusting

MAKES 1 LARGE LOAF   **PREPARATION TIME:** 20 MINUTES PLUS RISING
COOKING TIME: 30 MINUTES   **TOOLS** DOUGH HOOK

❶ Place the sultanas, currants and chopped peel in a bowl. Stir in the rum and set aside to soak. Lightly grease a baking sheet.

❷ Sift the flour and salt into the Kenwood Bowl. Add the sugar, cinnamon and yeast and stir to mix. Add the egg, milk and butter and using the Dough Hook mix to a soft dough. Knead for 4 minutes, on speed 1, until smooth and elastic.

❸ Remove the Kenwood Bowl complete with dough, cover with lightly oiled clear film and leave in a warm place to rise for 1½ hours, or until doubled in size.

❹ Using the Dough Hook, knock back and briefly knead the dough on speed 1 for 45-60 seconds. Turn out onto a lightly floured surface and roll into a 2.5cm (1 inch) thick rectangle. Sprinkle over the

soaked fruits, almonds and glacé cherries. Fold and knead to incorporate the fruit and nuts.

❺ Roll into a 23 x 30cm (9 x 12 inch) oval. Roll the centre slightly thinner than the edges. Roll the almond paste into a 20cm (8 inch) sausage shape and place along the centre of the dough. Fold the dough over to enclose it, making sure the top edge is set back slightly from the base edge. Press down to seal.

❻ Place on a lightly oiled baking sheet, cover with oiled clear film and leave to rise in warm place for 45-60 minutes, or until doubled in size. Preheat the oven to 190°C/375°F/Gas 5.

❼ Bake for 30 minutes, or until the loaf sounds hollow when the base is sharply tapped. Brush the top with melted butter, dust with icing sugar and transfer to a wire rack to cool.

IRISH SODA BREAD

MAKES 1 LOAF PREPARATION TIME: 10 MINUTES PLUS RISING
COOKING TIME: 35-40 MINUTES TOOLS K BEATER

INGREDIENTS

325g (12oz) strong plain wholemeal flour
115g (4oz) strong plain white flour
5ml (1 tsp) salt
5ml (1 tsp) bicarbonate of soda
5ml (1 tbsp) cream of tartar
25g (1oz) butter
50g (2oz) rolled oats
about 450ml (¾ pint) buttermilk

❶ Lightly oil a baking sheet. Preheat the oven to 230°C/450°F/Gas 8.

❷ Place the wholemeal and white flours, salt, bicarbonate of soda, cream of tartar and butter in the Kenwood Bowl. Using the K Beater on speed 1, rub in the butter.

❸ Add the oats and mix in. With the K Beater running on speed 2 add sufficient buttermilk to mix to a soft dough. Do not over-mix or the bread will be heavy.

❹ On a lightly floured surface shape into a large round. Place on the prepared baking sheet. Cut a deep cross in the top.

❺ Bake for 15 minutes, then reduce the oven to 200°C/400°F/Gas 6 and bake for a further 20-25 minutes, or until the bread sounds hollow when tapped on the base. Cool on a wire rack. Serve warm with a little butter if wished.

ZOPF

MAKES 1 LOAF PREPARATION TIME: 20 MINUTES PLUS RISING
COOKING TIME: 30 MINUTES TOOLS DOUGH HOOK

INGREDIENTS

450g (1lb) strong plain white flour
25g (1oz) caster sugar
7.5ml (1½ tsp) salt
7g sachet (1½ tsp) fast action dried yeast
1 egg, lightly beaten
150ml (5fl oz) lukewarm milk
75g (3oz) butter, melted
FOR THE GLAZE:
1 egg yolk
10ml (2 tsp) water

❶ Place the flour, sugar, salt and yeast in the Kenwood Bowl. Using the Dough Hook on minimum speed, gradually mix in the egg, lukewarm milk and melted butter to form a soft dough.

❷ Knead for about 4 minutes on speed 1, until smooth and elastic. Remove the Kenwood Bowl, complete with dough, cover with lightly oiled clear film and leave to rise in a warm place for about 1-1½ hours, or until doubled in size.

❸ Using the Dough Hook on minimum speed for 30-60 seconds gently knead the dough to knock back. Transfer to a lightly floured surface and divide into 3 equal pieces.

❹ Roll each piece into a long rope and then lay them side by side. Starting from the centre, plait together to the end. Seal the ends and tuck underneath. Turn the dough round and plait the remainder. Seal the ends and tuck underneath.

❺ Transfer to a lightly oiled baking sheet. Cover with lightly oiled clear film and leave to rise for about 30 minutes, or until nearly doubled in size.

❻ Preheat the oven to 190°C/375°F/Gas 5. Mix the egg yolk and water together for the glaze and brush over the loaf. Bake for 30 minutes, or until golden and the bread sounds hollow when tapped on the base. Cool on a wire rack.

CHELSEA BUNS

INGREDIENTS

500g (1lb 2oz) strong plain white flour

5ml (1 tsp) salt

7g sachet (1½ tsp) fast action dried yeast

75g (3oz) caster sugar

50g (2oz) butter, softened

225ml (8fl oz) lukewarm milk

1 egg

25g (1oz) butter, melted

30ml (2 tbsp) light brown muscovado sugar

5ml (1 tsp) ground mixed spice

75g (3oz) sultanas

50g (2oz) currants

25g (1oz) chopped candied peel

FOR THE GLAZE:

40g (1½oz) caster sugar

60ml (4 tbsp) water

5ml (1 tsp) orange flower water

MAKES 12 BUNS   **PREPARATION TIME:** 25 MINUTES PLUS RISING
COOKING TIME: 20-25 MINUTES   **TOOLS** DOUGH HOOK

1 Sift the flour and salt into the Kenwood Bowl. Add the fast action dried yeast, caster sugar and butter. Add the milk and egg. Fit the Dough Hook and mix to a soft dough on minimum speed.

2 Continue on speed 1 for 4 minutes, to knead the dough until smooth and elastic. Remove the Bowl with the dough inside, cover with oiled clear film and leave to rise in a warm place for about 1 hour, until doubled in size.

3 Lightly grease a 23cm (9 inch) square cake tin. Using the Dough Hook on minimum speed for 1 minute to knock back the dough. Transfer to a lightly floured surface and roll out into a 30cm (12 inch) square.

4 Brush the dough with melted butter and sprinkle with the muscovado sugar, mixed spice, sultanas, currants and candied peel, leaving a 1cm (½ inch) border along one edge.

5 Starting at a covered edge, roll the dough and fruit filling up, towards the empty edge. Press the edges together to seal. Cut the roll into 12 equal slices and place these cut side uppermost in the prepared tin.

6 Cover with oiled clear film and leave in a warm place to rise, for about 30-40 minutes, until the dough slices have almost doubled in size. Preheat the oven to 200°C/400°F/Gas 6.

7 Bake for 20-25 minutes, or until risen and golden. Leave to cool slightly in the tin before transferring to a wire rack to cool.

8 Make the glaze. Place the sugar and water in a small saucepan and heat gently, stirring to dissolve the sugar. Bring to the boil and boil for 1-2 minutes, until syrupy. Stir in the orange flower water and brush over the warm buns. Serve slightly warm.

Cook's Note: If using fresh yeast, blend 15g (½oz) yeast with the milk and leave for 10 minutes, then continue as above. Omit the fast action dried yeast.

MEDITERRANEAN FRUIT RING

MAKES 1 LOAF   PREPARATION   TIME: 35 MINUTES PLUS RISING   COOKING   TIME: 30 MINUTES   TOOLS DOUGH HOOK

INGREDIENTS

450g (1lb) strong plain white flour
5ml (1 tsp) ground cinnamon
2.5ml (½ tsp) ground ginger
2.5ml (½ tsp) salt
7g sachet (1½ tsp) fast action dried yeast
50g (2oz) chopped almonds or walnuts
75g (3oz) sultanas
50g (2oz) caster sugar
grated rind of ½ lemon
60ml (4 tbsp) olive oil
300ml (½ pint) lukewarm milk
beaten egg, to glaze

1 Sift the flour, cinnamon, ginger and salt into the Kenwood Bowl. Add the yeast, nuts, sultanas, sugar, lemon rind, olive oil and milk. Fit the Dough Hook and mix to a soft dough on minimum speed.

2 Knead on speed 4 for 7 minutes, until smooth and elastic. Remove the Bowl with the dough inside, cover with oiled clear film and leave to rise in a warm place for 1-1½ hours, or until doubled in size.

3 Lightly oil a baking sheet. Using the Dough Hook on minimum speed for 30-60 seconds knead the dough to knock back. Transfer to a floured surface and divide into 3 equal pieces. Roll each into a rope shape 62cm (25 inches) long. Lay them side by side.

4 Starting from the centre, working towards yourself, plait the pieces together, by folding the outside rope over the centre one, alternating sides as you go. Turn the dough around and repeat the plaiting process. Bring the ends together to form a circle and pinch to seal.

5 Place on the prepared baking sheet, cover with oiled clear film and leave in a warm place to rise, for 30-45 minutes, until the almost doubled in size. Preheat the oven to 200°C/400°F/Gas 6.

6 Brush with beaten egg, to glaze and bake for 25-30 minutes, or until risen and golden. Transfer to a wire rack to cool. Serve sliced.

CRANBERRY, HONEY AND OAT BREAD

MAKES 2 LOAVES   PREPARATION   TIME: 25 MINUTES PLUS RISING
COOKING   TIME: 20-25 MINUTES   TOOLS GRAIN MILL / DOUGH HOOK

INGREDIENTS

65g (2½oz) jumbo porridge oats
450g (1lb) strong plain white flour
2.5ml (½ tsp) salt
7g sachet (1½ tsp) fast action dried yeast
30ml (2 tbsp) honey
30ml (2 tbsp) golden syrup
50g (2oz) butter
120ml (4fl oz) milk
120ml (4fl oz) water
75g (3oz) dried cranberries
40g (1½oz) chopped walnuts
milk, for glazing
jumbo porridge oats, for sprinkling

1 Using the Grain Mill on maximum speed on setting 2, mill the jumbo oats straight into the Kenwood Bowl. Add the flour, salt and yeast.

2 Place the honey, golden syrup, butter and milk in a saucepan and heat gently until the butter melts. Stir in the water. The mix should now be just warm; if necessary leave to cool. Fit the Dough Hook.

3 Add the liquids to the dry ingredients and mix on minimum for 1 minute and 4 minutes on speed 1 to make a soft dough, which is smooth and elastic. Remove the Bowl with the dough inside, cover with oiled clear film and leave to rise in a warm place for about 1 hour, until doubled in size.

4 Lightly oil 2 baking sheets. Using the Dough Hook on minimum speed, gently knock back the dough. Mix in the cranberries and walnuts. Transfer to a lightly floured surface, divide in two and shape into plump rounds. Place on the prepared baking sheets.

5 Cover with oiled clear film and leave in a warm place to rise, for about 30-40 minutes, until they have doubled in size. Meanwhile preheat the oven to 200°C/400°F/Gas 6.

6 Brush with milk, slash across the top of each loaf and sprinkle with oats. Bake for 20-25 minutes, or until risen and golden. Transfer to a wire rack to cool.

Whether using the Multi-Mill to grind coffee beans for the perfect cup of coffee or using the Citrus Juicer or Non-Stop Centrifugal Juicer to make fresh fruit and vegetable juices or alcoholic fruit cocktails, there are lots of ideas to be found in this chapter.

Use the Liquidiser to make banana or strawberry milkshake, a fruit yogurt drink with raspberries and orange or a chocolate orange or ginger smoothie. The Liquidiser is also used to make a lemonade known as Kenwood lemonade, a recipe created years ago to demonstrate the sharpness of the stainless steel blades, and still impresses today.

KENWOOD LEMONADE

INGREDIENTS

1 lemon, thin-skinned variety, washed

30ml (2 tbsp) sugar

6 large ice cubes

600ml (1 pint) water, chilled

1 whole egg, complete with shell, washed

extra ice cubes and lemon slices, to serve

SERVES 4-6 PREPARATION TIME: 5 MINUTES

TOOLS LIQUIDISER

1 Cut the lemon in half and place in the Liquidiser with the sugar, ice cubes, water and whole egg. Blend at maximum speed for 10-20 seconds.

2 Strain through a sieve, into a jug, and serve with extra ice cubes and lemon slices, for decoration.

EXOTIC FRUIT COCKTAIL

INGREDIENTS

½ ripe mango, peeled

½ papaya, peeled

300ml (½ pint) natural yogurt

30ml (2 tbsp) clear honey

30ml (2 tbsp) lemon juice

SERVES 4 PREPARATION TIME: 5 MINUTES

TOOLS LIQUIDISER

1 Remove the stone from the mango and seeds from the papaya, if still present. Place the fruits, yogurt, honey and lemon juice in the Liquidiser.

2 Blend at high speed until thick and smooth. Pour into 2 tall glasses and serve immediately.

Illustrated opposite.

PEAR AND PINEAPPLE DROP

INGREDIENTS

2 pears

2 slices fresh pineapple

SERVES 1 PREPARATION TIME: 5 MINUTES

TOOLS NON-STOP CENTRIFUGAL JUICER

1 Cut the pears into quarters. Remove the skin from the pineapple and cut the slices in half.

2 Using the Non-Stop Centrifugal Juicer on speed 1, juice the pears and pineapple slices. Stir to blend the juices and serve.

Illustrated on page 154.

SUMMER COOLER

SERVES 2   PREPARATION TIME: 10 MINUTES   TOOLS NON-STOP CENTRIFUGAL JUICER

INGREDIENTS

1 cucumber, washed

4 apples, washed and quartered

4 mint leaves

2 sticks celery, washed

ice cubes, to serve

2 sprigs of mint, to garnish

1 Using the Non-Stop Centrifugal Juicer, juice the cucumber, then the apples and mint leaves and finally the celery sticks.

2 Stir to blend the ingredients then pour into 2 glasses, add a couple of ice cubes to each, garnish with sprigs of mint and serve.

Illustrated on page 154.

CITRUS PRESSÉ

SERVES 8   PREPARATION TIME: 10 MINUTES PLUS CHILLING   TOOLS CITRUS JUICER

INGREDIENTS

1 orange, halved

1 lime, halved

1 lemon, halved

1 grapefruit, halved

175g (6oz) sugar

900ml (1½ pints) boiling water

ice cubes and lemon slices, to serve

1 Extract the juice from the orange, lime, lemon and grapefruit using the Citrus Juicer. Pour into a large heatproof jug and stir in the sugar.

2 Add the boiling water and stir well to mix. Cover and leave to cool, then chill for 1-2 hours. Add a few ice cubes and lemon slices, just before serving.

ITALIAN TOMATO JUICE

SERVES 1   PREPARATION TIME: 5 MINUTES   TOOLS NON-STOP CENTRIFUGAL JUICER

INGREDIENTS

2-3 fresh basil leaves

3 ripe plum tomatoes, halved lengthways

5ml (1 tsp) lemon juice

few drops Tabasco

ice cubes, to serve

1 Using the Non-Stop Centrifugal Juicer, process the basil leaves and tomatoes on speed 1. Stir in lemon juice and Tabasco.

2 Place a few ice cubes in a glass and pour over the Italian Tomato Juice. Serve immediately.

Illustrated on page 154.

COFFEE LIQUEUR SMOOTHIE

SERVES 2   PREPARATION TIME: 5 MINUTES   TOOLS LIQUIDISER

INGREDIENTS
200ml (7fl oz) Espresso coffee
150ml (¼ pint) milk
30ml (2 tbsp) Irish Whiskey Cream
liqueur e.g. Baileys
5-10ml (1-2 tsp) sugar, optional
4 small scoops, about 200g (7oz),
vanilla ice cream

❶ Place the coffee, milk, liqueur and sugar, if using in the Liquidiser. Add the ice cream and blend at speed 1 for 10 seconds. Increase to maximum and blend until smooth.

❷ Pour into 2 large glasses and serve immediately.

CHOC-ORANGE SMOOTHIE

SERVES 2   PREPARATION TIME: 5 MINUTES   TOOLS LIQUIDISER

INGREDIENTS
400ml (14fl oz) orange juice
30ml (2 tbsp) orange liqueur e.g.
Cointreau
4 small scoops, about 200g (7oz),
chocolate ice cream

❶ Place the orange juice, liqueur and ice cream in the Liquidiser. Blend for 10 seconds at speed 1 or 2, then increase to maximum and blend for a few seconds until smooth.

❷ Pour into 2 tall glasses and serve immediately.

SPARKLING PEACH BELLINI

SERVES 6   PREPARATION TIME: 5 MINUTES   TOOLS NON-STOP CENTRIFUGAL JUICER

INGREDIENTS
3 ripe peaches, halved and stoned
45ml (3 tbsp) grenadine
1 bottle chilled sparkling dry white
wine

❶ Using the Non-Stop Centrifugal Juicer, juice the peach halves into a large jug. Stir in the grenadine and top up with the sparkling wine.

❷ Serve in individual wine glasses immediately.

IRISH COFFEE

S E R V E S 2   P R E P A R A T I O N   T I M E : 10 MINUTES
T O O L S MULTI-MILL / BALLOON WHISK

INGREDIENTS
45ml (3 tbsp) coffee beans
350ml (12fl oz) boiling water
90ml (3fl oz) double cream
60ml (4 tbsp) Irish whiskey
10ml (2 tsp) sugar
cocoa powder, for sprinkling

1 Grind the coffee beans in the Multi Mill, then prepare the coffee with the boiling water using a percolator or cafetière.

2 Using the Whisk, lightly whip the cream, until it almost holds its shape. Warm the glasses by filling with hot, not boiling water. Leave to stand for 1 minute, then drain.

3 Pour the coffee into the glasses, and then stir in the whiskey and sugar. Hold a teaspoon just above the coffee and pour the cream over the back of the spoon so that it floats on to the coffee to form a suspended layer.

4 Sprinkle with a little cocoa powder and serve the coffee immediately.

MOCHA FINO

S E R V E S 1   P R E P A R A T I O N   T I M E : 5 MINUTES   C O O K I N G   T I M E : 5 MINUTES
T O O L S MULTI-MILL

INGREDIENTS
45ml (3 tbsp) coffee beans
120ml (4fl oz) boiling water
120ml (4fl oz) milk
10ml (2 tsp) sugar
1.25ml (¼ tsp) cocoa powder
1.25ml (¼ tsp) ground cinnamon
15ml (1 tbsp) dark chocolate, grated

1 Grind the coffee beans in the Multi Mill, then prepare the coffee with the boiling water using a percolator or cafetière.

2 Meanwhile, pour the milk into a saucepan and heat until almost boiling. Place the sugar, cocoa powder and cinnamon in a cup and mix together. Pour over the hot coffee, stirring well.

3 Add the hot milk, sprinkle with the grated chocolate and serve immediately.

STRAWBERRY AND MELON FRAPPÉ

SERVES 1   PREPARATION   TIME: 10 MINUTES PLUS FREEZING   TOOLS LIQUIDISER

INGREDIENTS
125g (4oz) strawberries, halved
¼ Canteloupe or Galia melon, rind
removed and cut into chunks
2 ice cubes
10ml (2 tsp) caster sugar

❶ Place the strawberries in a small tray lined with plastic wrap and freeze for 1½ hours.

❷ Put the melon, strawberries, ice cubes and sugar in the Liquidiser. Add 30ml (2 tbsp) water and process to a crushed ice texture.

Variation For a creamier frappé add 15-30ml (1-2 tbsp) Greek yogurt and process with the fruit in step 2.

GINGER SMOOTHIE

SERVES 2   PREPARATION   TIME: 5 MINUTES   TOOLS LIQUIDISER

INGREDIENTS
300ml (½ pint) milk
6 pieces stem ginger in syrup
30ml (2 tbsp) syrup from stem
ginger
4 small scoops, about 200g (7oz),
vanilla ice cream

❶ Place the milk, stem ginger and syrup in the Liquidiser. Add the ice cream and process on speed 1 for 15 seconds. Increase to maximum for about 30 seconds, or until smooth.

❷ Pour into two glasses and serve immediately.

RASPBERRY AND ORANGE YOGURT DRINK

SERVES 4   PREPARATION   TIME: 5 MINUTES   TOOLS LIQUIDISER

INGREDIENTS
450g (1lb) raspberry yogurt
250ml (9fl oz) orange juice
150g (5oz) frozen raspberries
150g (5oz) frozen vanilla flavoured
yogurt dessert

❶ Place the raspberry yogurt and orange juice in the Liquidiser. Add the frozen raspberries and the vanilla flavoured yogurt dessert.

❷ Blend on speed 1 for 15 seconds then increase to maximum and blend until smooth and creamy. Serve immediately.

Illustrated on page 154.

FIZZY LEMONADE

S E R V E S 8-10   P R E P A R A T I O N   T I M E : 10 MINUTES PLUS COOLING   C O O K I N G   T I M E : 5 MINUTES
T O O L S CITRUS JUICER

INGREDIENTS
4 lemons, halved
225g (8oz) sugar
sparkling mineral water, chilled, to serve

1 Using the Citrus Juicer, extract the juice from the lemon halves. Pour into a small saucepan, add the sugar and heat gently, stirring continuously until the sugar has dissolved. Transfer to a jug, cover and leave to cool.

2 To serve, pour a little of the concentrate into a glass and top up with sparkling mineral water, diluting according to taste.

Illustrated below.

CARROT AND GINGER REVIVER

S E R V E S 1   P R E P A R A T I O N   T I M E : 5 MINUTES
T O O L S NON-STOP CENTRIFUGAL JUICER

INGREDIENTS
2.5cm (1 inch) piece fresh root ginger
3 carrots
1 orange, peel and pith removed

1 Using the Non-Stop Centrifugal Juicer, process the fresh root ginger and then the carrots and finally add the orange.

2 Stir the juices together to combine, pour into a glass and serve.

BANANA THICKSHAKE

S E R V E S 2   P R E P A R A T I O N   T I M E : 5 MINUTES
T O O L S LIQUIDISER

INGREDIENTS
2 bananas, peeled and cut into 4
200ml (7fl oz) milk
2.5ml (½ tsp) vanilla essence
4 scoops vanilla ice cream

1 Place the bananas, milk, vanilla essence and ice cream in the Liquidiser and blend at speed 1 to 2 until smooth.

2 Pour the banana thickshake into individual glasses and serve immediately.

The Kenwood Chef and Major will be used time and again to make basic recipes which form the basis of different dishes. This chapter covers these basic recipes. There is shortcrust pastry with variations including nut, oatmeal and sweet pastry with sugar for tarts and flans. It also includes puff pastry and choux pastry for profiteroles and gougère.

There is a basic everyday white bread recipe which is light and airy and a batter recipe for pancakes and crêpes. Lastly there are recipes for almond paste and royal icing for coating celebration fruits cakes, complete with quantities for 12cm (5 inch) to 30cm (12 inch) cakes.

BASIC RECIPES

BASIC WHITE BREAD

MAKES 1 LOAF   PREPARATION TIME: 20 MINUTES PLUS RISING
COOKING TIME: 25-30 MINUTES   TOOLS DOUGH HOOK

INGREDIENTS

15g (½oz) fresh yeast
or 7g sachet (1½ tsp) fast action
dried yeast
300ml (½ pint) lukewarm water
5ml (1 tsp) sugar
450g (1lb) strong plain white flour
7.5ml (1½ tsp) salt

*Cottage loaf illustrated
on page 162.*

❶ If using fresh yeast, mix the yeast with half the water and the sugar. Leave to stand for 15 minutes. Place the flour and salt in the Kenwood Bowl. If using fast action dried yeast add with the sugar to the flour.

❷ Using the Dough Hook on minimum speed, gradually mix in the yeast mixture and remaining water or water if using dried yeast, to a soft dough.

❸ Knead for 1 minute on minimum and 4 minutes on speed 1, until smooth and elastic. Remove the Kenwood Bowl, cover with lightly oiled clear film and leave to rise in a warm place for 1 hour, or until doubled in size.

❹ Using the Dough Hook on minimum speed for 30-60 seconds gently knead the dough to knock back. Transfer to a lightly floured surface and shape. Cover with oiled clear film and leave to rise for 30 minutes, or until doubled in size.

❺ Preheat the oven to 220°C/425°F/gas 7. Bake for 25-30 minutes or until golden brown.

Variations

Round Loaf Shape the dough into a round plump ball. Knead the edges into the centre, turn over, place on a greased baking sheet. Slash just before baking.
Cottage Loaf Increase quantities by 50%, leaving the yeast the same. Divide into ⅔ and ⅓ and shape into balls. Place on oiled baking sheets, cover and leave to rise for 20 minutes. Make a 4cm (1½ inch) cross-shaped cut in the top of the larger ball. Brush with water and place the smaller ball on top. Press a hole through the middle with two fingers. Leave to rise for 10 minutes then bake for 30-35 minutes.
Classic Split Tin Shape dough into a rectangle the length of the tin. Roll up lengthways, tuck the ends under and place in a 900g (2lb) loaf tin. Leave until doubled in size, sprinkle with flour and slash along the entire length.

CHOUX PASTRY

MAKES: ABOUT 30 PROFITEROLES OR 12-16 FINGERS FOR ÉCLAIRS OR 1 GOUGÈRE
PREPARATION TIME: 10 MINUTES   TOOLS FOOD PROCESSING ATTACHMENT

INGREDIENTS

225ml (7½fl oz) cold water
75g (3oz) butter
115g (4oz) plain flour
pinch of salt
3 eggs, lightly beaten

❶ Fit the Food Processing Attachment with the knife blade. Place the water and butter in a saucepan and heat gently until the butter melts, and then bring to the boil.

❷ Remove from the heat and tip in the flour. Beat with a wooden spoon until combined. Return to the heat and cook over a low heat for a few seconds until the mixture leaves the sides of the pan to form a ball. Do not over-beat.

❸ Transfer to the Food Processing Attachment. Turn on to minimum speed and gradually pour the eggs through the feed tube. Process until just mixed and the pastry forms a stiff, glossy paste. Do not over-process or it will become too thin. Use as required.

Cook's Note Choux pastry can be used for both choux puffs, profiteroles, eclairs and gougère. For sweet pastry 5-10ml (1-2 tsp) of sugar may be added and grated cheese, herbs or paprika for savoury items.

SHORTCRUST PASTRY AND VARIATIONS

MAKES 250G (10OZ) PASTRY SUFFICIENT FOR A 20-23CM (8-9INCH) FLAN CASE
PREPARATION TIME: 10 MINUTES PLUS CHILLING   TOOLS K BEATER

① Place the flour, salt and fat in the Kenwood Bowl. Using the K Beater at speed 2, mix until it resembles fine breadcrumbs.

② Sprinkle the water over the mixture, a spoonful at a time, whilst the K Beater is turning, until the pastry forms a dough.

③ Turn out onto a lightly floured surface and shape into a flat ball. Do not over-handle the dough. Wrap in clear film and leave to chill and rest in the fridge for 30 minutes before rolling out.

INGREDIENTS
175g (6oz) plain flour
 pinch of salt
85g (3oz) butter or margarine, cut into small pieces
or 50:50 butter or margarine and lard or white vegetable fat
30-45ml (2-3 tbsp) cold water

Shortcrust pastry flan illustrated on page 162.

Variations
Oatmeal Pastry: Replace 75g (3oz) plain flour with 50g (2oz) medium oatmeal and 25g (1oz) plain wholemeal flour.
Nut Pastry: Add 25g (1oz) very finely chopped or ground almonds, hazelnuts or walnuts to the breadcrumb mixture at the end of step 1.
Rich Flan Pastry: Use an egg yolk or whole egg, lightly beaten, to replace part of the water. In step 2 add the egg first, then add sufficient water to form a dough.
Sweet Rich Flan Pastry: Add 10-15ml (2-3 tsp) caster sugar at the end of step 1.

PUFF PASTRY

MAKES: ABOUT 1.2KG (2¾LB) PREPARATION TIME: 20 MINUTES, PLUS RESTING AND CHILLING
TOOLS K BEATER

Puff pastry vol-au-vents illustrated on page 162.

INGREDIENTS
225g (8oz) strong white flour
225g (8oz) plain flour
2.5ml (½ tsp) salt
450g (1lb) butter
10ml (2 tsp) lemon juice or white wine vinegar
280ml (½ pint) ice cold water

① Sift the flours and salt into the Kenwood Bowl. Add 50g (2oz) butter. Using the K Beater at speed 1 rub the flour and butter together. Shape remaining butter into a block 2cm (¾ inch) thick.

② Add the lemon juice and sufficient iced water to the flour to mix to a soft, elastic dough, using the K Beater. Turn out onto a lightly floured surface and roll into an oblong, slightly wider than the butter block and just over twice as long.

③ Place the butter on one half and fold the other half over. Seal the edges with the rolling pin. Wrap in clear film and chill for 15 minutes.

④ Press gently with a rolling pin, then roll out into a rectangle about 2cm (¾ inch) thick, and about twice as long as it is wide.

⑤ Fold the bottom third up and the top third down and seal the edges with the rolling pin. Cover and chill for 20 minutes.

⑥ Place the pastry on a lightly floured surface with the folded edges to the side. Repeat the rolling, folding and chilling sequence of steps 4 and 5 another 5 times, turning the pastry a quarter turn after each rolling and folding sequence.

⑦ If at any time the butter starts to show through the pastry sprinkle with extra flour and chill. Chill for 1 hour before rolling and shaping as required.

Cook's Note It is not practical to make a smaller quantity, but puff pastry freezes extremely well so it is worth making a larger quantity and freezing the excess for use later.

PANCAKES AND CRÊPES

INGREDIENTS

115g (4oz) plain flour
pinch of salt
1 egg
280ml (½ pint) milk
a little oil, for frying

MAKES 8 PANCAKES OR CRÊPES   **PREPARATION TIME:** 5 MINUTES PLUS STANDING
COOKING TIME: 15 MINUTES   **TOOLS** BALLOON WHISK

❶ Place the flour and salt in the Kenwood Bowl. Add the egg and a quarter of the milk. Using the Whisk at speed 1, mix until smooth. Gradually whisk in the remaining milk to make a smooth batter.

❷ Pour into a jug, cover and leave to stand for 30 minutes to allow the starch grains time to swell and soften and produce a lighter batter.

❸ Heat the minimum of oil in a 20cm (8 inch) heavy based frying pan or pancake pan. Pour in just enough batter to thinly coat the base of the pan. Swirl the batter around to coat the pan.

❹ Cook over a moderately high heat for about 1 minute, until light golden. Turn or toss the pancake, cook for 30 seconds, or until golden.

❺ Transfer to a plate. Repeat with the remaining batter to make 8 pancakes, stacking them on top of each other with greaseproof paper in between. Keep the pancakes warm in the oven whilst cooking the remainder if serving immediately.

❻ Serve sprinkled with sugar and lemon juice or use according to the recipe.

ALMOND PASTE

INGREDIENTS

225g (8oz) ground almonds
115g (4oz) icing sugar
115g (4oz) caster sugar
1 egg, lightly beaten
5ml (1 tsp) lemon juice
1-2 drops of vanilla or almond essence

QUANTITIES GUIDE FOR ALMOND PASTE

15cm (6 inch) round or
12cm (5 inch) square cake
350g (12oz) almond paste
18cm (7 inch) round or
15cm (6 inch) square cake
450g (1lb) almond paste
20cm (8 inch) round or
18cm (7 inch) square cake
550g (1¼lb) almond paste
25cm (10 inch) round or
23cm (9 inch) square cake
900g (2lb) almond paste
30cm (12 inch) round or
28cm (11 inch) square cake
1.1kg (2½lb) almond paste

MAKES 450G (1LB)   **PREPARATION TIME:** 10 MINUTES   **TOOLS** K BEATER

❶ Place all the ingredients in the Kenwood Bowl. Using the K Beater on minimum speed, mix together until the ingredients bind together to form a paste.

❷ Transfer to a work surface lightly dusted with icing sugar and knead into a ball. Cover until ready to use.

Cook's Note If you wish to avoid using raw egg to bind the ingredients together, replace with water.

To Cover a Cake with Almond Paste

❶ First make an apricot glaze. Melt 115g (4oz) apricot jam with 30ml (2 tbsp) water and bring to the boil, stirring. Sieve and use warm.

❷ Trim the top of the cake level, if necessary. Turn upside down so the flat bottom becomes the top.

❸ Measure around the cake with a piece of string to give the length of almond paste required. Cut another piece of string to the same height of the cake.

❹ On a surface lightly dusted with icing sugar roll out just under two-thirds of the almond paste, long enough to coat the sides of the cake, using the string as a guide. Trim the paste and roll up loosely.

❺ Brush the sides of the cake with apricot glaze and unroll the almond paste around the cake. Smooth the join, using a palette knife. Roll a straight-sided jam jar around the sides to adhere the almond paste to the cake.

❻ Roll out the remaining almond paste to fit the top of the cake. Brush the cake with apricot glaze and lift the paste onto the cake with the help of the rolling pin. Lightly roll the top, then leave to dry for 1-2 days before icing.

ROYAL ICING

MAKES 450G (1LB)   PREPARATION TIME: 15 MINUTES, PLUS STANDING   TOOLS K BEATER

INGREDIENTS

2 egg whites

450g (1lb) icing sugar, sifted

5ml (1 tsp) glycerine

QUANTITIES GUIDE FOR ROYAL ICING

15cm (6 inch) round or

12cm (5 inch) square cake

450g (1lb) royal icing

18cm (7 inch) round or

15cm (6 inch) square cake

550g (1¼lb) royal icing

20cm (8 inch) round or

18cm (7 inch) square cake

700g (1½lb) royal icing

25cm (10 inch) round or

23cm (9 inch) square cake

1kg (2¼lb) royal icing

30cm (12 inch) round or

28cm (11 inch) square cake

1.4kg (3lb) royal icing

❶ Place the egg whites in the Kenwood Bowl. With the K Beater running at minimum speed, gradually add the icing sugar, a little at a time.

❷ Continue adding the icing sugar until the mixture is stiff and stands in soft peaks, suitable for coating a cake. If required for piping add a little more icing sugar as the icing should be slightly stiffer.

❸ Add the glycerine to keep the icing from becoming hard. If it is required to cover a tiered cake a hard surface is needed to support the tiers so omit the glycerine.

❹ Transfer to an airtight container, to prevent the icing drying out, until it is required. Leave to stand for a few hours to allow any air bubbles to rise to the surface.

For Peaked 'Snow' Icing

Make sure the icing is stiff enough to pull into well-formed peaks with the back of a spoon. Spread the icing all over the cake and then create the peaks with a spoon. Leave for 24 hours to dry.

To Flat Ice a Cake

❶ Apply on top of almond paste. Spoon almost half the icing on top of the cake and spread it evenly with a palette knife, using a paddling motion to help remove any air bubbles.

❷ Draw an icing ruler at an angle of about 30° across the top of the cake applying light, even pressure. Remove any surplus icing. If possible leave to dry for 24 hours.

❸ To ice the sides, place the cake on an icing table. Spread the icing on the sides and smooth roughly with a small palette knife. Hold a cake scraper or palette knife at an angle of 45° and draw it towards you around the cake to smooth the surface.

❹ For a square cake apply each side separately. Neaten the edges with a palette knife and leave to dry for 24 hours.

❺ For a really smooth finish apply a second thinner coat. Use fine sand paper to rub and smooth down any imperfections before re-coating. Brush off any loose icing with a clean pastry brush.

A guide to cooking terms, methods and ingredients which may be less readily available in certain countries.

Acidulated Water – Water with a little lemon juice or vinegar added, into which fruits and vegetables that discolour quickly are submerged e.g. apple, Jerusalem artichokes, and celeriac. Allow 15ml (1 tbsp) lemon juice or vinegar to 1 litre (1¾ pints) cold water.

Al Dente – An Italian term used to describe correctly cooked pasta; which is cooked until tender but still firm to the bite.

Amaretto di Saronno – An Italian liqueur flavoured with almonds, apricots and aromatic extracts.

Anchovy Essence – A rich anchovy based sauce, used as a flavouring. It can be substituted with an anchovy purée made from canned anchovies, mixed with a little water, to make a smooth paste.

Arrowroot – Can be used as an alternative to cornflour as a thickening agent in liquids, such as sauces and glazes. Arrowroot will produce a clear sauce, unlike cornflour, which will give an opaque sauce.

Aubergine – Also known as egg plant or brinjal.

Bain-Marie – A cooking technique used to avoid direct contact with heat, where a deep dish or roasting tin is half-filled with hot water and delicate dishes such as custards, terrines and egg-based dishes are cooked, without overheating.

Baking Blind – The method used for baking a pastry case without a filling; the pastry case is lined with greaseproof paper and weighed down with dried beans or ceramic baking beans.

Baking Powder – A raising agent consisting of an alkali, such as bicarbonate of soda (baking soda) mixed with an acid, usually cream or tartar (tartaric acid). These produce carbon dioxide which expands during cooking and makes cakes rise.

Baking Soda – Another name for baking powder.

Balsamic Vinegar – Italian oak-aged vinegar with a slightly sweet flavour and is dark brown in colour.

Batch – The correct quantity of ingredients, which can be comfortably mixed or processed in a bowl or attachment.

Bicarbonate of Soda – A main ingredient of baking powder, but can also be used on its own as a raising agent.

Blanching – Briefly immersing food such as vegetables, fruit or nuts in water to help remove the skin, e.g. tomatoes, almonds, peaches; or to serve as a first stage of cooking, in the preparation of many dishes.

Blue Cheese – a soft blue-veined cheese, mostly made from cows' milk e.g Stilton, Gorgonzola, Roquefort, Dolcelatte.

Bouquet Garni – Small bunch of herbs, usually a mixture of parsley stems, thyme and a bay leaf, tied in a muslin and used to flavour stocks, soups and stews.

Brie – A French full-fat cheese made from cow's milk, which has a soft creamy texture encased in a soft white crust.

Brioche – A butter, egg and sugar enriched French yeast bread, baked in the shape of a cottage loaf, either as an individual bread or a large loaf. Often eaten for breakfast, it is also ideal to use as a replacement for sponge or bread in trifles and bread and butter puddings.

Buckwheat – Also called Sarrazin, Blé Noir, Beaucuit or Bucail. It is a small triangular grain-like seed, which has a flavour reminiscent of beech nuts.

Bulghur Wheat – Also called bulgar, bulgur wheat, burghul or cracked wheat. It is a whole-wheat grain including the wheat germ, which has been cooked, dried and cracked.

Cajun Spices – A ready mixed blend of New Orleans style spices including chilli powder, pimientos, pepper, garlic, ginger and allspice. It can be substituted with any type of Mexican, Jamaican or Creole spice blend.

Caper – A flower bud which is either pickled in vinegar or preserved in brine and used as a condiment in many dishes.

Caramel – The result of cooking sugar or sugar syrup very slowly to a rich brown colour.

Caster Sugar – Also known as Superfine sugar, it is a refined white sugar, finer than granulated but coarser than icing sugar.

Celeriac, Celery Root or Céleri-rave – A root vegetable with white flesh and a sweet, nutty celery-like flavour.

Charred – Cooked until blackened in colour.

Cheddar Cheese – A full-fat medium hard cheese from England, but is produced world-wide. It can be substituted with Gruyère, Emmental or Monterey Jack.

Chives – A green herb related to the spring onion family, whose leaves are snipped into short lengths and used as a seasoning.

Cider – A sparkling alcoholic drink produced from the fermentation of apples, it can be substituted with still or sparkling apple juice, in many dishes. Add a splash of brandy or calvados as well if wished for extra flavour.

Clear Film – A clear flexible film suitable for covering foods during storage or resting.

Coconut Milk Powder – A dried powder made from coconut milk, used to flavour a variety of dishes. Use creamed coconut as an alternative.

Conserve – Whole fruit jam.

Coriander - A leafy green aromatic herb, also known as cilantro or Greek parsley.

Cornmeal – A golden coloured cereal from Italy, called polenta, which is also used to make a soft savoury mass known as polenta.

Coulis – A French term referring to a smooth purée of fresh fruit or vegetables.

Couscous – A staple of North African cuisine, it is a granular, small pelleted form of Semolina.

Creaming – The method of beating fat and sugar together to obtain a light airy texture and pale colour. Used in cakes and puddings which contain a high proportion of fat. It helps to incorporate air.

Crème Fraîche – A French variety of cream made from cow's milk, with a thick consistency and sharp flavour. If unavailable use soured cream as a substitute.

Crêpe – French term for a pancake; made from a pouring batter which is cooked in a shallow frying pan.

Curd Cheese - A soft smooth full fat soft cheese with a slightly sharp flavour. It can be substituted with cream cheese mixed with a few drops of lemon juice if curd cheese is unavailable.

Curdle – To cause sauce or creamed mixture to separate once the egg is added, either due to over-heating or beating the egg into the mixture too quickly.

Demerara Sugar – A golden brown sugar with quite large sparkling crystals, good for decorating cakes and biscuits.

Deseeded – Fruit or vegetables with the seeds removed.

Digestive Biscuit – A sweetmeal biscuit with a nutty flavour.

Double Cream – A full-fat thick cream which can be whipped. Adds texture and flavour to a wide range of dishes, particularly desserts. Can be substituted with whipping cream.

Dropping Consistency – Describes the texture of cake or pudding mixture prior to cooking. A spoonful of mixture, held on its side above the bowl, should fall off, on its own accord, within 5 seconds.

Dust – To sprinkle lightly with icing sugar, cocoa or flour, usually using a sieve or strainer.

Emmental – A full fat medium hard cheese originating from Switzerland. It has a firm smooth texture, and a flavour which is mellow and sweet with a lingering hint of hazelnut.

Feta – A full fat white cheese traditionally made from the ewes' milk, but now more usually cows' milk and preserved in brine, originating from Greece.

Filo Pastry – Also known as phyllo. A popular Greek / Middle Eastern pastry made in wafer thin sheets. It can be bought frozen or chilled as ready prepared sheets.

Flaked Almonds – Thinly sliced blanched almonds.

Flambé – Flavouring a dish with alcohol, usually rum or brandy, which is then ignited so that the alcohol content is burned off.

Flan Tin – Usually circular, a shallow sided tin often with a loose base, for baking pies, pastries and flans.

Folding In – A delicate method of combining a whisked or creamed mixture with other ingredients by cutting and folding, so that the mix retains its lightness. Used mainly for soufflés, meringues and certain cake mixes. A large metal spoon, which has a thinner edge than a wooden spoon, is normally used.

Fudge – A soft non-sticky caramel made from sugar, butter and condensed milk.

Gelatine – An animal derived setting agent available as a powder or as leaf gelatine.

Ghee – Clarified butter, used extensively in Indian cookery. Use clarified butter as an alternative. To clarify butter, heat until melted and the bubbling ceases. Remove from the heat and leave to stand until the salt and sediment have sunk to the bottom. Gently pour off the fat and strain it through muslin. Discard the sediment.

Glacé Cherries – Cherries preserved in syrup.

Glaze – To apply a glossy coating to sweet and savoury foods, usually, egg or milk on pastry or bread before cooking. After baking, cakes can be glazed with honey or sugar syrup.

Gluten – A protein constituent of wheat which is viscous or sticky. The amount present in flour varies and produces the different textures of cakes and breads.

Glycerine – A thick, clear liquid with a slightly sweet flavour used to preserve the soft texture of royal icing. It is available from large supermarkets and most pharmacies.

Greek-style Yogurt – A thick natural yogurt, ideal for those allergic to cows' milk. It tastes rich, yet has the characteristic slightly acidic flavour.

Grilling – Also known as broiling, it is a method of cooking using radiant heat directed either from above or below.

Icing Sugar – Also called Confectioners' Sugar. A powdered sugar used for making icings.

Kirsch – A German white brandy distilled from cherries.

Knead – A gentle but firm action used with bread dough, to develop the gluten in the flour.

Knock Back – To knead yeast dough for the second time, to ensure an even texture.

Loaf Tin – Rectangular high-sided tin for baking bread or cakes.

Lukewarm – About blood heat, approximately 37°C/99°F.

Malibu – A white rum flavoured with coconut. Can be substituted with coconut liqueur.

Marinade – A sauce used for marinating – a process in which meat or other foods are soaked for a period of time prior to cooking, to tenderise or flavour.

Mascarpone – An Italian soft cream cheese which has a silky smooth texture and light whipped cream taste.

Marmalade – A preserve or jam usually made with citrus fruits.

Non-stick Baking Parchment – An opaque paper used to prevent sticking, primarily used for lining tins before baking cakes.

Oiling – Brushing a tin or baking sheet with vegetable oil, butter or margarine to prevent the food sticking during cooking. Also referred to as greasing.

Orange Flower Water – An aromatic liquid made from the fragrant flowers of the Seville Orange and used as a flavouring in cakes and biscuits.

Pare – To thinly peel the skin or zest from fruits, particularly citrus fruits and vegetables.

Pearl Barley – A cereal which has been hulled and milled until the barley grain resembles small pearls. The polished, refined grain cooks more quickly because the husk has been removed. It is an excellent addition to soups.

Pith – Innermost white lining under the rind of a citrus fruit.

Prosciutto – An Italian cured, dried ham similar to Parma ham.

Prove – To leave yeast dough to rise after shaping.

Purée – Fruits, vegetables, meat or fish which have been blended, sieved or pounded to a smooth textured pulp.

Puy Lentil – Tiny green lentils from France. Considered to be the most superior of all lentils, but if unavailable substitute with any green or brown lentil.

Ramekin – A small round straight-sided dish or pot made of earthenware, china or glass used for individual dishes such as soufflé or pâté.

Red Pepper – A large sweet, fleshy capsicum with a mild flavour, not to be confused with the small hot chilli pepper; also available green, yellow, orange and white.

Reduce – To make a sauce or liquid more concentrated by fast boiling in an uncovered pan.

Refresh – To cool hot vegetables very quickly by holding under cold running water in order to stop the cooking process.

Rest or Relax – A process used when making pastry or bread dough to allow gluten in the flour to contract, thereby making rolling out the dough easier and also to avoid shrinkage in pastry, when cooked.

Risotto – An Italian dish of rice cooked in butter or oil with stock, meat, seafood or vegetables and often Parmesan cheese.

Rocket – A tasty salad herb, very common in French and Italian dishes. It has a distinctive peppery taste.

Runner Beans – Long green beans picked when young before the bean pods have developed. Usually sliced then steamed, boiled or stir-fried.

Rye – A cereal grain with a low gluten content, so is often mixed with wheat for making breads and crispbreads, especially in Europe.

Sauté – To cook food in a small quantity of fat which quickly browns the food.

Searing – Quickly browning meat in a little hot fat.

Seasoning – Adding condiments, usually salt and pepper to a dish to enhance the flavour.

Self-raising Flour – Flour to which a raising agent has been added in order to facilitate the rising of cakes. Can be substituted with plain flour and baking powder.

Simmering – Cooking food and liquids slowly and steadily over a gentle heat and keeping just below boiling point.

Single Cream – A low fat runny, pouring cream, used in soups, sauces, coffee or as a topping for desserts and pastries.

Soft / Stiff Peaks – Refers to the beating or whipping of cream or egg whites. Soft peaks will form a peak but will flop over whilst with a stiff peak there is no movement and you could turn the bowl upside-down without the contents falling out.

Squid Ink – A black substance obtained from squid and used as a natural colouring usually for sauces and pasta.

Stem Ginger – Fresh ginger root preserved in syrup.

Stir-Frying – A quick method of frying ingredients, at a high temperature and with only a little oil, usually in a wok; the ingredients are moved around constantly until cooked.

Stock (Bouillon) – A flavoured liquid base made from either meat, poultry, fish or vegetables and used for making sauces, stews, soups and other savoury dishes.

Strong Plain Flour – A flour with a high protein content and good gluten content, making it perfect for bread.

Swede – A root vegetable with orange-yellow flesh and a slightly sweet flavour. Used in casseroles and stews, savoury dishes and mashed as a side vegetable.

Whipping – Beating air rapidly into a mixture, using the Whisk.

White Fish – When a recipe stipulates white fish any local firm white fish, such as halibut, huss, cod, hake, whiting, coley, plaice or sole can be used.

Wilt – The term 'to wilt' is used to explain how to cook green leaves like spinach or pak choi or herbs. The green leaves are placed in a pan with the moisture left from washing them, still left clinging to the leaves. They are then cooked briefly, stirring and turning until the leaves release their natural juices and become floppy, but still retain their colour.

Zest – The oily outer part of the skin of the citrus fruit, without any pith, used for flavouring.

INDEX BY ATTACHMENT OR TOOL

This index is arranged to show which tool or attachment is used in the preparation of the recipe. Some recipes require more than one tool or attachment.

INDEX

INDEX

INDEX